*Fifty Years
at Jesus*

Fifty Years at Jesus

The Diaries of Frederick Brittain, Litt.D.
Fellow of Jesus College, Cambridge

(covering the years 1919 ~ 69)

Edited by Muriel Brittain

MURIEL BRITTAIN • CAMBRIDGE

I would like to thank the publishers Heinemann Educational Books Ltd. for their kind permission in allowing me to adapt and use material from Freddy's autobiography *It's A Don's Life* (1972).

Muriel Brittain
Jesus College, Cambridge.

First published in Great Britain 2001
Muriel Brittain, Jesus College, Cambridge CB5 8BL

ISBN 0-9541760-0-6

© 2001 Muriel Brittain

A CIP catalogue for this book is available from the British Library.

All rights reserved. No part of this publication may be reproduced in any form or by any means – graphic, electronic or mechanical, including photocopying, taping or information storage and retrieval systems – without the prior permission in writing from the publishers.

Printed and bound in Great Britain by Bell and Bain Ltd, Glasgow

Contents

Acknowledgements page iv
Introduction page 1

1919 .... *page 3*	1945 .... *page 159*
1920 .... *page 9*	1946 .... *page 164*
1921 .... *page 17*	1947 .... *page 169*
1922 .... *page 29*	1948 .... *page 172*
1923 .... *page 38*	1949 .... *page 176*
1924 .... *page 47*	1950 .... *page 181*
1925 .... *page 53*	1951 .... *page 187*
1926 .... *page 58*	1952 .... *page 192*
1927 .... *page 67*	1953 .... *page 201*
1928 .... *page 71*	1954 .... *page 206*
1929 .... *page 74*	1955 .... *page 214*
1930 .... *page 80*	1956 .... *page 221*
1931 .... *page 86*	1957 .... *page 225*
1932 .... *page 90*	1958 .... *page 227*
1933 .... *page 96*	1959 .... *page 231*
1934 .... *page 101*	1960 .... *page 240*
1935 .... *page 107*	1961 .... *page 246*
1936 .... *page 111*	1962 .... *page 252*
1937 .... *page 114*	1963 .... *page 261*
1938 .... *page 116*	1964 .... *page 270*
1939 .... *page 123*	1965 .... *page 277*
1940 .... *page 128*	1966 .... *page 284*
1941 .... *page 134*	1967 .... *page 293*
1942 .... *page 139*	1968 .... *page 300*
1943 .... *page 144*	1969 .... *page 304*
1944 .... *page 152*	

Frederick Brittain's Published Works *page 307*
Index *page 309*

Introduction

FREDERICK BRITTAIN, always known affectionately as Freddy or FB to his friends, was born on 24 October 1893. Until he enlisted in the Royal Army Medical Corps in 1914, he had only ever travelled within a twenty-five mile radius of the quiet and little-visited part of south-east England that lay partly in Hertfordshire and partly in Bedfordshire. It was here that his ancestors had lived for centuries, mostly working on the land, as farm labourers, market gardeners, or farmers, and where both his parents were born.

FB was the second child of the five children of William Brittain and Elizabeth Daniels who were married in 1891. His first school was the church day school for infants in Barnet and he also attended Sunday school. By all accounts he was a noisy, talkative child. In 1900, when he was six, FB was promoted from the infant school to the boys' school where there were seven teachers plus the headmaster for 400 boys. The teachers performed miracles with very little space and equipment and class sizes of between fifty to sixty pupils, with two or even three different lessons taking place in the same room.

The Education Act of 1902, which took the first step of bringing secondary education within the reach of working-class children proved to be beneficial for FB. Local authorities were empowered to grant a few scholarships each year to enable boys and girls to go from elementary schools to secondary schools. In the summer of 1906, after a written examination at Barnet and an oral examination at Hatfield, FB was awarded a Hertfordshire County Scholarship to Queen Elizabeth's Grammar School, Barnet. His first term commenced in September that same year and his fascination with languages was kindled at Queen Elizabeth's where he spent the next five years being instructed in, among other things, French, Latin and German

When FB left school in 1911, his prospects were narrow. His ambition was to go to a university but such an ambition was financially impossible for a boy from a working-class family because the few scholarships that were available did not meet the whole cost. It was decided that the best course of action would be for him to become a student teacher at Christ Church School for a year, during which time the Hertfordshire County Council made him a grant of £20, and on this he managed to live. At the end of the year he became an assistant master at Christ Church, at a salary of £70 per annum.

At the end of the school term in July 1914, FB gave up teaching and on Monday 10 August, a few days after the start of the First World War, entered the Second Division of the Civil Service, having passed the entrance

~ Introduction ~

examination the previous autumn. He was appointed to the Accountant General's Department of the General Post Office at St. Martin's-le-Grand but did not find the work stimulating.

On Friday 2 October, 12 days before his 21st birthday, he received permission from the Civil Service to enlist in the ranks of the Royal Army Medical Corps. He was posted to the Second London General Military Hospital in Chelsea where he worked in the medical wards for about two months before being transferred to the surgical side. From 31 August 1915 and for the greater part of the next three and a half years, the hospital ship *Egypt* under the command of George Montford, became his floating home. A transcript of the diaries that FB kept during this time were accepted into the Imperial War Museum's archive in June 2000.

When the War ended FB was able to set about realizing his overmastering ambition of taking a degree at Cambridge University, the vision of which had never faded from his mind since a visit to Cambridge in 1914. For the first time in history, the State would be making financial grants available to ex-Servicemen for that purpose. Even if he had failed to get a grant, he had received most of his Civil Service pay throughout the war and had saved it, with Cambridge in view. The Chaplain aboard the *Egypt* at the time, the Rev William Hodges, was a Cambridge man. He had taken his degree from Jesus College, and on his advice FB wrote to Arthur Gray, the Master of the College, and was accepted to read for a degree in modern and medieval languages commencing with the autumn term of 1919.

~ 1919 ~

Wednesday 16 April
Received a letter from Arthur Gray, the Master of Jesus College, as a result of which I went to Cambridge and was interviewed by him. He advised me not to begin this term as the definitive grant is not commencing until October and the interim grant does not cover much.

> [Arthur Gray was nearer 70 than 60. He had entered the College in 1870 and had been a Fellow since 1875. Utterly devoted to the college, he was elected to the Mastership in 1912, the first layman to hold the office. He had written histories of both the Town and the University of Cambridge, as well as of his own college, and had made Jesus College the setting of a book of ghost stories titled, *Tedious Brief Tales of Granta and Gramarye*. One story was called 'The Everlasting Club' in which the characters were named after Jesus men who were up in the mid-eighteenth century, thus fooling some of the more gullible readers. FB knew very little of this when Arthur Gray received him in the Conference Room of the Master's Lodge, with its windows looking into the cloister at one end and into the three-sided outer court of the College at the other. FB remembers him as being very kind and they talked for some time, with the Master appearing to be always on the point of breaking into a smile. As FB discovered later, this was a permanent characteristic due to his cheekbones being unusually high. Some time later FB noticed that one of his ears was higher then the other, which also added to the 'smiling' effect. When asked what career he hoped to follow on leaving Cambridge if he was admitted, FB replied that he did not know. He had the vague idea that he might return to the Civil Service, if they would have him, but he hadn't really looked that far ahead. He only knew – and of this he was certain – that he wanted three years at Cambridge. Before dismissing him the Master made some notes in a book and told him that he would be hearing from him later. FB was too timid to explore the college, and even came away wondering whether the parish church of All Saints, just across the road opposite the entrance gate, was the college chapel.]

Good Friday 18 April
South Mymms. Walked to St Giles for the Liturgy. The Three Hours, Evensong and Stations and Tenebrae, were very impressive, especially at the end with

all lights extinguished except for the flickering candle behind the altar and one half-obscured under the choir stalls lighting up the faces of old White, T. Rowbotham and P. Penketh, and dimly revealing the chapel screen behind.

Easter Sunday 20 April
At Evensong the sun shone through the west windows and its rays lit up the clouds of incense.

Tuesday 22 April
Went to the Social at Mymms* and was introduced to Benbow – the new stalwart – and a socialist. I was glad to meet many old friends again – Mrs Blake has placed a room at my disposal whenever I wish it. The vicar welcomed me and others back and I had to say a few words in reply. We wound up a most sociable evening in the old style with 'Sir Roger'. We found the last bus had gone, so had to walk home.

[*FB adopted the medieval spelling of Mimms from this point on.]

Thursday 1 May
Spring-cleaned my bedroom and then went to Hyde Park for the May Day demonstrations – a long procession with banners, etc –addressed by George Lansbury, Margaret Bondfield and Sylvia Pankhurst.

Tuesday 6 May
Resumed duty at the Accountant General's Department of the Civil Service and was posted temporarily to the Cashiers' Department.

Wednesday 7 May
Went to a Fancy Dress Social at Mymms and helped to judge the dresses. I liked the look of Elsie Bull as Cinderella and wished she were four years older, as I afterwards discovered she was. I'm afraid I kept giving her admiring glances.

Friday 9 May
Attended the Independent Labour Party Meeting where I was forced into the Chair. I raised the question of Jack Brown as a candidate for Parliament. Someone was deputed to raise the question at the next meeting of the Trades Council in order to get their support.

[J. W. Brown had been interned in Germany during the war. He was unsuccessful in politics and afterwards became Secretary of the British Film Institute.]

Monday 26 May
Participated in the Rogation Procession from St Giles. The vicar blessed and censed the crops and we came back through the upper village with Stations at intervals.

Tuesday 15 July
St Swithin's Day, but he let us off without rain, perhaps because we have had our forty wet days in advance. Went with A. K. Williams down Galley Lane across the fields by the brook to the Roman Camp. We sat on the bank and AK read and criticised a literary effort of mine. It was a quiet and peaceful scene with the sun setting a silvery gold over Dyrham Park's trees. Came back through the hayfields, some are already in cocks, others not yet cut, it's a bad year for hay.

Monday 21 July
About twenty-five of the Barnet Labour Party went to the Divisional Demonstration in St Albans Market Place to protest interference in Russia and conscription. I was called on to speak at the last minute and didn't feel at all nervous.

Thursday 24 July
The Board of Education wrote to say that I have been awarded a grant of £203 per annum to go to Jesus College, Cambridge on October 1st!!! *Deo Gratias*.

Wednesday 30 July
Met Rouse and together we went to the Lyceum to see *The Marriage of Figaro* and enjoyed the exquisite music immensely. I would like to see it again.

[FB attached his copy of the programme into the diary]

Sunday 3 August
Uncle George was demobilized on Friday and he and Aunt Rose came for the weekend. Went with him to Mass and walked home by footpaths and then by the Wash and Dancers Hill big field where the ripening barley hissed like a sea in the breeze, the sun lighting the elms with vivid green and yellow. In the afternoon I had a nap and then went to Evensong and back to music at home.

Wednesday 20 August
General Meeting of the Barnet Labour Party. A new man called Tuft seems to me to be a *hunter*. He bragged of being a Socialist, yet professed ignorance of the Labour Party's programme. Audibly (to me) he ridiculed people who

were using ungrammatical English. I don't regard him as *my* acquaintance.

Thursday 21 August
Met Mother and took her to see the Carl Rosa Company's production of *Aida* at the Lyceum.

> [FB's mother had been asking him whether he was being rash in abandoning a Civil Service post with a regular income and good prospects, for an unknown future. This was very much on his mind so that he returned mechanical answers to her enthusiastic comments and questions about the opera during the interval. He decided that he must go to Cambridge whatever happened, but for the rest of his life FB could never hear the music of *Aida* without recalling the mental agony he suffered at that time.]

Thursday 4 September
Went direct from the station to the (Barnet) horse fair – fewer horses this year. Then to the pleasure fair which has no big shows at all but small ones such as the Fat Woman, Siamese Twins, dwarf horse etc. Went on the slippery cakewalk. The latest rage is throwing pennies on to linoleum of black and white squares for prizes or for gambling at the horse fair. Met Ethel and May, also "Caxton", and we all went to the African show where a native walked on broken glass and ate fire. Here we met APD and Mrs Dent and went on the roundabout showering confetti in "Stall Alley". In fact we entered into the fun of the fair with zest and enjoyed it. It attracted a dense crowd today.

Thursday 11 September
Went to see Mr Abbott, Senior Tutor of Jesus College, to arrange lodgings.

> [FB went for this interview, as he had previously gone to see the Master, in fear and trembling, but was reassured when he found himself facing a gentle, shy, nervous man with blue eyes and a pointed beard. He soon realised to his astonishment that he was as frightened of FB as the latter was of him.]

Tuesday 16 September
We are still sending out The Egyptonian – No. XXIII was published and despatched today.

> [*The Egyptonian* was the newspaper that FB started aboard the Hospital Ship *Egypt* during the war.]

Thursday 25 September
At 12 noon I finished up with the Civil Service and said goodbye to friends.

~ 1919 ~

Friday 26 September
Jack and I went out at midnight to meet the unemployed ex-soldiers marching from Manchester to London. We met them with a band and gave them supper at the Co-op Hall where Jack welcomed them on behalf of the Labour Party. While there Harold told me that the railwaymen throughout the country came out on strike at midnight.

Thursday 2 October
Went to Hatfield and back by pony to see the Secretary of the Trades' and Labour Council at the NUR Strike Room.

Monday 6 October
Said goodbye and left home at 10 a.m. for Cambridge on cycle, [because of the strike and having sent his luggage in advance by a friendly car. FB's lodgings were at 56 Cam Road on the Chesterton side of the river with Midsummer Common between him and Jesus College.] I was surprised to find that someone had already paid me a social call, for a black-edged visiting card, with two crests on it, was lying on the table when I arrived. It read "Mr R H Edleston, 57 Jesus Lane" and I wondered who he was. My landlady could only say that he was a middle-aged gentleman, dressed in black and that he had a big moustache and a funny little beard.

Tuesday 7 October
Went to a shop and bought a cap, gown and surplice for a total cost of £3. 13s 6d and emerged a fully decked undergraduate. Saw my tutor, Mr Elliott, who was very kind. I signed the "redeat". [C. A. Elliott had gone to Jesus from Eton via Trinity and was to return to Eton in 1933 to be headmaster and subsequently Provost.] I went to Hall at 7.30 p.m. with trepidation but, to my surprise and relief, they were all very friendly and no one was in the least inquisitive about who anyone was or where he had come from. The menu was moderately thick soup, roast veal and ham with baked potatoes and cabbage and then stewed figs and custard.

Thursday 9 October
After difficulty I found Adams Road and called on Mr Braunholz, my Director of Studies.

> [FB was to read for an honours degree in modern and medieval languages and literature, a Tripos which had not been introduced into the university curriculum until late in the 19th century. The number of men reading for it in any one college was small and Jesus, a conservative college, had not yet elected a Fellow to deal with it. So he was sent to E. G. W. Braunholz of King's College whose linguistic knowledge was unparalleled in

Cambridge. There can have been few European languages that he could not read and enjoy. A most gentle and modest man, none of his pupils could ever forget his humility or the charming courtesy with which he treated them.]

Saturday 11 October
The Boat Club captain called a meeting of the Rowing Club in the Common Room and about thirty persons were present. I was told that I would be able to row about three days a week.

Sunday 12 October
Attended Evensong in the College Chapel, sitting with other freshmen in the transept. It was sung under the tower with a choir of boys and a few men. During the psalms the clerk walked round with a big board checking off the names of those present.

Friday 17 October
Spent the morning in lectures and the afternoon in sliding seat pairs on the river. Later attended "white" chapel.

[White refers to the fact that on Saints' days (17 October commemorates St Etheldreda, the patroness of Ely Cathedral), eves of Saints' days, Sundays and Saturday evenings, surplices substituted the wearing of gowns in chapel.]

Wednesday 22 October
At 11 a.m. we met in the College Hall, where the Praelector, after showing us the various paintings of old worthies, called our names over, his Scottish accent and unconscious humour causing much amusement, e.g. when he called one name the porter replied "gone to Australia". We then followed the Praelector through the streets to the Senate House and matriculated by signing the University book.

Sunday 2 November
Attended a meeting at the Guildhall of the Cambridge South London Mission – the big hall was packed. The Vice-Chairman was in the chair supported by other dons looking gorgeous in scarlet robes, as today is a Scarlet Day. The guest speakers were the Bishop of Woolwich and H. H. Thomas, MP. The Bishop said that he had lived in South London for over thirty years and found people still living in conditions not fit for dogs, therefore he was glad to find such seething interest. H. H. Thomas was well received in spite of the recent railway strike. He spoke on "What Labour Wants", e.g. equality of opportunity. He appealed to Varsity men to try to

understand the feelings of Labour, saying that intelligence is not the monopoly of one class. It was an earnest, even eloquent speech, even though he dropped all his "H's".

Friday 7 November
Rowed 2 in our VIII to the railway bridge and then saw the Coxswainless IV's semi-final race in which Jesus I were beaten by Christ's I by about a second. We rowed on after as far as Horningsea where Steve Fairbairn took us in hand and gave us a gruelling all the way home.

> [Steve Fairbairn had been a rowing Blue and Captain of Jesus College Boat Club in the 1880s. After taking his degree he had gone back to his native Australia to be a grazier, but from the beginning of the 20th century he began to spend more and more time in England, living in Cambridge during term and coaching the boats of his old College.]

[There are no further entries for 1919.]

~ 1920 ~

Thursday 15 January
Arrived in Cambridge for my second term. Unpacked my box and went to see my Tutor and the Dean. There are about twenty freshmen this term, I hear, which makes me feel senior.

Tuesday 21 January
Attended a meeting at Trinity called by the STC [Society of the Confraternity of the Holy Trinity] to meet Bishop Gore who spoke on the forthcoming Mission.

Thursday 30 January
Having unaccountably been left out of the rowing this term, I went out sculling in a "whiff" (31 ft long) for the first time in a very strong wind. Ran into the bank just below Trinity Hall boathouse and tipped while trying to move. Waded out and emptied water from the boat. Steve Fairbairn came along and gave me a fresh start and excellent coaching to Barnwell Pool.

~ 1920 ~

Sunday 1 February
The weeping willows above and below Garrett Hostel Bridge are in leaf, about 1 inch long, and look beautifully veiled especially those at a little distance.

Sunday 8 February
I was too late for the St Clement's Church service so went to the Roman Catholic Church for High Mass at 11 a.m. It's peculiar how extremes meet; here most people sat for the Creed and the choir did not turn east. The long Epistle and Gospel were read in English from the pulpit before the sermon. After Hall I went to the Mission; it was very fine and I was much moved by Bishop Gore's broad Catholicity and sincerity.

Tuesday 10 February
Too rough to scull today. After Chapel I went to the Union Debate on the motion "That this House considers the pre-war policy of the Liberal Government both deceptive and dangerous". For the motion – Sir Ernest Wild, KC 316 votes. Against – Lord Haldane 441 votes. He gave many interesting sidelines on pre-war and wartime difficulties.

Ash Wednesday, 18 February
Attended the University Litany at Great St Mary's Church, the Vice-Chancellor, Proctors etc. attended in robes.

Saturday, 21 February
After the 9 a.m. lecture I went sculling and it was pretty rough. Steve Fairbairn revealed that I had improved somewhat since he first took me out three weeks ago.

Tuesday 24 February
Attended the Union Debate (which was joint with the Oxford Union) on the motion "That the time is now ripe for a Labour Government". The House was crowded one hour before time, Winston Churchill (against the motion) being the great attraction.

> [Sir Winston Churchill (1874–1965) was, at this time, Secretary of State for War and Air, a post he held from 1919 to 1921. *Granta*, the University paper that week said, "We didn't believe all he said, but there is a magnetic, boyish, over-the-hills touch of greatness about him that made us shout for joy". Louis Mountbatten [1900–1979] also opposed the motion, accusing the Labour Party of "diplomacy, ducal and dog-gone incapability". In 1947, as Admiral Lord Mountbatten, the Labour Government appointed him the last Viceroy of India.]

Saturday 6 March
The Misses Cade and Rankin came up for the day, we lunched at Matthews, then sat awhile in the sun on the Backs looking at the pleasure boats which have already come out. The willows are a vivid green and the crocuses (which I hadn't seen for five years) are all in bloom.

Wednesday 11 March
Received a box of wild daffodils from the woods at Mymms. They are glorious, and are one of the chief joys of life. After the lecture I went out in a "funny" for the first time, taking it carefully at first but soon got into the swing and found no difficulty in balancing. It was a most delightful sensation when moving along. Later I went to see the Dean and he says that I should go into the Church.

Wednesday 18 March
At Barnet for the Easter vacation. Cycled to Mymms and spent all day covering the greater part of the woods alone. Went to the edge of Mymmshall Wood, back to Green Path and down Larch Glen to Bluebell Corner. Sat under a larch and listened and looked at the birds (goldfinches etc.) then along the edge of the pasture and cornfields to Cinder Path, and back along the rough pasture to Daffodil Wood where I picked daffodils. Along, through the bracken and down to Primrose Wood, Boundary Path to Dark Lane and back to Mymms at 4 p.m., not having spoken to anyone since entering the woods this morning. Had tea at Mrs Saines' before going to Stations of the Cross and then home.

Wednesday 7 April
The first reunion of the Old Egyptians was held at the Colonnade Restaurant in the Strand. Commander Montfort came up from Plymouth and took the Chair. Dinner was followed by a concert, greatly marred by the lack of a promised piano. There were many toasts, the Chairman proposed "the Secretary" and I was quite overcome with its reception.

Tuesday 13 April
Went to Mymms for the first meeting under the Church Enabling Act. I was elected to the Parochial Church Council.

> [The Enabling Act caused Parochial Church Councils to come into being, thus giving the laity a voice in church affairs for the first time.]

Wednesday 14 April
(South Mymms) I received a wire from Mr Gowar, Headmaster of St Giles' School, asking me to go and teach there temporarily. Cycled over and taught at afternoon school – my very first experience of teaching girls.

~ 1920 ~

Friday 28 May
Cambridge. Wrote to P & O about a post in Italy during the Long Vacation, but no luck.

Sunday 30 May
At 8.30 p.m. five of us "Kept a Lodge"! The Master was not in, but we had quite a good time in the delightful old house. Malcolm Gray (the Master's son) showed me round the house and through their private door into the charming Old College Library with its old books, skeleton in a case, etc.

Tuesday 1 June
The Union Debate on Home Rule for India was only defeated by the casting vote of the Acting President. An article of mine in *Granta* – *The Perils of the Deep* – was published today.

Monday 7 June
"May" exams (French and Italian) all day at the Sidgwick Museum.

Tuesday 8 June
At 7.30 a.m. attended STC Mass at St Botolph's. Double-sculled with VBH to Baitsbite Lock, easying at the bridge, Ditton, Baitsbite, Horningsea and Clayhithe. Lunched at the Green Man, did some walking and passed a big field of beautifully scented broad beans in full bloom. The Fen country is quite enchanting, giving such a feeling of breadth and immensity. On return we easied at the same places, except that we "did a course" in fair time.

Wednesday 9 June
Finished my "May" exams. It is the first day of the May races, we started 2nd behind 3rd Trinity and bumped them below the Glasshouses.

Friday 11 June
Coombe and I went to St Ives, through the long, old-fashioned street to Market Hill and past Cromwell's statue to the church, which we found was only re-opened yesterday after two years, the spire having been knocked into the nave by an airman during the war. It is a very fine, spacious church with a painted screen surmounted by an organ with a rood before it. The High Altar has gold statues, candles, chandeliers, etc., and the same in the north aisle. The pillars of the nave each have two modern statues attached. We crossed the old bridge with its chapel and after lunch at the Temperance Hotel, hired a tub and sculled upstream. There was greenery everywhere, beautiful woods and islands overgrown with reeds and rushes. We went as far as Hemingford Grey Mill, then to the right of a branch stream, the tall spire of Houghton Church visible across the fields and isles.

Saturday 12 June.
Jesus finished Head of the River with Playford grinning all over his face. There was no bonfire tonight, as it began to pour with rain, also because our Bursar (Goodwin) died today.

> [Humphrey Blake Playford, Captain of the College Boat Club and a Blue, became a priest-schoolmaster. His tall, handsome figure was a familiar sight over many years in the Stewards' Enclosure at Henley Regatta where he was an umpire and a judge. FB took the credit for introducing him, much later on, to Betty Birks, an art mistress at Kings College Choir School, whom he married in 1960.
> It is the custom for the College rowing Head of the River to have a bonfire and to burn an old boat in celebration.]

Monday 14 June
I was very reluctant to leave Cambridge for the Long Vacation, though pleased to go home.

Saturday 19 June
Attended Vespers at St Giles and then helped the Vicar to pick gooseberries. As he would inquisitively interfere with the "dear bees", he got stung under the eye.

Thursday 24 June
Teaching all day at Mymms, then to the Social at the Parish Hall where I recited *Gore* (under pressure) and danced the Valeta and the last waltz (ladies privilege) with KD.

Dedication Festival, Sunday 11 July
At Evensong we almost went into convulsions in the vestry over a garment (presumed to represent a cotta) worn by the preacher, the Rev Archdale King. Pascoe Bligh thought he might be married and that it was one of his wife's garments!

Monday 19 July
Mr Gowar being away, I acted as Head Master.

Thursday 22 July
School broke up for the holidays with many expressions of regret from my pupils and I shall be sorry to part with them. Apart from the strain, I have really enjoyed these weeks teaching and loved the children.

> [On 26 July FB left for Paris where he was met by Signor Brookes. He then

embarked on a tour of Italy, which included Milan where the Cathedral, "with its tomb of St Charles Borromeo, had no tawdriness, not one image, only a picture of Our Lady". In Mandello he was introduced to Sr Brookes' mother and two sisters. Coming out of church there he felt as if he was acting in *Cavallaria Rusticana* – minus the killing. He found Venice beyond his expectations, particularly St Mark's, and quoted "Earth hath not anything to show more fair". At Florence the beauty of the Cathedral was marred by the presence of spittoons round the altar and the choir, and the loud use made of them by the celebrants during the High Mass, and by the Canons during the Office and after it. At Pisa he got a room for 3 lire and discovered tips were abolished. He travelled on to Parma then back to Mandello, where the chief topic of conversation was the mind of social revolution which had broken out all over Italy. The employees had turned out the employers and established a Soviet system and were managing the businesses themselves. At Lecco he saw "Viva Lenin" scrawled everywhere, numbers of young men with arm bands and red ribbon in their hats but no signs of violence, though the people were obviously poor, living on an average of 20 lire a day, the cost of a modest meal in a restaurant. At Milan red flags were in evidence, together with barbed wire and sandbags on chimneys and roofs.]

Saturday 11 September
Returned from Italy last night. Cycled to Hatfield to join in a demonstration to celebrate the formation of the Hatfield Labour Party. We marched through the town with seven banners.

Friday 1 October
While I was showing my Italian pictures to the children at school, Mrs. Trotter walked in.

[The Trotter family who lived at Dyrham Park, were suspicious of high church practices at South Mimms. In the big schoolroom, with its ink-stained desks and scrubbed floor, hung a big coloured engraving, which Mrs Trotter, always on the look-out for popery, once denounced as a picture of the pope, though in fact it was a copy of Bellini's well-known portrait of Doge Loredano of Venice.]

Harvest Festival, Thursday 7 October
We had a parochial tea in the Parish Hall followed by Evensong. Mrs and Miss Trotter enjoyed the service. At 8.45 p.m. there was a concert and dancing in the Parish Hall. I was MC.

~ 1920 ~

Friday 8 October
Arrived back at Cambridge, beautiful with autumn tints. Owing to repairs to locks the river has sunk 5 ft and is half its usual width, so sculling is out of the question.

Wednesday 13 October
Double-sculled with VBH to Upware (only five houses and a school) and had an excellent lunch at the Five Miles From Anywhere – No Hurry Inn. The dialect here is something like Bedfordshire with middle consonants, especially "it's", elided.

Monday 18 October
A sudden change to cold weather and I lit a fire for the first time, though the coal strike begins today. Set out with some trepidation in a light pair with VBH for the first time but got on better than expected. Hughes tells me a man remarked to him that I couldn't do a stroke of work, as I am "always on the river". The man can't know me at all, as I'm sure I do more than the average man and am considered "a swot" by those who live near. At Hall, a man next to me (up before the war) was quite sure I was Australian. He addressed me as Digger and on my asking if he was Australian said, "No, but I know one when I see one".

Wednesday 27 October
The thickest fog I've ever seen in Cambridge. Went to visit Wynn for the first time.

> [Edward Wynn, a Scholar and then Chaplain of Jesus College just before the First World War, was at that time Vice-Principal of Westcott House, the theological college opposite Jesus College. He went on to become Dean of Pembroke College and then Bishop of Ely, which made him automatically Visitor of Jesus College. FB and he became close friends.]

Thursday 11 November
Went to 10.30 a.m. Requiem Mass at St Giles, Cambridge, for those who fell in the war. After Hall went to see the Armistice Rag in the Market Place. A cab full of tar was set alight and dragged round the streets to the Market Place. There was a big crowd for the fireworks.

Tuesday 16 November
It was such a lovely day and so blue a sky that after the 9 a.m. lecture VBH and I went to Ashwell and up Clay Bush Hill to the lonely elm with its superb view of three counties. After lunch at the Three Tuns, we went down by the brewery to look at the young stream [the source of the River Cam], which

is a clear brook here, and then along a beautiful leaf-strewn lane to the road.

Sunday 21 November
A biting morning with beautiful rime frost. A heavy fog came down in which a Pembroke VIII ran into a tub with Steve Fairbairn in it and capsized. Three or four couldn't swim but were rescued – the water must have been near freezing point. I hear we had 17° of frost the other night – remarkable for November.

Thursday 2 December
Went to the Jesus Classical Society for a paper by Mr Edmonds on "Books and Libraries in Ancient Greece and Egypt".

> [J. M. Edmonds, the classical scholar, had entered the College in 1894. Between his graduation and his returning to Cambridge he had been a master at The King's School, Canterbury. His kindness of heart was shown there in his class lists, which were notorious for the large number of names bracketed together in equals. This feature was particularly helpful to boys in the lower part of the list. If, for instance, there were thirty boys in the class and the last six of them were bracketed equal, each of them could write home saying that he was twenty-fifth among thirty. Some members of the school used to hope eagerly that in one of the end-of-term lists the headmaster would read out, "All boys in Mr Edmonds' class are bracketed equal first". When Edmonds returned to Cambridge in 1908 he was appointed to a University Lectureship. His publications included several volumes of Greek verse with elegant translations. During the First World War he also contributed a number of striking epitaphs to the columns of the *Times* and the *Times Literary Supplement*. One of them, for a British graveyard in France, has achieved world-wide fame, being frequently quoted in books, painted in memorial windows throughout the English-speaking world, and carved on innumerable war memorials, seldom with any acknowledgement of its authorship or request for permission to use it. Perhaps this neglect of the usual courtesies was sometimes due to its air of timelessness, which led many borrowers to imagine it to be a translation from the Greek Anthology. Others have ascribed it to A. E. Houseman or some other modern writer. Field-Marshall Lord Wavell mis-attributed it in print to General Edmonds, who was a member of his staff during the Second World War. J. M. Edmonds, always courteous, used to say that he would not have minded the mis-attributions of authorship or the breaches of his copyright, if only the text had not been commonly misquoted, as it is, for instance, on the Kohima Memorial and even in the Ashendene Press edition of his epitaphs. The correct version runs:
>
>> When you go home, tell them of us, and say
>> "For your tomorrows these gave their today".]

~ 1920 ~

Saturday 4 December
Formed a College Italian Society – the Dean was elected President and myself Secretary.

Monday 6 December
"Went down" for the Christmas vacation.

Monday 20 December
Barnet. Saw Dr Nunn about my cough, but he says it's nothing serious and gave me throat-paint.

Friday 24 December
A beautiful Midnight Mass with very good congregation but to my disappointment there was no procession. Walked home with Edie and Miss Buttivant, arriving about 2.30 a.m.

Monday 27 December
The Christmas Social attracted a big company, especially of children. The Vicar led 'Blind Man's Buff', musical chairs, dances etc. I had the last waltz with Elsie Benbow. It was a good "Old English" gathering, which all seem to have enjoyed.

Tuesday 28 December
The Christ Church Old Boys' Dinner was not as good as usual and some of the songs were vile.

[No further entries for December]

~ 1921 ~

Saturday 1 January
Served Mass at 9 a.m., about 20 attended. Decorated the hall for the Marguerite Christmas Revels. We had a very enjoyable time till little after midnight and finished with 'Auld Lang Syne'. I had a little fun under the mistletoe with Else Benbow and Mrs Blake. The Vicar told ghost stories, and said how he saw again yesterday the ghost, which he saw years ago on Wash Bridge.

~ 1921 ~

Saturday 8 January
Walked with Maud to Wash Bridge but there was no sign of the ghost.

Saturday 15 January
Cambridge. After Hall I went to a meeting in the Dean's rooms to discuss starting a Sung Mass with a server in Chapel on Sundays. After some Protestant demur he agreed.

Sunday 23 January
Served at the 11.15 a.m. Sung Mass in the College Chapel. This was an honour, as I am no doubt the first server at the first Sung Mass there for centuries. Merbecke fits our beautiful old Chapel. The Dean is again under the impression that I am an ordinand. After Hall I thought of going to the Roosters, but couldn't resist going to Father Wynn's again; he has a great attraction. There were nearly 20 present, of all religions and none. Father Wynn entertained us with stories, drifting on to King Charles, Fathers Stanton and Ignatius, etc.

Monday 31 January
Sculled to Post Reach and back, the water smooth as glass and the crocuses by the glasshouses open to the sun. So finishes an extraordinarily mild January without one cold day.

Friday 4 February
Preparation service for Holy Communion. Ashwin remarked that I look "perfectly priestly" in my "square" [cap] which is not surprising as it is someone else's, (mine having been taken by mistake) and being much too small, is cut open an inch in the front and three inches or more at the back. My week's work was 43 hours.

Tuesday 15 February
At the Union Debate Hilaire Belloc supporting the motion for "Increase in the power of the crown" used a good phrase, "enough to make a jackass weep".

> [Hilaire Belloc (1870–1953), the French born writer and poet became a naturalized British subject in 1902. He was elected a Liberal MP in 1906 but did not seek re-election in 1910. His disapproval of modern industrial society and Socialism led him to write *The Servile State* (1912), which advocated a return to the system of medieval guilds, but he is best remembered for his nonsensical verse for children.]

Sunday 20 February
A gorgeously sunny, spring like day, followed by clear moonlight. Got up late. Went to Sung Mass and stayed some time afterwards in Chapel looking at the stained-glass windows, particularly the big one in the south transept, the bright colours of which show radiantly and the figures are so clear except the one at the top, which was a dazzle of gold, no doubt William Morris's intention. Walked round the Backs, the crocuses in Trinity Avenue are a glorious sight. There was a delicate white haze over the sunlit lawns.

Thursday 24 February
Not spring like today, but summer like. I cycled to Trumpington, Harston, Foxton and Shepreth, which has many thatched roofs and well-timbered houses, water mills, a brook running through the village and a moat close to the road. I saw a blackthorn bush smothered in blossom.

Sunday 27 February
When the Dean of St John's was called for early service this morning his gyp found the door had been screwed down during the night and the heads of the screws filed off. The gyp telephoned the Dean from the Porter's Lodge and told him he need not get up yet! The door had to be opened with crowbars.

Friday 4 March
Went to see the Greek play *Agamemnon* – very fine acting, dresses and music. It lasted from 8 p.m. till nearly midnight.

Thursday 10 March
Had a lecture at 9 a.m. and at 10.45 a.m. went with VBH in a light pair to Horningsea. The water looked dark blue in the sun but a strong wind right across the stern made it glitter with thousands of wavelets. Very sore on getting back on account of the peculiar seat with holes in it.

Friday 11 March
Full term ends today. Went to the Senate House to see Wyld take his degree. I expected a quiet affair but it was quite lively as there were about forty degrees conferred, including an honorary one on a Harvard man and a doctorate on the Master of Downing who walked up the House accompanied by a long wire of bunches of flowers, the end of which were carried along the side galleries as he walked. There were showers of confetti and pieces of paper, coloured streamers, toy balloons, rattles, trumpet blasts, screeches, cheers, stamping of feet etc. Latin speeches by the Public Orator (Glover) were accompanied by ironical cries of "hear, hear" etc. I was surprised to see the ceremonial, the numerous raising of hats and candidates received kneeling. In Hall Ashwin and I saluted Wyld as "Dominus" acting as train-bearers

and ragging him generally on his "wedding day" as Carter observed, Tommy Watt, the Praelector, having "given him away".

[John Campbell Watt a tough, squat, red-faced Glaswegian, was always referred to as Tommy. He had been one of the Fellows of the College in the days of compulsory celibacy and was the only resident one among them who had remained unmarried when the statutes were relaxed in 1882. He had done no teaching for some years before FB went into residence, but was nevertheless a great asset to the College, quite apart from his official duties as Praelector. The alternative native title of this office 'Father of the College' suited him well, for he was devoted to it and the undergraduates were his family. His duty was to present them for their degrees in due course. On such occasions he fussed round them like an old hen with her chickens, and if one of them was late at a meeting place he would get redder and redder in the face and express his feelings with a broader and broader Scottish accent until the culprit arrived. He kept open house and people called at his rooms at any hour of the day. He would often rebuke others for their extravagance but was a generous host himself. Once, when he had been entertained royally by Sir Arthur Quiller-Couch, he was heard to say, "That was a very fine breakfast ye gave us Q, but what I keep asking myself is, can ye afford it?" He was so tender hearted that, if any man failed in an examination or did not get as high a class as Watt's patriotic over-estimate of all Jesus men's abilities led him to expect, he would express his disapproval of the examiners in language that was always vehement and often unparliamentary.]

Passion Sunday, 13 March
South Mymms. On coming out of Evensong at St Giles a crowd of children asked me to teach, but Mr Gowar is unable to take me on, as the County Council is economising.

Palm Sunday, 20 March
Asperges were performed for the first time, blessings and distribution of palms going outside the tower as usual.

Easter Eve, 26 March
Sat up all night at St Margaret's, going for a walk about 1 a.m. At above 5 (dawn) Mr Fuller and I caught a duck and pushed it into Mrs Saines's bedroom. Great glee when it began quacking loudly!

Easter Monday, 28 March
Sung Mass at 9 a.m. – good choir and congregation. Not bad for a Bank Holiday!

Wednesday 30 March
Snow in the morning. Went with VBH to watch the Varsity Boat Race. Oxford won the toss and chose the Surrey side. The boats were level at Hammersmith Bridge then Oxford led by a length, but we finally won by a length.

Monday 4 April
Vespers of the BVM [Blessed Virgin Mary] at 6 p.m. As we came out, Father Clarke was just coming up in his trap. Commenting on Mrs Mitchell [a parishioner] Father Clarke said she had called him round a few days before and had told him he was as bad as the Vicar of South Mymms and they ought to be boiled together!! The Vicar is still urging me about the diaconate.

Friday 8 April
An annular eclipse of the sun, visible at Greenwich as a partial eclipse was at its height at 9.45 a.m. Cycled to North Mymms, the fringe of the wood looking lovely with young larches vivid green rising above the surrounding trees still leafless, and the cherry blossom like snow. Continued to Bluebell Corner, up the glade and back along Boundary Path. It was not quite dark and the wood was still except for owls hooting.

Tuesday 12 April
Easter term begins. The 8.34 a.m. train was cancelled owing to the rail strike, so I caught the 11.29 a.m.

Wednesday 14 April
Cambridge. Wrote notes on Foguet's *17th Siecle*. Saw the Dean [Dr Nairne] who says that his sympathies are all with the miners.

Thursday 22 April
Went with Wyld and Father Ward to the county prison, which is used at present as a store for wartime records. I was shown round the cells, chapel, yards, gallows and burial place of executed men. Then we went up Castle Mound with its glorious views of Cambridge and Ely Cathedral, which is very plain.

Monday 26 April
I took my oral examination in French diction, and was disappointed at being as far from the examiner as I possibly could be and the echoing hall being a further disadvantage. Did better in the conversation and reading. Heard Philip Snowden in the Union Debate "That political power in the immediate future lies with the Labour Party" – very good.

[Philip Snowden, Chairman of the Independent Labour Party, 1903–1906, was Chancellor of the Exchequer in 1924 and from 1929–1931. He was created 1st Viscount Snowden in 1931 and he died in 1937.]

Saturday 7 May
At 1 p.m. I went to Parker's Piece to the lunch picnic of the Cambridge University Pavement Club. There was a huge crowd composed of Varsity and Town, a jazz band and a few people wearing costumes. The party soon began to sit down and roared to the others to do so, pelting them if they didn't. Soon about 600 or 700 sat down, including women and children, but there was still a ring of people standing up all round. There must have been 1,500 present. Those who had brought food went on eating, the band playing meanwhile from its coal cart stand, with the speeches at intervals. My total work for the week was 54 hours – my record so far!

Sunday 8 May
Ashwin and I went to the Guildhall for the SCM (Student Christian Movement) address by Mr Studdert Kennedy ("Woodbine Willie") on "Catholicity" – it was extraordinarily fine. He pointed out that ritual is not an extra but necessary to many in order to help the *complete* Christian life.

Thursday 19 May
Cycled alongside Campbell and Playford who were rowing in the final of the Pairs. They won easily (nearly 100-yards) in spite of running into the bank at Ditton.

Saturday 21 May
Attended the ordination of two priests in Ely Cathedral – very reverently carried out. The Bishop looked kindly and has a fine voice. After the Litany we all went into the choir for Mass and the laying on of hands, the Bishop and Canons changing into copes for this.

Monday 23 May
Modern and Medieval Languages Tripos Examination begins. We had French composition in the big examination hall this morning and French translation in the afternoon. The essay is tomorrow.

Friday 27 May
Tripos continued in the Senate House with Italian translation.

Saturday 28 May
Tripos concluded in the Engineering hut near the Arts School with Italian essay from 9 a.m. to 12 noon.

~ 1921 ~

Monday 30 May
Mr Edleston took me to see the Assizes and got me a seat on the bench next to the Sheriff, next but one to the Judge, and just in front of the Chaplain. There was only one case, adjourned to the next Assize. The proceedings closed with the clerks calling out "God save the King and his Majesty's Justices". After general bowing all round the Judge left between files of police and the trumpeters in knee breeches played at the door. The party then drove off to Trinity where the ceremony was repeated. I was surprised to hear that the Judges take their own linen, plate and cutlery about with them and have their own cooks. The Judges' dress was rather odd; gown, red capes and a kind of priest's scarf. Later, participated in ragging about on the Close and then visited Mr Edleston's who entertained me with anecdotes of Lord Alfred Douglas, Napoleon III, etc.

Thursday 2 June
My brother Frank and I took two canoes up the Granta to Grantchester and on to Harston where we had lunch and rested. Then we sat under the fine tunnel of chestnut trees to Harston Mill where we took our boats up to the higher level and on to the outskirts of Barrington. There was plenty of deep water all the way with great tall reeds and rushes, and yellow irises in flower and forget-me-nots, making a delightful picture.

Friday 10 June
Meeting of the Pavement Club. About 500 of us on cycles made our way from the Senate House along Trinity Street, Sidney Street, Downing Street, Sidgwick Avenue and several times through Newnham College where a meeting was held.

Sunday 12 June
Chapel at 11 a.m and Dr Foakes-Jackson celebrated.

> [Foakes-Jackson was in some ways the eccentric and absent-minded don of popular legend. Even Nairne, who had been one of his pupils in the 1880s found him trying at times. One morning, when Foakes-Jackson discovered that he and Nairne had both been invited to a feast at the same college, he called on him and asked him whether he was going to accept the invitation. Nairne replied that he had not yet decided and Foakes-Jackson went away. An hour or two later he came back and repeated his question. Nairne replied that he still had not decided and asked Foakes-Jackson to go away as he was busy. To his surprise, Foakes-Jackson came back a third time before lunch and asked the same question. Nairne, becoming suspicious, asked him why he was so anxious to know, and Foakes-Jackson answered, "Well, you see, I thought that if you weren't going you would lend me your

scarlet gown". "I didn't want to go to the feast at all", said Nairne when telling the story afterwards, "but I decided at once that I must go because if I hadn't gone I should have had to lend him my beautiful scarlet gown, and I knew he would clean his false teeth on it before he left the table."]

Friday 17 June
Went to the Senate House to see that I had got a second in the Tripos lists. After Hall went to see Braunholtz. He characteristically referred to the results by saying, "of course you have seen the lists" and then rather upset my ideas by proposing that I should read some French in Part II. The Dean, to whom I went next, advised me to keep to my original ideas. I read Dante with him.

Saturday 18 June
The baggage, which has arrived on the common for Midsummer Fair keeps growing thicker.

Monday 20 June
Went to the Senate House with Mr Watt and about twenty-eight other "supplicants" to sign the book and pay the University degree fee of £4.

[Under special University legislation on behalf of ex-servicemen, sitting for the first part of his Tripos entitled FB to the degree of BA without further examination. He decided to take the degree but to stay in residence for a third year to sit the second part of the Tripos and so complete the usual course.]

Tuesday 21 June
Mother arrived to see me take my BA degree. She was pleased to see the Vicar there, it is thirty-one years since he took his degree.

Sunday 26 June
South Mymms. Attended Evensong at St Giles and had quite a struggle with the Vicar who tried to get me to wear my hood. I found out afterwards that he had been telling the children at Catechism to look out for it.

Thursday 7 July
Cambridge. It rained during the night, the first for months. In the afternoon I went with Mr Edleston to the flower show in the grounds of St John's where we had tea and walked round their Fellows' garden ("The Wilderness"), then to Peterhouse garden to look at the deer.

Monday 11 July
The temperature is 94°F in the shade. No real wet weather since a year last April, it is said to be the driest for 50 years. Read feebly on account of the heat. Baxter and Phillips were gated for nailing up Barton's door (he was to read in Chapel).

Saturday 16 July
I hear that McLean and Forsyth were sent down yesterday for being drunk and hindering the police in their duty and that Abbott [the senior tutor] was called out at 1 a.m. to bail them out.

Monday 18 July
Attended a lantern lecture by Cardinal Gasquet in the Examination Hall on "The Revision of the Vulgate".

Thursday 21 July
In the morning I read Vulgate Latin. At 2.30 p.m. stroked a Clinker Four to Ditton and back. Read *Petronius* aloud with Warren. We were both struck with its humour, its descriptive power and its apparent modernity.

Monday 8 August
Went with the girls to the Varsity Botanic Garden.

[Phil Tracey and Eva Saines were having a holiday in Cambridge.]

Monday 15 August
Finished packing, distributed "largesse", and left the College at noon.

Sunday 21 August
South Mymms. Attended 11 a.m. Mass at St Giles, the Vicar preached on Bolshevism, his *bête noire*, and read a letter from the Bishop of London accusing him (Allen Hay) of disloyally securing the ordination of lay-reader Walsh. His reply denied all knowledge, after which the Bishop apologised and enclosed £10 for the clerical holiday fund. On giving out the banns, the Vicar added, "This is the first marriage in this church this year – the outlook is bad." I canted and had to wear my hood.

Monday 29 August
Cycled to see Grandfather who has been in bed for three weeks – he is thin but in full possession of his faculties. He tells me that his Grandfather was the orphan son of the owner of Radwell Mill so we are a Hertfordshire family after all.

Thursday 8 September
Hottest September day for twenty-five years.

Friday 16 September
Went to the woods at 8 p.m. in glorious harvest moonlight, the trees throwing their shade on to the stubble and the moon glittering through the breaks in the trees and falling on the bracken and the yellowing leaves of the hazels. In some places the moonlight on the path and on the bracken seemed a tangible thing. I could almost believe in fairies tonight.

Saturday 17 September
A letter arrived to say that Grandfather died at midnight on Thursday. RIP.

Saturday 24 September
Grandfather's funeral with twenty-six relations following the coffin. On counting up we found he had fifty-eight living descendants.

Friday 30 September
Rode in a "one horse shay" to Welham Green and took the chair at the Labour Party concert.

Wednesday 5 October
Cambridge. Full term begins.

Friday 14 October
The water felt really cold for washing this morning. After Hall, went with Marsden to the Varsity Observatory, a lovely moonlight walk. We looked through the telescope at the nearly full moon, the double star of Andromedae, and the star cluster in Perseus.

Wednesday 19 October
Heavy rain and everyone talking about it, it is so unusual to see rain this year.

Thursday 20 October
Voting took place at the Senate House today as to whether women shall have membership of the Varsity with a few limitations or merely titular degrees. The town is fairly full of non-resident voters. At 12.15 p.m. a non-placet procession started from Castle Hill (there was a counter-attraction at the Assize where Clavering was acquitted of murder). There were Pipers in kilts, a female "Proctor" and "bulldogs" in tall hats and with Victorian ringlets, male "bedders", two hideous "girls" with a banner proclaiming "Now you've seen us give us our degrees", next a woman dragging a man on a chain labelled "Mere Man" and a hearse with coffin of "St Male Undergrad" drawn by a

crowd of "undertakers" in tall hats, a coach of "mourners" in fancy dress, then a long line of followers shouting, "We don't want women" as they passed the Senate House. I was hanging on to the Senate House railings "not like a respectable BA", as I was told by Father - - - - - -, who said his father (the Dean of Ely) and his brother had all voted for "reason, enlightenment and progress", i.e. for the women. Returned to the Senate House with Wyld and Page at 8.30 p.m. and found a large, cheering crowd. Membership of women lost by 300, titular degrees carried by 100. Wyld was disappointed.

Tuesday 25 October
Attended Low Mass at All Saints' at 7.30 a.m. and lectures from 9 a.m. – 11 a.m. At 2.30 p.m. stroked the VIII to the Ditch and back. Heard stories about E. Matthews (who always looked too quiet). It appears he often used to get "binged" and on one such an occasion when he and a friend were propping up a wall, the Proctor asked for his name. He replied, "Allow me to introduce you to my friend Robinson of the Guards". "What Guards?" "Of the Mud Guards!"

Wednesday 2 November
As it is All Souls' Day when the Everlasting Club meets, we decided to rag Baxter who keeps in Cow Lane. On going there we found a small crowd already assembled listening to voices coming from the Everlastings' room and trying to break open the door with feet and pokers without success. We decided this was not a good plan for respectable bachelors!

> [Arthur Gray had made the room at the top of Cow Lane, officially marked G staircase, the scene of his best ghost story *The Everlasting Club*, included in his book *Tedious Brief Tales of Granta and Gramarye*.]

Thursday 3 November
Found I was sitting next to Allum in Chapel. On my remarking that I was surprised to see him there, he replied that he was boxing at 8.30 p.m. and that he had come to take his mind off it. Then to our amusement the Psalm was XVIII containing "He teacheth my hands to fight . . . Thou shalt make room enough under me for to go that my footsteps shall not slide . . . I will beat them as small as the dust before the wind." Allum won his fight.

Saturday 5 November
I was elected a member of the Roosters who debated "That self-government is better than good government".

Friday 11 November
Heavy white frost. The Backs are frozen over from bank to bank. Astonishment at Jesus on finding that our German gun had disappeared from the Close during the night and equal astonishment at Caius College when the same gun was found in one of their courts. Its iron stays had been torn away and part of the iron removed to get it out and then replaced. A number of men must have been in on it to drag such a heavy gun through the streets. Great crowd for the Armistice Day Rag and there was a fire burning in the big bronze vase on Senate House Green. Caius men were all gated at 8.30 p.m. on account of the gun.

Thursday 24 November
A meeting of the Psychical Saints had been advertised all over the town, to be held in the Guildhall where "Sir Arthur Conan Doyle will vindicate materialisation". The place was packed, including dons. Twenty minutes after the appointed time, a notice was shown stating that Conan Doyle had failed to materialise and people realised the meeting was a hoax.

Friday 25 November
Stroked the VIII for the final of the College VIII's. Felt absolutely done in the gut as if the oar would drop from my hands, but was encouraged by the cheers of "tens" from the bank. Kept the rate of stroke up and increased it with my second wind. Felt doubtful but when we received the order to easy I was pleased to see the other boat was still rowing. So we won in record time for the crocks – 8 minutes and half a second.

Monday 28 November
The elms round the Backs are still lovely but there is a carpet of thousands of golden leaves, brought down by the frost lying beneath them. A fine sun and that grand odour of decaying leaves, yet the weeping willows along the bank are still as green as in spring.

Sunday 4 December
I had tea with Mr Edleston, Miss E., Miss Acland and Prince Fourinvsky (a cousin of the last Czar).

Friday 16 December
On my cousin's farm in Bedfordshire. Began to learn horse riding on a quiet horse called Major. Learned to keep on at a trot, to mount and dismount and to saddle a horse. Rode down to the coursing meet, but there was only one hare caught owing to recent shooting. Spent the evening amusing Will Brittain by drawing up a family "pedigree" and talking about William I of Stotfold, John II of Radwell etc. with considerable hilarity.

Monday 19 December
Sang a Requiem for Archbishop Mathew at St Giles, South Mymms.

Saturday 31 December
This has certainly been *annus mirabilis* for weather, practically no rain and a most wonderful summer equal to an Italian one. Nothing like it in living memory.

~ 1922 ~

Tuesday 10 January
South Mymms. A glorious spring-like day so I went to the wood where the golden sun was dazzling over it. The winter oats are thick green, the young wheat is rising and hawthorn catkins are scattering clouds of pollen. It was sunset as I loitered, taking farewell of it for the time being, then I went in the church among the dim sanctuary lamps with a white moon outside.

Sunday 15 January
Cambridge. The west organ was removed from Jesus Chapel a few days ago.

Friday 20 January
Went to see the Dean. He made me promise not to worry about financial matters and the haziness of my future, but to concentrate on getting a First, when, he said, "You will have a very good future before you".

Sunday 22 January
Opened the Rooster debate "That the twentieth century woman has shown that the saying 'the hand that rocks the cradle rules the world' does not apply to her".

Tuesday 24 January
Rowing at 8.30 a.m. The spray was frozen hard on the blades of the oars and the bilge was frozen inside the boat.

Wednesday 8 February to Saturday 11 February
The Lent Races.

> [FB rowed at 3 in the Jesus IV, which started 4th in the 4th division. They made a bump each day and so were the sandwich boat on Friday.]

In spite of rough water and fresh wind we soon drew on to Trinity Hall III. At First Post Corner the crowd were calling "half a length, quarter of a length" then "pull her round bow and 3" but I had hardly got us two "thick 'uns", when we bumped them right on Grassy Corner. On Saturday we unfortunately got an obstruction from a Sidney boat, our bow oars hitting the bank, mine being knocked out of my hands. A re-row was allowed at 5.45 p.m., when it was almost dark, but a splendid full moon glistened finely on the water, leaving the big stars visible. Unusual conditions for rowing a race! We did not gain more than half a length on Christ's III, but we had made four bumps without and so won our oars. The first boat rowed over Head and the second boat finished fourth on the river. At the bonfire after the Bump Supper the general feature was to smack everyone on the back and say, "Well rowed Sir, jolly well rowed Sir" and try to take his tie. Adami was very happy and beating a tin kettle, Randall was solemn and Masefield pretty drunk. There was general dancing round the fire singing "Oh he might have been at Pemmer, at Caius, the Hall or Emma, or become a Pothouse man, but in spite of all apologies, that are due to other colleges, he remains a Jesus man". We adjourned to Layng's and Harriss's rooms, where JSH was sick in the grate after which we all solemnly carried him to bed. Finch, Halward and I went out just before midnight. Halward would shout "jolly old Prog" to the Proctor who was just outside, but fortunately he took no notice.

Sunday 12 February
In Chapel we were going to sing the "Dies Irae" (how appropriate) but I was so hoarse that we cancelled it.

Wednesday 15 February
Meeting in the Master's Lodge on "Industrial Homes for Tramps" with an address by Brother Giles, OSF and the Earl of Sandwich in the Chair.

Thursday 23 February
The Cambridge University Italian Society met at Caius. Mr Bullough's paper was very interesting though, inveterate smoker that he is, while reading from his manuscript he took out a tobacco pouch and cigarette papers, made a cigarette, lit it and puffed at it, all the while still reading. Professor Okey told us the paper reminded him of his early days when he and others ran a newspaper called *The Republican.*

> [Thomas Okey was one of the eight children of a poor basket-maker in the East End of London and had only received an elementary school education. He left school at the age of 11 and worked for many years as a basket maker, teaching himself Italian and other languages during his mealtimes or, before or after his long working day, which began at 6 a.m.

and lasted until 8 o'clock at night. He became well known as an Italian scholar but when he was informed of his election to the Chair of Italian at Cambridge he was terrified at the prospect and all but declined the offer. He looked the part and might well have been an Italian scholar who had suspended his lectures for a time in order to fight under Garibaldi, yet he was as English as anyone could be. A most affable and warm-hearted man, the charming simplicity of his character is reflected in his autobiography, which he appropriately called *A Basketful of Memories*.]

Saturday 4 March
At 8 p.m. went with the rest of the Roosters and guests to a debate at Newnham "That life on a desert island offers more opportunities for self-expression than life at Cambridge". The motion lost by 41 to 54.

Wednesday 19 April
Spring is more forward in Cambridge than at home but on the whole this is the latest spring we have had for years, at least since I returned to England. No bluebells or cherry blossom to bring back from home this year.

Monday 22 May
I was very sorry to read in this morning's paper of the sinking of my old ship the *Egypt* by collision off Ushant with considerable loss of life. In addition to that it is sad to lose the ship in which I lived so long and liked so much.

[FB is referring to his World War I service aboard the hospital ship *Egypt*, 1915-1919.]

Wednesday 24 May
The weather is very hot. "Tripping" again, this time Modern Italian, after which I walked out feeling like a released man.

Sunday 4 June
At 2.30 p.m. I attended the Varsity sermon by the Bishop of St Albans, who deprecated trying to make "an African Anglican, a Chinese Congregationalist, a Mongolian Methodist, a Basuto Baptist, or a South Seas 7th Day Adventist . . ."

[The Right Revd Michael Furse, KCMG, DD (Dublin), an Oxford man, was Archdeacon of Johannesburg, then Bishop of Pretoria, before he was translated to St Albans in 1920.]

Saturday 10 June
Last day of the May Races. The first three boats finished up with no change, this has not happened since 1903. (1. Jesus, 2. First Trinity, 3. Pembroke). Our second boat is still 7th on the river. There was the usual bonfire on the Close. Shenton was whirling round and round with burning bottle cases of straw in each hand. Finch did him a good turn by going up and knocking him over. Plenty of the same burning torches snatched from the fire and flourished everywhere. Playford was carried round in an old basket.

Sunday 11 June
Served at 8 a.m. Mass as Father Westcott, the Dean, was away and attended Mattins at 10.15 a.m. Went to the Union then wrote some letters. Wyld came to Lunch. At 3.45 p.m. had tea with the Roberts' and at 4.45 p. went with them in their car via Great Shelford, Sawston, Little Chesterford, Saffron Walden and Howlett End to Thaxted church for 6.30 Evensong. The Vicar (Conrad Noel) wearing a cassock and surplice and a quaint hood, sat in a plain household elbow chair in the gangway of the nave, facing east with a stool beside him for the books. The first part of the service was conducted by the curate who, with nothing over his cassock, sat in the nave chairs with the back row of the singers. After the 'Gloria Patri' Conrad turned round and gave out notices. All then sat while two of the Psalms for the 10th evening were said. A layman in secular dress read the first lesson from the lectern. Magnificat was beautifully sung to plainsong, with women in descant on the even verses. (No old office hymn before, as might be expected, but 'Holy, holy, holy'). The curate then read the second lesson from the lectern, dressed as before. The 'Nunc dimittis' was sung as Magnificat, but the fourth verse was rendered, 'To be a light to lighten the nation'. Conrad sang the rest of the office un-accompanied. The collection took place during the hymn after the third collect, then the curate from the gangway right among the people near the west end said prayers and intercessions, e.g. for the famine stricken, the unemployed, the departed, and the general Thanksgiving. The curate read the sermon after another hymn, Conrad having moved to a chair in the nave, without surplice at the end of the sermon. A prayer from the pulpit was followed by a fourth hymn. People meanwhile had come in and out as they wished, and servers in scarlet cassocks and sleeveless rochets had lit all the candles in the Sacrament chapel. There was no Grace or Blessing and about half the congregation (or more) now left. The rest moved into the chapel for Devotions, which consisted of the Benediction without monstrance or Blessing, and were led entirely by a woman in the front room, the vicar and curate being seated among the congregation. A thurifer was, meanwhile per-fuming the chancel and east chapels. There was no Litany, but intercessions and prayers. Everything was beautifully sung with descants in places. 'Adoremus in Aeternum' and Psalm 117 were in Latin, but the rest was in

English. During this a server went inside the altar rails, pulled back the curtains (no doors behind) of the tabernacle, revealing the Host in a metal and glass pyx, and lit five small candles before it, while the thurifer knelt outside the rails, censing. Afterwards, the curtains were replaced and the candles extinguished by the server, we went out, while the organist played a voluntary. Spoke a little while with the Vicar. There were a few things I did not like such as psalms not sung, no old office hymn, Latin in a parish church and Italian pronunciation of Latin. But it was a wonderful service. Obviously nothing was done for show and the people really liked it. There was no fuss, all so very smooth and nice. I noted the absence of sacerdotalism; the clergy and laity (men and women) seemed all on a level, the clergy retaining their proper part of leading and instructing the people. It was not continental, not insular, but apparently in the best pre-reformation style. One would have thought it impossible for modern English people to behave as this congregation did, all of whom were obviously villagers, nearly all ordinary working class. A wonderful church and service, which all ordinands ought to visit to see what an English church congregation is capable of. Afterward we went to the Swan for a drink and the landlord proved to be an old chorister of Father Roberts of years ago at St Benet's, Kentish Town. We returned via Newport and Audley End (beautiful view of the Essex Granta spanned by bridges!) The Granta is a tiny but pleasant stream over at Newport, and borders the road for some distance. Home via Ickleton, Duxford, Whittlesford, Little and Great Shelford and Trumpington, reaching Cambridge about 9.15 p.m. In to supper.

Wednesday 14 June
Wyld went to see the Tripos results (I dare not go myself) and came back with the news that I had a Second. Everything went black. Went to see Elliott who sympathised and said he had expected a First. The Dean was also surprised and told me to take no notice of the result. He had discussed my future with Manning and they tried to persuade me to become ordained.

> [Bernard Manning, who was less than a year older than FB, came from Caister, a little market town in Lincolnshire, and was the son of a Congregational minister there. He came up to Jesus with a scholarship in history, took a very good degree and had been appointed Bursar of the College in 1920. He was a staunch Nonconformist and a Liberal in politics yet he and FB became close friends. FB's memoir of Manning, following his (Bernard's) death, is said by some to be his best book. A semi-invalid, Bernard was very well known and popular among the undergraduates, few of whom had any knowledge of his disability.]

~ 1922 ~

Saturday 17 June
Went to the Senate House to hear the final Tripos lists read and again later to see the Degree Congregation but was turned out as I was wearing a blazer.

Thursday 22 June
Packing most of the day, a big and tiring job. At noon went to see the Midsummer Fair opened by the Mayor in scarlet robe and cocked hat and the Town Clerk in his gown and wig. The Mayor raised his hand at which whistles blew and the organs played. The Mayor and Alderman then scattered new halfpennies among the crowd.

Friday 23 June
Left for Hertford by cycle with Warren, through Trumpington and Fowlmere and up stiff hills to Heydon, which is a delightful village with magnificent views, especially to the north. After bread and cheese and beer at the William IV we went on to Great Chishall, where the church stands on a promontory among rolling hills covered with corn, it was delightful with a mist of rain fine in the distance over the copses on the heights.

Sunday 2 July
South Mymms. Thunder at 11 a.m. I attended Mass at St Giles and when the Vicar began talking about the royal visit to the hill country (of Judaea) people thought he was referring to our own royal visit at North Mymms Park, where the Princess Mary and Viscount Lascelles [King George V's daughter and son-in-law] are spending the weekend as the guests of Mr and Mrs Walter Burns. It turned out that he referred to the visitations of the Virgin, on which he then preached. (He told me beforehand that he was going to preach on the royal visit and hoped my democratic susceptibilities would not be upset!) I was afraid at first that he would compare Mr Walter Burns to Zacharias. KD has her hair up and looks very fine. Grandmother died this morning, aged 84 last birthday.

Monday 7 August
Cambridge. P. Gardner-Smith was elected Dean of the College.

> [Percival Gardner-Smith had come to the College as an undergraduate in a horse drawn cab in 1906. He took a double First in Theology and of his supervisors it was Professor W. R. Inge, later known as the Gloomy Dean of St Paul's, who most influenced his thought. He was ordained from Ridley Hall and became a successful parish priest until he was asked to become Dean of the College after Alexander Nairne's appointment as Regius Professor of Divinity. At that time the Deanship was not an enviable office, for some of the Fellows were unsympathetic – wishing to

abolish it as a step towards the secularisation of the College. PGS, as he was known, remained during practically the whole of the next three Masterships. He was celebrated throughout the University and beyond it as a teacher of Theology, a witty and stimulating lecturer, and a preacher of the first order.]

Monday 21 August
Arrived at Brighton where I am to tutor C. M. H. Harmsworth (nicknamed Joe after his godfather, Joseph Chamberlain) in History for Little-go. I met Lady Harmsworth and her mother at 2 Fourth Avenue, Hove, who are both very nice and I was invited to tea. Joe's father, Sir Hildebrand, brother of Lord Northcliffe, the first Lord Rothermere, is a great humourist. He prefers to sit about in his shirtsleeves, eats jam with a spoon, and drinks his tea from the slop basin to annoy his mother-in-law.

Sunday 27 August
Attended High Mass (Patronal Festival) at St Bartholomew's with Gounod's 'Messe Solemnalla' very finely rendered. To my surprise Father John How was sitting next to me. In the afternoon I went to Ditchling by bus and on the way back a very nice girl sat next to me whose dog wanted to come on my knees, so we could not help talking.

[John How, formerly Precentor of Trinity College, was a member of the Oratory of the Good Shepherd and was at that time presiding over the Cambridge members of the Oratory House, afterwards St Francis' House, and now part of Lucy Cavendish College in Lady Margaret Road. He left Cambridge in 1923 for parish work and later became Bishop of Glasgow. When they left the church How asked FB where he was going to "keep" next term, and finally managed to drag out of him the confession that the only thing he wanted to do was to stay at Cambridge, and that he would almost as soon be dead as doing anything else. Thereupon How invited FB to live at Oratory House and said that he would be able to earn a living by coaching and supervision work from the colleges. Although FB found it difficult to believe, starvation at Cambridge seemed bliss in comparison with affluence anywhere else and he accepted the invitation, which seemed to have dropped from the clouds.]

Tuesday 29 August
The usual coaching from 9.30 to noon. When walking along the front, to my delight I met the girl on the bus (Muriel) again, her little cousin Joan, and the useful dog. Later met her, her aunt and Joan and we sat on the West Pier talking and listening to the band.

~ 1922 ~

Saturday 9 September
Tuition 9 a.m. – 12 noon and 3 – 4 p.m. At 6.30 p.m. met Muriel (sola) and sat on the front, then walked towards Portslade and sat in a shelter till we discovered it was 9.30 p.m. and had to hurry back.

Monday 18 September
A most beautiful day and the usual tutoring. Muriel leaves Brighton today. Addio! Finished reading W. O. C. Morris's *Napoleon*. A keen appreciation of the greatest stress is on the military side.

Thursday 5 October
Arrived at Cambridge and went to the Oratory House ("the House") to take up residence. Unpacked and went to Pembroke to see Joe Harmsworth whom I am to tutor in Spanish for four hours a week.

Thursday 12 October
Mr Abbot came to see me about pupils in French and Latin and Professor Okey has arranged for me to see Mr Keynes at King's College about the translation from the Italian of a book by Nitti called *The Decadence of Europe*. At 8.30 p.m. I was elected President of the Roosters. Attended the debate "That beauty is better than brains".

> [John Maynard Keynes (1883-1946), created first Baron, the Cambridge born economist whose *Economic Consequences of the Peace* published in 1919 had made a great stir, was educated at Eton and King's College Cambridge. He pioneered the theory of full employment, became chairman of the Liberal periodical *Nation* in 1923 and strongly attacked Churchill's restoration of the gold standard in 1925. His two great works, *A Treatise on Money* (1930) and the revolutionary *General Theory of Employment, Interest and Money* (1936) were inspired by the unemployment crisis. He was also the founder of the Cambridge Arts Theatre in 1936.]
>
> Francisco Nitti, a former Prime Minister of Italy, had written a powerful book, mainly devoted to a severe criticism of the Peace Treaties of 1919. Recognising a kindred spirit in John Maynard Keynes, he sent him a copy of his book and asked if he could find an English translator for it.

Wednesday 18 October
At *"the House"*. We were called in solemn yet jubilant tones, "7 o'clock and four rats in the bathroom trap".

~ 1922 ~

Tuesday 24 October
Working hard at the Nitti translation – it contains nearly 100,000 words and I post each chapter as I finish it. The proofs of early chapters are arriving at the same time, which means that I often work until 2 a.m.

Sunday 5 November
Attended Mattins in College Chapel with a sermon by the new Dean on Sunday observance and – much needed – on chapel attendance. Walked through the town with Dr Nairne who was going out to lunch (which he said, he hated). He was resplendent in cassock, scarlet gown and DD cap but stopped to ask me in agonised tones, "Have I got a clean collar on?" He thinks it is as well that he applied for the Regius Professorship of Divinity at Cambridge and kept his rooms in College, rather than living all the time as a Canon of Windsor, as his mother would then have made him have lunch every day instead of his usual stale bun, which he takes when he feels like it.

Thursday 16 November
Went to the Union to see the General Election results. Many Labour gains.

Sunday 3 December
11 a.m. meeting with Professor Okey to read translation. Warren came to lunch and we went to Evensong at King's (Brahms' 'All Flesh'.) After Hall I was re-elected President of the Roosters with a combined bombardment of the Chair with the usual red herrings and elected to "The Order of the Red Herring".

Friday 22 December
South Mymms. Tea at Mrs Blake's. I was surprised to hear that I am engaged, at least, so they tell me! The lady herself told them, though I was not aware of it in the least. In fact the person in question "can wait till the blue moon".

Tuesday 26 December
Danced chiefly with KD at the Social. She seems more beautiful than ever now that she has grown up.

[No further entries for December]

~ 1923 ~

Monday 1 January
Barnet. Worked at Old Provençal. Cycled to Mymms via North Mymms. The Colne is full of water even above the swallow holes under the brick bridge in the park where its bed is always grass grown. Had supper at the Clarke's but ran off at 7.25 to meet KD in the churchyard and walked as far as Warrengate with her. Back by 10 p.m. or just after. Moonlight, white frost, but at thaw point.

Monday 8 January
My translation of *The Decadence of Europe* was published by Fisher Unwin today.

Wednesday 10 January
Caught the 11.36 a.m. train from New Barnet and arrived in Cambridge at 1.50 p.m. Went straight to the Oratory House where my new quarters (no. 1) are newly decorated. Busy getting straight.

Monday 18 January
Cambridge full term begins. Morning - Chaucer and in the afternoon sculled to Ditton and back.

Friday 19 January
Attended the STC High Mass at St Michael's Church. Had tea with Professor Okey at Caius College.

Saturday 20 January
At 8.15 p.m. I went to the Rooster Debate on the motion "That the playing of musical instruments, church bells and gramophones, should be prohibited within a radius of two and a half miles of Great St Mary's".

Sunday 21 January
I went to the Guildhall at 8.15 to hear G. K. Chesterton but was unable to get in owing to the huge crowd.

> [G. K. Chesterton (1874–1936), the English critic, novelist and poet who achieved wide popular appeal with his creation of the amiable detective-priest, Father Brown, in 1911.]

~ 1923 ~

Thursday 25 January
After Hall Warren and Marinari came in and we worked "gregariously". Nitti sent me an autographed copy of *La Decadence dell Europa* and a large autographed photograph of himself with a complimentary inscription.

Saturday 27 January
After dinner attended the Roosters debate on the motion "Training in domestic arts should form a compulsory part of male education".

Thursday 1 February
On coming out of the House Chapel early this morning, I noticed yellow crocuses in bloom for the first time. Later noticed a large number along the south bank of Trinity Avenue, the mild weather has brought them out suddenly.

Saturday 3 February
Met K in Town [London] at 2 p.m. and we went to the opera *The Immortal Hour* at the Regent Theatre.

Saturday 17 February
Went to the Lents tea on the towpath with the Dean and Mrs Gardner-Smith. We finished Head easily.

Saturday 3 March
Saw the Cambridge Amateur Dramatic Society's production of *The Mikado*. Robey was a scream as Pooh-Bah.

> [Edward Robey, who became a well-known barrister and a Metropolitan Magistrate, was the son of Sir George Robey, the comedian who claimed to be a member of Jesus College, but was not.]

Wednesday 7 March
The Roosters Bicentenary – we celebrated 184 years in advance "to save posterity the trouble". Very good dresses, impersonations and speeches.

Saturday 17 March
Went to Mymms, then by bus to St Albans with K. Had tea at the Dolphin, then over the river through Verulam Woods and into the fields beyond. Later we saw *Four Horsemen of the Apocalypse* at the Cathedral Picture House.

Tuesday 27 March
Cycled to Mymms. K volunteered the information that she liked me but is filled with doubts about the future and admitted that she is afraid of me.

Tried to remove her fears and said we must go slowly. Had a bad night but "Faint heart never . . ."

Wednesday 28 March
Felt "down". Precented at Tenebrae at 7.30, then went for a walk with K who was looking charming with her hat in her hand. I felt calmer.

Saturday 31 March
Attended 8 a.m. Mass. (Violet of Easter Eve only). Went with K, who was looking very beautiful, to the Strand Theatre, and saw the play *Treasure Island*. Returned for Blessing of New Fire and Paschal candle and Evensong. Went to Confession.

Wednesday 4 April
Met K in the churchyard at 7.10 a.m. We walked to Potters Bar Station and caught the 7.49 a.m. train to Cambridge. Looked round the colleges, finishing at Jesus. Had lunch at Matthew's then canoed along the Backs. Arrived back to Mymms at 10.15 p.m. and cycled home after a tiring but *most* enjoyable day.

Thursday 5 April
Walked through the woods with J. S. Heber. Anemones everywhere, the larches a glorious green, and the cherries in their first blossom. Fed at the Waggon and Horses.

> [This was the first Trust House in England. It stood at the top of Ridge Hill and commanded an immense view to St Albans and beyond to Bedfordshire to the North and to Barnet and London to the south. It was demolished when the top of Ridge Hill was levelled for the construction of the M25 motorway in the mid-1980s.]

Saturday 7 April
Travelled to Wales to tutor G. Davies. He met me at Carmarthen, and drove me to his house – Alltypferin – 9 miles away in delightful surroundings. Remnants of a house party were still in progress but most left in the evening.

Sunday 8 April
I had a delightful walk to Alltypferin Church, down the wooded ravine and over the river.

Friday 13 April
Two hours work in the morning then caught the train to Cardiff where I stayed the night with Uncle George who is now living there.

~ 1923 ~

Friday 11 May
Cambridge. Coaching. After lunch Jerry Young took me in his car to Newmarket, Ashley, Cheveley, Stetchworth and Dullingham. We did 55 miles an hour in places!

Thursday 24 May
Joe Harmsworth tells me strange things about Colville – that he fell in love with a Swedish girl in France and she was with him without revealing to him for two months that she was married. She now compels him to go up to London every other day to see her and take her about and this is to continue until she returns to Sweden. Hence his apparent neglect of work. I feel sorry for him.

Saturday 26 May
Had tea at Miss Lattimer's with Creswick, an Old Elizabethan at Trinity.

> [H. R. "Dick" Creswick had the unusual distinction of being University Librarian of both Oxford and Cambridge at different times. He was made a Professorial Fellow of Jesus College in 1949 and died in 1988.]

Wednesday 30 May
A warm, summer like day such as we have not had for weeks in this dreadful May.

Wednesday 6 June
Saw Sir Arthur Quiller-Couch this morning. At the May Races, our second boat bumped LMBCI and became 6th on the river.

> [Sir Arthur Quiller Couch (1863–1944), was educated at Clifton College and Trinity College, Oxford, where he was a lecturer in classics from 1886–87. After some years of literary work in London and in Cornwall, where he lived from 1891 and writing many best-selling novels under his pseudonym of Q, he became Professor of English Literature at Cambridge in 1912 and was a Fellow of Jesus College. He was to become one of FB's closest friends.]

Saturday 9 June
Our first boat was bumped again, this time by 1st Trinity, so we finished third. Pembroke are Head for the first time in history.

Sunday 10 June
Went to College Mattins at 10.30 a.m. and Dean Inge of St Paul's delivered a sermon. There was no sung Mass as attendance has been poor recently.

~ 1923 ~

Thursday 14 June
Mother came to visit me in Cambridge. I took her round the Varsity Library etc. and to lunch at the Union. Joe and G. Clark got 3rds and Colville a 2nd in the English Principal exam.

Tuesday 19 June
Went to the Senate House to see degrees given and dropped confetti on to the Jesus men as they came out into Senate House passage.

Sunday 24 June
A lovely hot day so went to sung Mass at St Edward's in flannels and summer blazer.

Monday 2 July
Arrived home and went down to Mymms with considerable mental anxiety as I had decidedly cooled off with K and didn't know how to tell her. To my relief she was before me with a similar confession.

Tuesday 3 July
"Spring cleaning" my books and then tea at Gaffer's, who retired last week. "Listened in" at their wireless telephone to a very enjoyable lecture on Byrd with songs and instrumental pieces. It was perfectly clear. Everyone seems to be adopting it now, but it was my first experience of it.

Wednesday 4 July
At 10.15 p.m. I walked back from Mymms via Wash Farm, the first field lying in haycocks except one in swathes, the third still uncut. It was delightful in the afterglow.

Saturday 7 July
Met K. I go down like a ninepin before her beauty. It is strange how my feelings change. Before I dreaded meeting her, yet today I longed for 4 o'clock and felt so glad when I saw her. Possibly Mrs D's opposition to me and my sympathy for K help to spur me on, coupled with her beauty. Why should Mrs D. be so hostile? We agreed to keep in touch.

Saturday 21 July
Cambridge. Robey, Hilliard, Henwood and myself all dressed in tourist style, carrying attaché cases, guide books etc. and with some approach to an American accent went to the Senate House and soon succeeded in ensnaring one of the local guides. We told him we particularly wanted to see Jesus College, of which we had heard so much at Yale, and he took us there. He showed us round the Hall, Chapel, and the courts and took us to the close,

where a cricket match was going on. James Hoppett, the head porter, was watching it and he recognised us but did not give us away. I said, "Say guide, I guess that's the Master" at which the guide got anxious though Hoppett looked pleased. We then told the guide we had been invited to tea at the College and paid him off.

Sunday 22 July
On my way to breakfast with the Dean of St Catharine's the Rev H. J. Chaytor, an authority on Old Provencal, I ran full tilt into the guide; he recognised me and looked sheepish, but neither of us spoke. At 9.30 p.m. Battersby and I introduced a milk can into Barratt's bed.

Thursday 26 July
Went to Dr Nairne's 'At Home' in the Fellows' Garden; after tea Pars and I played Warren and Slater at bowls and beat them.

> [L. A. Pars had become a Fellow of the College as soon as he graduated in 1918. He was a brilliant mathematician, a pianist, and a devotee of the theatre. He combined these qualities with athletic pursuits, especially tennis and mountain climbing. He out lived FB by many years, dying shortly after having to leave his College rooms in 1985 at the age of 89.]

Friday 10 August
Excitement! Speed's map of Cambridge has arrived. Warren started colouring it forthwith.

Saturday 11 August
Father Wynn introduced me to Mr Comber, Director of Studies in Modern Languages and a Fellow of Pembroke College.

> [FB counted Henry Gordon Comber as one of his chief benefactors and never forgot his first view of Comber's rooms at Pembroke. The outer room had a highly polished floor and furniture, and its walls were lined with books, particularly Spanish classics. This was not remarkable in a don's room, but what was striking was the numerous vases of cut flowers on the tables, the row of miniature trees growing in little wooden tubs on the window ledges, and the shoal of goldfish swimming in an enamelled bath on a chair just inside the door. In the inner room there were more books and flowers, rows and rows of framed photographs of men, a large cage full of whistling canaries, another cage full of lovebirds, and a tall cabinet packed with curios mostly from South America, where Comber had been born. As Father Wynn and FB entered Comber was standing at the far end of the room, watering another row of miniature trees from a

long-necked watering can. He was a big stout man, weighing about eighteen stone, with black, beady eyes, a big black moustache, and a completely bald head except for some black hair at the back, below the crown. FB was nervous and stammered when he was introduced to him, but his kindly expression and manner soon put him at his ease. Edward Wynn left as soon as he had introduced FB, who then spent the next hour and a quarter alone with the 'Old Man' as he was invariably called at Pembroke. The result of the interview was that from that autumn until his death twelve years later, FB was his assistant, taking classes several times a week in his outer room and occasionally in the college library.]

Monday 13 August
South Mymms. The harvest is in full swing with oats standing in shocks and the wheat a golden bronze in the fields leading to the gate of the wood. Went to the Vicarage and received conflicting advice on the matter of K.

24 August to 22 September

[FB was again in Hove tutoring Joe Harmsworth and his brother Anthony. Sir Hildebrand celebrated Joe's success in the English Principal by sending him and FB to order a new suit each at his expense. He also said FB could go from his lodgings to the Harmsworth home in Fourth Avenue to do his own work whenever he liked. They went to several Gilbert and Sullivan operas in Brighton and to *The Beggars' Opera* twice.]

Monday 1 October
Took Mother to the Blakes' for a holiday and rest. I was back home by 5 p.m. to commence my duties as housekeeper.

Saturday 6 October
Attended the 350th Anniversary Commemoration of the foundation of Queen Elizabeth School. There was a church service, a reading of the Charter in the grounds, a fair in the playground and three performances of tableaux, culminating with dancing and 'Auld Lang Syne' round the mulberry tree at 11 p.m.

Monday 8 October
Back to Cambridge and to Pembroke College to discuss lectures with Comber. After tea with Warren went to see Joe Needham in his laboratory.

[Joseph Needham, a layman member of OGS living at the Oratory House, soon began to make his mark in the world of science. A warm-hearted man of unusual character, an original thinker and an omnivorous reader, he was elected a Fellow of Caius College in 1924. He later became a Doctor of Science, University Reader in Biochemistry, a Fellow of the Royal Society, a prolific writer and (*inter alia*) an authority on Chinese subjects. He was elected to the Mastership of his college in 1965.]

Tuesday 16 October
I am to conduct lectures and classes at Pembroke every day this term and have other pupils for twenty hours a week.

Wednesday 24 October
Cycled to Madingley. The land is beautiful with autumn tints and the setting sun throwing dark shadows on the new clods of earth in the ploughed fields.

Thursday 1 November
Attended the Old Elizabethans' Annual Dinner at the Holborn Restaurant. I was Vice-Chairman and proposed the health of Mr F. A. Milne, Chairman of Governors. He made very complimentary remarks about me in his speech, as did Mr Lattimer. AKW and I sang from *The Beggars' Opera* all the way back, and also through the streets of Barnet. I was in bed by 1 a.m. but did not sleep till 4 a.m.

Friday 6 November
Up at 6.30 a.m. and in Cambridge by 9.30 and got to Pembroke at 10.

Saturday 17 November
After dinner went to Newnham where we met the bus full of Roosters and entered for the debate "That it is better to be amiable than sincere" on which I spoke from an unusual position.

Thursday 22 November
At noon went to see Mr Whibley who was very kind – he asked me if I intended to stay at Cambridge. I said there was nothing I should like so much but some people advised me to think of the future. He said that as I liked the work and was happy, he advised me to stay by all means. There was no more fear of the workhouse here than elsewhere and that Dr Nairne, whose opinion was the same, was a practical man and not a mere mystic, and that one thing leads to another, etc.

[Charles Whibley encouraged FB in a practical way by giving him small paid jobs such as reading the proofs of his edition of the Posthumous Collected Essays of his Tory hero, W. P. Kerr, whom he praised for refusing to have electric light in his rooms at Oxford. A die-hard Tory, Whibley asserted once that we must get rid of "the foul principle of democracy" and hark back to the golden days before the Reform Bill of 1830. His stout, thickset figure, fresh complexion, rather long thin hair, smallish eyes and high stiff collar are admirably captured in Gerald Kelly's superb portrait at Jesus College. Whibley was distinguished as a literary critic, editor, anthologist, political writer, translator, wit, conversationalist and diner-out. As his obituarist put it in the *Times* when he died in 1930, "he had a real hatred of Whiggery and indeed of liberalism in any form".]

Friday 23 November
Cycled to Ditton and back with the Jesus boats and with two of the trial VIII's, which had a breast race up Long Reach.

Sunday 2 December
The Roosters debated Tariff Reform with a settlement of Europe as a cure for unemployment, and also "That modern dancing is unworthy of civilised man". I proposed the formation of a new office, limited to first-year men, the holder to be addressed as the "Pious Almoner and Philanthropist".

Friday 21 December
Caught the 10 a.m. train for home in snow which settled thickly. Went to Mymms about 7 p.m. and met Katharine and Monica (Allen Hay's daughters) who pelted me with snowballs and screamed with laughter when I slipped down. The village looked just like a Christmas card, deep in snow, especially when a white moon rose over it. Found them all at home sitting up listening to the *Messiah* on the wireless.

Saturday 29 December
Sang in the chorus of *The Three Roses*, the Nativity play in the Parish Hall. A very good performance but my eyes were chiefly on K although she looks more beautiful off the stage than on. She needs no paint or dressing up. Could not help thinking of the many times when that head, those lips . . . ! I would have spoken to her after but the Dragon [Mrs D], now with bobbed hair, was waiting on guard and prevented me from doing so.

Monday 31 December
This has been a year of unrest abroad and unemployment in England. It has been a very bad summer except for the heat wave and we have had an early severe winter so far. Personally though, a fruitful year, for which *Deo gratias*.

~ 1924 ~

A newspaper cutting stuck inside the cover of this diary recalls the words of the Duke of Wellington who said, "third-class facilities are a premium to the lower orders to go wandering aimlessly about the country".

The printed matter at the beginning of the Boots Home Diaries which FB used is full of useful information, for example the ABC of Health

THE ABC OF HEALTH

As soon as you are up, shake blanket and sheet,
Better be without shoes than sit with damp feet.
Children if healthy are active, not still,
Damp beds and damp clothes will both make you ill.
Eat slowly, and always chew your food well,
Freshen the air in the house where you dwell.
Garments must never be worn too tight,
Homes should be cheerful, and airy and light.
If you wish to keep well, as you do I've no doubt,
Just ope' all the windows before you go out.
Keep all the dark corners most carefully clean,
Let dust on the furniture never be seen.
Much illness is caused by the lack of fresh air,
Now to ventilate properly must be your care.
Old rubbish and rags must be burnt and not kept,
People should see that their floors are well swept.
Quick movements in children are healthy and right,
Remember the young cannot thrive without light.
See that the cistern is clean to the brim,
Take care that your dress in the morning is trim.
Use your nose to find out if there be a bad drain,
Very sad are the fevers that come in its train.
Walk as much as you can without over-fatigue,
Xerxes could walk full many a league.
Your health is your wealth, which your wisdom must keep,
Zeal will help a good cause and the good you will reap.

Published by the Ladies Sanitary Association

Tuesday 8 January
Mother and I went to see Loughton's opera *Bethlehem* at the Regent theatre. It was a wonderful performance and a beautiful opera. Thick snow fell as we returned.

Wednesday 9 January
The snow is deep. At 2.30 p.m. went to the matinee of *Bethlehem* (solus in the gallery).

Friday 15 January
Cambridge. Father Wilfred Knox is Warden at the Oratory House this term and Malcolm Muggeridge has joined us (from Selwyn).

> [Wilfred Knox came of a very able family, being the son of E. A. Knox, Bp. of Manchester, and a brother of Ronald Knox and of E. V. Knox, the editor of *Punch*, and he possessed his full share of the family brilliance. He was not a handsome man, and his complete indifference to his outward appearance did not help to make him look any more so. Slim, of average height, he had a large head, and hair that curled slightly. He was shy with strangers; and his high-pitched voice, which rattled away like a machine-gun, and his extremely nervous laugh accompanied by a hysterical intake of breath, were the reverse of attractive. He generally wore a pair of stained grey flannel trousers, very baggy at the knees because they were never pressed, a grey woollen pullover, and a black jacket with the usual clerical collar and stock. Out of doors he wore a somewhat greasy and battered black trilby hat, and if the weather was wet, a cheap raincoat. All his clothing was cheap, as it was apparently part of his rule of life not to spend an unnecessary penny on clothes. He used to go into outfitters' shops asking for "the sort of shirt a workman wears". He was sometimes accused of robbing the scarecrow in the Oratory House garden and the jest may have had some justification. FB's most important office at the House was as Wilfred's vicar choral. The title was never formally conferred on him, but he carried out the duties of the office for years, even after he had left the House, for musically Wilfred Knox was completely tone-deaf.
>
> Malcolm Muggeridge (1903–90) was born in London and became a journalist and broadcaster. He was the Moscow correspondent of the *Manchester Guardian* from 1930–33, assistant editor of the *Calcutta Statesman* (1934–35) and a member of the editorial staff of the London *Evening Standard*. He served in the Intelligence Corps during World War II and received the Legion of Honour and the Croix de Guerre with Palm. After the war he became a household name as a television reporter, interviewer and sage. He was a regular contributor to *Panorama* (1953–60), had his own series *Appointment with . . .* (1960–61), and *Let Me Speak*

~ 1924 ~

(1964–65), in which he quizzed the great figures of the day and challenged minorities to defend their beliefs. He was usually controversial but greatly respected. His books include *The Earnest Atheist* (1936), *Tread Softly for You Tread on My Jokes* (1966) and *Chronicle of Wasted Time* (1982). In 1982 he became a Roman Catholic.]

Friday 8 February
I am staying with the Dean and Mrs Gardner-Smith at 3 Chesterton Lane, after ten days in the Priory Nursing Home with influenza.

Saturday 16 February
Met Marie at Walnut Tree Avenue and we saw the last race (Lent Bumps) in which Jesus finished Head.

Saturday 23 February
Took Marie to the theatre where we saw *The Green Goddess* – and went for a short walk afterwards.

> [Marie was FB's new girlfriend. They met nearly every day, the usual place being Victoria Bridge, and went for walks, cycle rides, to the theatre and dancing. At the Leap Year dance at the Liberal Club she wore a "magnificent orange frock".]

Wednesday 19 March
Joe and I left for France to stay a month in Boulogne.

Friday 21 March
Bought a Rooster in bronze.

> [This was the first of what was to become the famous Britannic Cockerel collection, though he did not buy another one all his life. FB's friends, thinking that he was collecting cockerels, presented them to him.]

Friday 28 March
Paris. We are staying at the Hotel Monte Carlo. In the afternoon we visited Napoleon's tomb at Les Invalides and explored Notre Dame. In the evening we went to the Folies Bergère, a good and very artistic performance, though no doubt Queen Victoria would not have approved of some of it.

Sunday 30 March
Attended High Mass at Notre Dame. There was no sermon and hardly any kneeling, not even during the Consecration. We returned to Boulogne.

~ 1924 ~

Monday 14 April
Caught the boat for Dover and arrived at Victoria at about 3.30 p.m.

Tuesday 17 June
South Mymms. I was cantor at the Solemn Requiem and funeral of Mrs Hay, senior. Lunched at the Vicarage then went to the Regent Theatre at Kings Cross and saw *Romeo and Juliet* with John Gielgud and Gwen Françon-Davies in the leads.

Wednesday 18 June
I was best man at Vincent Robinson's wedding at St Giles church

Sunday 22 June
Cambridge. At 6.30 p.m. (rather than 7.30 due to a misunderstanding) cycled with Marie along the towpath to have supper at Clayhithe. On the way back we dismounted a while into the tall wild flowers next to the ditch. She was still annoyed with me, but came round.

Thursday 26 June
Sikes came to lunch.

> [J. B. Sikes was handicapped from birth. He could not lift a cup to his lips and had to type every letter he sent. He must have been one of the first spastics to enter the University, although the term was not in use at that time. The gallant, cheerful and uncomplaining fight, which he put up against all his disabilities, won him the admiration and affection of everyone who knew him. He gave promise of becoming an outstanding medieval historian, but his mind gave way some years later and he came to a tragic end.]

Saturday 28 June
Marie saw me off for home at 6.20 p.m.

Tuesday 1 July
Travelled to France and went via Boulogne to Poitiers where I joined some pilgrims at St Radegund's tomb.

> [St Radegund, the Patron Saint of Jesus College, was born in the sixth century. She became Queen of France but fled the Court to found an abbey at Poitiers, where she was said to have healed a sick nun. Her other attributes included saving oarsmen from shipwreck and helping people to pass examinations – so she was a tailor-made patron for the College. Plaques at the Cathedral recorded thanks to the Saint for favours received.

~ 1924 ~

A Jesus visitor, noticing that one was signed S. F., accused Steve Fairbairn of having placed it there but Steve replied that he had never had any trouble with examinations.]

Friday 4 July
Left Bordeaux and entered Spain. It is interesting to note that several small towns, e.g. Miranda, use the railway platform as a public promenade; the girls in the Post Office not only sell stamps but also stick them on; there are letter boxes on the tram cars and practically all women carry fans.

Sunday 10 August
I'm back in Brighton where I am coaching Joe for his next Cambridge examination and giving Lady Harmsworth lessons in Italian.

Monday 25 August
Lady Harmsworth received a wire from Stresa to say that her eldest son, Sonny, is ill there so she decided to go with Joe and myself at once to Italy via the Simplon-Orient Express.

Tuesday 26 August
When we arrived in Stresa I was introduced to Lord Rothermere who took us on a voyage in a motor boat, which was very enjoyable in the fresh breeze and sun.

Wednesday 3 September
I received a letter from Signor Nitti, who is now in Zurich as an exile from Fascism, asking me to translate his new book *La Tragedia dell'Europa*. I decided to go and see him.

Thursday 4 September
Arrived in Zurich about 7 p.m. and after dinner talked with Signor Nitti, his wife, two daughters, sons and their girl friends. His Excellency is a very interesting, amiable man with, I should say, a quick insight. He has a great liking for the English. I felt at ease with him at once. He was a chain-smoker and a non-smoker in alternate years. This was one of his non-smoking years.

Saturday 6 September
I arrived back late to Stresa. Joe tells me his brother has been worse. Joe and I ragged Attilio about Fascism in the dining room.

[When FB returned to England with the Harmsworths he took the manuscript (once more on the advice of Professor Okey) to the firm of J. M. Dent and Sons. The head and founder of the firm, the great Joseph

Mallaby Dent, himself interviewed FB, frowning at him down his white beard and making him feel very small. Like Fisher Unwin, he offered him a choice between a lump sum and a small royalty for his translation, and with his former experience in mind, he confidently chose the royalty. It was 27 September when the details of publication were settled; and as the book, like its predecessor, dealt with current international affairs, both Nitti and the publisher wanted it to appear as early as possible – by the middle of November if that could be done. Further, the book was estimated to run to 300 large pages, and FB therefore set to work at top speed. There was a difficulty about the title. A literal translation of the Italian would have been "The Tragedy of Europe", but that would have looked depressing and was also liable to be confused with the title of the previous book. FB therefore, with the *Solitudinen faciunt, pacem appellant* of Tacitus in mind suggested *They Make A Desert*, which was accepted by both Nitti and the publishers. After a great effort on the part of the printers and the translator, the book appeared on 12 November. As with *Decadence of Europe*, FB had reason to be pleased with the reviewers' remarks about the translation. On the other hand, in choosing a royalty rather than a lump sum he had backed the wrong horse a second time; for *They Make A Desert* dealt with the same subjects as *Decadence of Europe* and appeared too soon after it. It therefore sold badly and FB would have done much better by accepting a lump sum. His total payment was no more than £11. 7s 3d, which worked out to about nine pence a page for translating, proof-reading and indexing!]

Sunday 28 September
South Mymms. The Vicar was in form today. Leslie Powell, who appeared in the choir tonight, the first time for years and not since he moved to Barnet, was greeted with "Is it your birthday?" Also the Vicar asked everyone, "Have you read Signor Nitti's latest book? No, you must, but it's not out yet".

[Leslie Powell was the eldest of a large family of brothers, all of whom he kept in order just as he kept everybody in order at Chipping Barnet Parish church when be became Verger there later on. Members of that congregation used to say, "Our Rector is Leslie Powell's right-hand man".]

Wednesday 8 October
Cambridge. Interviewing pupils and correcting proofs today.

Wednesday 29 October
At the General Election there were large Conservative gains and the Liberal Party collapsed.

~ 1924 ~

Wednesday 12 November
Extract from Henwood's paper on Julius Caesar – "Olympus was the God of Sport"!

Friday 21 November
Went to the Registry at 11.30 a.m. to pay my MA fee of £3 to the Varsity and at 2 p.m. to the Senate House to be admitted MA, being presented by Pars who has succeeded Watt as Praelector. Dr Nairne was also present and our Dean, as Senior Proctor. Dined at High Table, sitting between Watt and Pars. At 8.30 p.m. read my paper on St Radegund to the College Theological and Essay Society in the Dean's rooms.

Saturday 22 November
The first Cambridge Old Elizabethans Dinner in Creswick's rooms, P, Great Court Trinity. There were six present and Mr Lattimer was in the chair.

Boxing Day, Friday 26 December
Barnet. Got up late and went to Mymms with Mrs Hay where I watched the two Bull girls leave the church after their double wedding. Spent the afternoon in the Vicarage study where the Vicar got on with his stamps – stamps everywhere, including the floor – and I worked at St Radegund.

Sunday 28 December
As I am President of the newly formed Mymms Labour Party I went to Flint Lodge for a discussion with Mr Hastings, who is Chairman.

Wednesday 31 December
Frank and I "listened in" to the New Year – Big Ben striking and the bells of St Martin's ringing.

~ 1925 ~

Friday 9 January
Attended a Labour Party Committee at Mymms. Afterwards bumped into K by the church and we talked for a while. Met her later under the Cypress tree in brilliant moonlight, the moon being right overhead. The meeting revived old feelings in us.

Saturday 10 January
Attended the institution of the new Rector of Barnet by the Bishop of St Albans. He was huge with his cope, mitre and crozier.

> [The Right Revd Michael Furse had been a Colonial bishop before being translated to St Albans. At his retirement party he deplored people who stayed in jobs until they dropped and he told the story of a village cleric who boasted to a farmer friend that he intended to die in harness. "Ah", said the farmer, "I had an old mare once wot died in 'arness, but I don't know as 'ow it did the 'arness much good!"]

Sunday 11 January
The fog was so thick there were no buses. I was godfather to Daphne Mary Blake, Phil and Mrs Cunnington being godmothers.

> [Phil was Miss Dorothy Philpot, a charming lady of ample proportions who taught at the village school, was also the devoted sacristan of the church and later its considerable benefactor. The Vicar used to say that she was worth her weight in gold and that was a considerable amount! Mrs Hilda Cunnington would have become FB's mother-in-law in 1959 had she not died at the age of 59 in 1949.]

Sunday 25 January
Cambridge. The chief subjects of discussion at dinner in Hall were (1) whether golf is worse than popery, Manning and I maintained that it was but the Dean was to the contrary; and (2) the inordinate length of today's Hulsean Lecture by Dr Bouquet. The Dean said Bouquet "ought to be hanged from the tower of Great St Mary's". Mr Watt said "damn him" and the Dean countered with "Amen".

> [Dr A. C. Bouquet, or DB, was lecturer in the History and Comparative Study of Religions and was known as 'the comparatively religious Dr Bouquet'.]

Friday 6 February
Took Marie to the pictures and to tea at Matthews, then for a walk. She takes up a new post in London tomorrow.

Friday 27 February
Read a paper to the Jesuits [Jesus College Historical Society] on the Journalists of Medieval France, i.e. the Troubadours.

~ 1925 ~

Monday 9 March
Sat on the roof of the Victoria Cinema to watch the Archery "Rag" in aid of Fruiting Campaign Funds.

> [Situated in Market Square, the Victoria Cinema was demolished in 1989 and replaced by a Marks & Spencer store.]

Easter Day, 12 April
Mymms. At Mattins before Sung Mass Mr White was reading the lesson and seemed to be going on forever. The Vicar tapped on the screen, etc. but White sailed on, taking no notice. He had just said "and the Lord said" when the Vicar rose and interrupted with "Here endeth the first lesson. We praise thee, O God".

Friday 15 May
Cambridge. Cycled to Histon, Impington and Milton to see the apple blossom, then through masses of buttercups to Baitsbite and back along the towpath.

Monday 8 June
My book *Saint Radegund* is published today by Bowes and Bowes. I had a dancing lesson, as every afternoon for the past two weeks.

Wednesday 10 June
Went to the matinee of *Beaux Stratagem* at the ADC Theatre, then to Ditton in the ramshackle Ford with Milner-White, George Tibbatts and Holm to see the May races from the Jesus Paddock.

> [Eric Milner-White and George Tibbatts were both clerical members of the Oratory. Milner-White became Dean of King's College, Cambridge. He left his fine sense of liturgical fitness clearly stamped on the services there when he became Dean of York twenty years later. George Tibbatts became Vicar of St Luke's, Cambridge.]

Thursday 11 June
I went to the Hawks Club Ball at the Guildhall with my Danish pupil and two Newnhamites.

> [FB had never been able to afford the luxury of going to a May Week Ball in his undergraduate days. He approached the evening with some trepidation, because in spite of having taken two weeks of dancing lessons beforehand, he imagined that all Newnhamites were expert dancers, and was convinced that so handsome and accomplished a man as the Dane must be the same. Therefore he was delighted to see Joe Harmsworth

already there, because he knew that, on account of his weight, he would do more sitting out than dancing. FB rapidly explained the situation and begged him to help him in keeping his party away from the dance floor for as long as possible. Joe rose to the occasion magnificently by keeping them all in fits of laughter with his stories, until at last one of the girls said, "Come on, we must dance". FB followed reluctantly, feeling like an ox going to be slaughtered but, to his astonishment and relief, the other three turned out to be such poor dancers that he felt embarrassed on their account rather than on his own. To add to his embarrassment his partner engaged in the trick of flinging first one shoulder and then the other up and down. That had been all the rage a year or two previously but was now taboo, as was obvious from the glances that everyone threw in their direction. FB attempts at restraining her proved fruitless and he was glad to avail himself of Joe Harmsworth's services as an entertainer as frequently as possible during the rest of the night.]

Wednesday 29 July
Nitti and his wife arrived to stay at the Lion Hotel for the Liberal Summer School.

[The famous 16th century Lion Hotel in Petty Cury was demolished in the early 1960s along with many other historic buildings in the street, to make way for the locally disliked concrete and glass monstrosity known as the Lion Yard Shopping Arcade.]

Friday 31 July
Went to the Guildhall to hear Nitti's speech. He and Keynes seemed to be the only live Liberals there. Guided Nitti and Signorina Nitti round the colleges.

Thursday 6 August
South Mymms. Met Marie at the Waggon and Horses and we walked in the woods together. Stayed the night with the Vicar and told him I would write my next book on St Giles. We started forthwith looking out dedications in Crockford, which we continued, a letter each, till 1 a.m., discovering 130.

St Radegund's Day, Thursday 13 August
Cambridge. Sung Mass (entirely from the Latin Prayer Book, plus the proper of St Radegund from my edition). Dr Nairne was present and delighted. Later sculled on the river.

Assumption of the BVM, Saturday 15 August
Cycled with Gardiner to Thaxted for the 3.30 p.m. sermon by Conrad Noel and the procession for Lady Day in Harvest, which was led by a group of

little girls carrying a statue of Our Lady. Four held ribbons and a lighted candle each and four others a small sheaf of corn. It was delightful, as also were Devotions afterwards before the monstrance at the High Altar. Gardiner was greatly impressed and moved.

Monday 17 August
Worked on *St Giles* in the Varsity library, then sculled.

Saturday 22 August
Mother and I went to stay in Dick Turpin's Cottage at Thaxted for a week, which was lent to me by a friend. A most enjoyable and inspiring stay, that turned out to be a new revelation to me of the possibilities of Anglo-Catholicism and its real meaning and value and of the uselessness of so much that passes as such.

Tuesday 8 September
Made my first visit to Oxford. The streets are wider than in Cambridge, but no red brick, no market square and no "Backs". Went to St Giles' Fair and to tea with the Cowley Fathers.

Sunday 13 September
South Mymms. The Vicar published three sets of banns this morning and announced that it was unique in his ministry at Mymms and exhorted other young men to follow the example of these three.

Monday 5 October
Cycled to the woods in glorious sunshine. The chestnuts are golden, the sycamore gold and green, and the bracken looked like chunks of gold in the sun.

Sunday 11 October
Father McKenny's sermon was on somewhat old-fashioned lines. It was not appreciated by Pascoe who said he seemed "cocksure of God, cocksure of the devil and on equally good terms with both".

Monday 12 October
Mrs Hay was loquacious about Father McKenny, calling him an old fool, and saying she wouldn't mind the Vicar having his old friends to stay but did object to his spending all his time dodging them and leaving her to entertain the old fools and bores. He retorted that he self-sacrificingly denied himself of their company and allowed her to enjoy their charming conversation. She replied that she had great difficulty of getting rid of Father McKenny as he wanted to stay another night and was only persuaded to go when she repeated for the sixth time the times of the trains to town.

Saturday 5 December
Cambridge. At the Roosters Annual Dinner I proposed a motion demanding restitution of the Eleven Days stolen from the country by the so-called reform of the calendar in 1752.

Friday 11 December
Full term ends today. I have spent practically every afternoon in the Varsity library this term.

[No further entries for December]

~ 1926 ~

Wednesday 13 January
South Mymms. Freezing all day but sunny and delightful. Took the train to Knebworth and then walked back via Welwyn, Lemsford, North Mymms and through the wood. Had tea at the Waggon and Horses before going home. Walked about twenty miles in total, my feet were sore but I enjoyed the walk more than anything I had done for a long time.

Friday 15 January
Went to Bedford Square for an interview with the Readers' Board for the London Diocese, and then to the Labour Party Social at St Albans, with singing and fun on the bus on the way home.

St Radegund's Day, Thursday 11 February
Cambridge. Special Collect, Epistle and Gospel of St Radegund (taken from my book) at 7.45 a.m. Mass in the College Chapel. As a result of my researches, the College observes the Feast of St Radegund for the first time, not knowing before of any feast of hers except the one during the Long Vacation (13 August). A number of guests attended the Feast in Hall including Lord Chalmers, the new Master of Peterhouse. It was a good dinner with port of 1884 vintage and Madeira of 1821, also sherry, hock and champagne. Manning and the Dean addressed me as "the father of the feast" and introduced me to others as such. Afterwards went to Manning's rooms for tea and talked with him until 12.45 a.m.

~ 1926 ~

Saturday 13 February
Attended Dr Braithwaite's Commemoration feast at Caius as the guest of Joe Needham. I sat next to the Dean, (Hunkin).

[Joseph Wellington Hunkin, OBE, MC, DD, became the Bishop of Truro in 1935.]

Wednesday 3 March
The crocuses are glorious in Trinity Avenue, especially on the town side of the river, where I believe there were none before but they are as thick as a carpet this year.

Monday 8 March
E. V. Knox arrived for the 'Union for Getting Back the Eleven Days' (UGBED) inaugural dinner at the Lion Hotel. A Court of Enquiry on the Eleven Days was held at College.

U.G.B.E.D.
(UNION FOR GETTING BACK THE ELEVEN DAYS)

Remember, remember, the 3rd of September
The Popish treason and plot;
We see no reason why this ELEVEN-DAYS' treason
Should ever be forgot.

GIVE US BACK OUR ELEVEN DAYS!
(Thurs., Sept. 3rd to Sunday, Sept. 13th, 1752, inclusive)

OBJECTS AND METHODS

(1) The Ugbed was founded in order to press for the restitution of the ELEVEN DAYS stolen from the nation by the so-called Reform of the Kalendar in 1752.
(2) Anyone is eligible to become a Member of the Ugbed ("Mugbed"), provided he passes the necessary test; and everyone becomes a Vice-President on joining.
(3) The following are admitted without test: (a) Those who are convinced of the elementary fact that the earth is flat; (b) Anglo-Israelites; (c) strict vegetarians; (d) absolute abstainers; (e) genuine Jacobites; (f) Sir Wm. Joynson-Hicks, Mr Winston Churchill, and Mr S. Saklatvala.
(4) Mugbeds are required to observe the Eleventh Day of every month with special solemnity, and to rise not later than 11 p.m. daily. They are also recommended to partake of Elevenses daily when possible; if not, when impossible.
(5) In order to drive home to the national conscience the importance of

recovering the ELEVEN DAYS, Mugbeds will first press for the institution of an Eleven-day Week, each day consisting of 15$\frac{3}{11}$ hours.

(6) The working day would then sometimes fall during the night. This would help to solve the national unemployment problem, as many more men would be employed in the making of electricity, gas, oil and candles.

(7) Further, the night would sometimes fall during the day. This would solve the world-old difficulty of getting up in the morning, and would also assist the great cause of national economy, as less money would be squandered on artificial light, such as night-lights for children and nurses, motor car headlights, etc.

(8) The Ugbed would also urge the introduction of an Eleven-Day Month. This would give 33$\frac{2}{11}$ months in a year – only 5/33 less than the number of marks required for passing University Examinations.

(9) The Ugbed stands for No Popery in our beloved national church, and therefore spurns the Popish innovation of Pope Gregory XIII, which was foisted on us as a "Reformed" Kalendar.

(10) The present so-called Kalendar is unpatriotic, as it makes it impossible to wear roses on St George's Day, which now falls on April 11th (Old Style) instead of on May 5th (New Style). Thus we are faced with a difference of 24 days between these two dates – 2 months and 2 days (Ugbed Style). Can we expect the roses to be ready?

(11) The Ugbed stands for strict observance of the Sabbath, but would point out that the present increasing disregard of the Sabbath is not to be wondered at, since what is now called Sunday is really Thursday. The Ugbed therefore insists that desecration of Thursday is not desecration of the Sabbath, and protests against the desecration of the real Sunday. It calls upon all loyal Mugbeds to observe the present so-called Wednesday as the Lord's Day, though those who find it difficult to find employment on the present so-called Sunday will not be censured if they keep two rest-days per week.

(12) The Ugbed indignantly protests against the existence of the Football Club known as Sheffield Wednesday, as that day is really Sunday.

(13) As is well known, the world was created in the year 4004 B.C., on Friday, March 25th at 9 a.m. It is obvious that the human frame was arranged to work in accordance with this date, and that the digestion was by Providence ordained to be at its best on Christmas Day. Consequently, the Ugbed deplores the harm wrought by the so-called Reformed Kalendar, which has sentenced millions of youth to the pangs of indigestion, due to their eating plum-pudding ELEVEN DAYS before the appointed time, and pancakes ELEVEN DAYS before Shrove Tuesday.

(14) To those who deplore the excesses of Bolshevism, Botulism, Fascism, Communism, Sinn Fein, Popery, Cross-word puzzles, and golf, the Ugbed would respectfully point out that these movements would in all probability

never have taken place if their founders had been born at the proper time.

(15) The Ugbed accepts no legal responsibility for the non-payment of rents at the present so-called Quarter Days, nor will it do so for those Mugbeds who try to reclaim their lost ELEVEN DAYS in a cinema, restaurant, or public house.

(16) Those who experience any difficulty in grasping the Ugbed Chronology will find their difficulty disappear if they constantly repeat to themselves the Ugbed formula, "Next Wednesday is really last Sunday week."

(17) Do not neglect the warning given in 1918, when the war ended at the Eleventh hour on the eleventh day of the Eleventh month. The war would not have broken out on August 4th, 1914, if we had had our ELEVEN DAYS.

(18) The Ugbed regrets that it can admit only one lady at a time to membership, in accordance with the prophecy contained in Mr Kennedy's fine poem:

> "*Dies* in the singular
> Common we decline;
> But its plural cases are
> Always masculine."

(19) ELEVEN is the perfect number. The nation was therefore deprived of perfection in 1752. This is not light matter, and must be remedied. Let us labour for the happy return of the ELEVEN DAYS, when every man will dwell under his own palm-tree, and every landlady dance round her own aspidistra.

JOIN THE UGBED!

Do not delay until the Eleventh hour.

F.B.

Sunday 14 March
Checked into the Priory Nursing Home for three weeks and was operated on for piles. Father Wilfred visited me every day.

Easter Sunday 4 April
Left the Priory. Went to Little St Mary's Church, but it was packed out so I went to St Giles (Cambridge) instead.

Monday 12 April
South Mymms. Spent all day wandering in the woods – the anemones and blackthorn are superb and a few bluebells are out, extraordinarily early this year. At the Easter vestry meeting I moved the resolution about the Archdeacon's horse.

[At the Easter Vestry and annual meeting of the Parochial Church Council at South Mimms the Vicar asked for comments on the previous year's church accounts. FB asked for an explanation of the item 'Visitation Fee, 18s.' which appeared in the expenditure column. The Vicar replied that it was an annual fee paid to the Archdeacon and that it was a very ancient one, paid by every parish in the country. He believed that it originated in the distant past, to compensate the Archdeacon for feeding and putting up his horse when visiting the parishes in his jurisdiction. Upon FB asking when the Archdeacon last visited South Mimms on a horse, he was told that it had not happened within living memory. The churchwardens, in fact, added that nowadays they had to go up to the Archdeacon in London, and pay their own fares into the bargain although the affair was still called a Visitation. In view of these facts, FB proposed a resolution that as long as the fee was levied and paid the Archdeacon should be requested to visit the parish at least once a year on horseback. Archdeacons, FB pointed out, with their gaiters, breeches and short cassocks still wore riding dress. They should live up to their gaiters and cease to be walking sartorial falsehoods. FB's proposal having been seconded, was put to the meeting and carried unanimously. A reporter for the local paper, who was covering the meeting, brought the resolution to the notice of his chief. The latter, thinking that it might interest the British public communicated it to the Press Association who distributed the story to the British Press.]

Saturday 17 April
Saw the first post-cremation funeral I have seen. In the Vicarage I was shown a *Times* leading article on the Archdeacon's horse, which they accused me of writing, but I had not.

[The first intimation the Archdeacon had of the new duties expected of him were communicated to him by the press who kept telephoning him to ask when he was going to visit South Mimms on a horse. Puzzled by this, he decided to leave the house to avoid further enquiries, only to walk into a bevy of Press photographers and journalists waiting outside. The next day all the London papers and most of those in the provinces came out with a report on the situation, under such headlines as 'Strange Request to Archdeacon' and 'Archdeacon Requested to be Equestrian'. South Mimms became the centre of interest in the country, particularly when a few days later the *Times* published a delightful fourth leader on the subject. It was an excellent piece of humorous writing and was afterwards reprinted in anthologies of English prose. Naturally FB was flattered when people accused him of having written it and he wished he had done so.]

~ 1926 ~

Monday 3 May
The coal strike began and the General Strike begins tonight. Printers refused to produce the *Daily Mail* because of an unfair article on the miners.

Thursday 6 May
Pupils disappearing on account of strike duty. Cambridge is getting emptier.

Wednesday 12 May
The General Strike ended suddenly at 1 p.m. today.

Tuesday 18 May
Went to Hall at 7.30 p.m. and afterwards stayed talking with Duckworth after all the others had gone.

> [W. L. H. Duckworth had been born on St Boniface's Day 1870 and was therefore christened Wynfrid – the Saint's original name – though his family always called him by his second name, Laurence. Everybody liked him. Tall, spare and very abstemious, he was a mirror of old-fashioned courtesy with a gentle humour of an unusual kind. He had been admitted to the College in 1889, had been a Fellow since 1893, and had great knowledge of the College and its traditions. A Doctor of Medicine and a Doctor of Science, the precise language, which he used in his lectures, had become absorbed into his ordinary speech. The result was that he never seemed to say anything in one word if he could say it in six, or use a short word if a long one would do. For example, he described a boys camp as a "camp for juvenile individuals" and translated a tenant-farmer's application for a new cowshed as "a request for additional shelter for the accommodation of his herd".]

Sunday 23 May
A number of the Order of the Red Herring came in for wine and coffee, then we had a group photograph taken in the Common Room.

Saturday 19 June
Lady Margaret Boat Club went Head of the River for the first time since 1872 so there was a big bonfire at St John's tonight, which lit up their Chapel tower finely.

Saturday 26 June
Went to Hampstead and was interviewed by the Bishop of Willesden from his bed.

Monday 28 June
Admitted to the Office of Reader by the Bishop of London at St Paul's Cathedral.

Sunday 4 July
South Mymms. Cycled to St Giles, breakfasted at the Vicarage and stayed the day. At 11 a.m. Mass I read my Declaration as Reader. At Solemn Evensong at 6.30 p.m. I held forth [i.e. preached] chiefly on the subject of last week's Anglo-Catholic Congress (re-housing and unemployment). Coates and I had supper at the Vicarage before going home.

> [Coates played the organ when Mrs Hay was not available. He was known as 'Old Coates' or more often as 'Womp', because of his tendency to produce a loud noise from the organ during the spoken parts of the service. The lessons therefore, went something like this - "And the Lord said unto WOMP, thou shalt do no WOMP".]

Sunday 8 August
Cambridge. Cycled left-handed round Madingley. Saw wheat cut and standing in shocks. The scabious was very pretty and everywhere.

Thursday 19 August
Caught the train to Bury St Edmunds with Nigel Williams then cycled to Lavenham and Long Melford and went into the magnificent church. It has a Lady Chapel of unique plan, like a cloister with the garth covered in and forming a chapel. Enjoyed an excellent hot lunch at the Bull, and was offered two helpings of everything by a most courteous waitress. On to Sudbury, thence to Foxearth and Cavendish and back to Cambridge feeling much pleased with our excursion. West Suffolk is a comparatively unspoilt area with very little motor traffic, even on main roads.

Wednesday 15 September
Accompanied Marie to Golders Green near the new Circular Road – she was going on night duty.

Wednesday 22 September
South Mymms. At the Vicarage we discussed holding a meeting to settle on a wedding present of a horse to the Archdeacon.

> [When the press reported the news of the Archdeacon's engagement, the Vicar decided to hold a meeting of the Church Council to consider the situation, but as he had to leave for Switzerland to visit a sick relative, FB was given instructions to hold the meeting in his absence. FB read out the

notice of the Archdeacon's engagement and reminded the meeting that he had not carried out their request to visit the parish on a horse. Therefore FB proposed they should give the Archdeacon a wedding present and that it should be a horse. This resolution was carried unanimously and a Horse Committee was elected but most of the members of the Church Council contemplated nothing larger than a model silver horse as a wedding present for the Archdeacon. The newspapers chose to think otherwise and took the matter very seriously. A number of them published illustrated interviews with the Archdeacon, some of the details being obviously journalistic fakes, though others were clearly due to the Archdeacon's sense of humour. Where, he reasonably asked, was he to keep a horse in Piccadilly? How was he to make his way on horse through the ceaseless motor traffic of Central London? Besides it was so long since he had ridden a horse that he trembled at the prospect. As one journalist put it, the prospective horse was to him nothing but a nightmare with which he was loath to be saddled at a time when he was just going into double harness.]

Monday 11 October
Went with the Fenwicks, Benbow and Douglas Plank and a photographer to Fraser's Farm, where the Archdeacon's Horse was photographed.

[The Vicar, who was following the newspaper correspondence from abroad, apparently decided that things were getting embarrassing for the Archdeacon. Early in October the *Times* published a letter from him, stating that, since the Archdeacon had shied at the horse, and since the horse would undoubtedly shy at the motor traffic in Central London, the Horse Committee had decided to give him a car instead, and subscriptions could be sent to FB as treasurer. The Horse Committee, however, had not been consulted about the proposed change and were reluctant to adopt it. They were also being besieged daily by Press reporters and photographers, clamouring to be present when the horse was presented to the Archdeacon. Knowing that they would have to capitulate before long, but determined to get even with some of the serious-minded journalists who regarded the Horse Committee as unsophisticated simpletons, they announced on 10 October that they were going to Dyrham Park Farm the following afternoon to select a horse for the Archdeacon. They found a bevy of reporters and photographers waiting for them when they arrived and the farmer, William Fraser, who was in collusion with the Horse Committee, produced one or two cart-horses, quite unsuitable steeds, for them to consider. They were examined with deliberation and the reporters solemnly wrote down that they were found 'unsuitable for the purpose in view'. The committee then went back to the farmyard, where they saw a horse looking out of his stable door. His name, Tony, was chalked on the lower flap, and by a stroke of luck a piece of chalk was lying on the ground in front of it. FB decided this would be a good horse and the committee approved changing the name on the door to 'Gaiters', which FB duly did. Gaiters was brought out of his stable and was trotted up and down the farmyard. One of the reporters asked his age. M. H. Benbow, who was a farm bailiff, a member of the Horse Committee and their Equine Adviser, looked at Gaiters' teeth and pronounced him to be "a bay gelding, rising five years". This, the reporters solemnly wrote down though for all most of the company knew Gaiters might have been sinking sixty-five. After he had been photographed in various attitudes the committee adjourned. The next morning's papers were full of portraits of Gaiters.]

Wednesday 13 October
Pictures of the horse in today's papers

[One of the papers inevitably showed the Horse Committee's Equine Adviser "looking a gift horse in the mouth", while in another, the curate was shown giving him a feed from a sieve, the legend being "Filling the Archdeacon's Gaiters".]

Friday 15 October
A friend rang up to say it was announced on the wireless last night that the Archdeacon had declined the horse as a wedding present.

Monday 18 October
Letter to FB from M. H. Benbow, Equine Adviser to the Horse Committee.

Well my Gad I have had a D- of a time. Poor owd Gerken gone nearly mad. I had no business having anything to do with a *hoss*. I said "Dear Mr G. surely you know I was appointed to Inspect a Hoss", then he went on again . . ." The idea making all of such people look D- fools in the eyes of the country . . ." I met the dear wife of our dear church warden and of course, as you are aware, he wears Gaiters Day and Night and, of course, poor old chap walking up and down Potters Bar Station everybody kept calling out saying "What you, Gaiters" and of course poor owd Cobbe not buying a *Sketch* could not see the joke at all. When he got to London he speculated in a *Mirror* then he did lead off "It would be better to speculate in coal to warm the dear church than in Hoss flesh . . ." Ma Cobbe, meeting dear little Mrs Booth, started pulling Mrs Booth's nose, calling her everything but a lady so how its all going to end I don't know. I was thinking could you arrange to be here in case I had a nasty poke in the eye . . .

I have sent about 30 letters on to you, not to Cambridge, I told them

Oxford College so you won't be bothered… I wished you had been here this weekend you would have killed yourself looking at the dear people's dials.

    Best wishes
    Malcolm the Hoss Buyer

Wednesday 27 October
Sculled to the Horse Grind in a hard white frost but bright sun and with mist rising off the water.

Thursday 4 November
My edition of *The Lyfe of Saynt Radegunde* was published by the Cambridge University Press today.

Saturday 4 December
No reading today as I had drops put in my eyes. At the Rooster dinner I opposed the motion "The house approves of early rising, early lectures and early birds."

[No further entries for December]

~ 1927 ~

St Agnes's Eve, Thursday 20 January
Cambridge. Looked for snowdrops in the garden but not one flower and only about two even showing a tip of white in their buds. After dinner went to the Workers' Educational Association Social in the Co-op Hall in Burleigh Street, where we played "winking" etc. with a large company.

Saturday 19 February
This is the last day of the Lents. The first boat finished Head easily and the second boat is 3rd on the River.

Saturday 26 February
The Roosters held a mock trial of the Mistress of Gurnham for breach of promise. Robey proved an excellent judge.

Monday 21 March
Arrived at York and was met by Oldham. The Minster is the most beautiful Cathedral I have yet seen in England with nine altars, i.e. High, Nave, Crypt, East end, South choir aisle, South choirside (Zouche chapel), South transept, North transept (facing north) and North transept (facing east). A verger showed me the vestments, including chasubles, worn daily at every Mass. Spent the night at the Station Hotel.

Tuesday 22 March
Travelled to Gainford to stay with Edleston and Miss Edleston. He gave me letters of introduction to the Bishop and the Dean of Durham.

Friday 25 March
On my arrived in Durham I went to the Deanery, where I was entertained in a most hospitable manner by Bishop Welldon, the Dean a fair-haired giant of a man, and shown round the castle library, Cathedral and Deanery. Lunched tête-à-tête with Bishop Welldon. In the afternoon caught the bus to Auckland Castle to see the diminutive Bishop of Durham, Hensley Henson. He gave me tea and showed me his beautiful private chapel, where one of the objects of interest was a large palm branch, which had been sent to Bishop Westcott (a former Bishop of Durham) by Lord Halifax, the distinguished Anglo-Catholic layman, and which had been blessed by the Pope. "I don't suppose one will be sent to me", Bishop Henson added.

> [Hensley Henson's ecclesiastical opinions were making him obnoxious to the Anglo-Catholic party in the Church.]

Tuesday 5 April
South Mymms. Went to the Prince's Theatre in London to see *The Medea of Euripides* with Sybil Thorndike in the title role.

Saturday 23 April
Cambridge. Attended the Jesus College Boat Club Centenary Dinner in Hall, which was chaired by the Master and there were 116 present. Steve [Fairbairn] proposed the toast of the prosperity of the Club, later his health was drunk with enthusiasm and he received an ovation on rising to reply. The evening finished with an unofficial bonfire in the middle of Chapel Court.

Friday 20 May
The Patriarch [the Rev Allen Hay, the Vicar of South Mymms] arrived in his new car with Bishop Smyth, having left Mymms against the advice and bewailing of all the family, as it was his first drive. Mrs Hay warned the Bishop of impending death but he replied that in any case his time was short

~ 1927 ~

and that he would as soon die on the road to Cambridge as in any other way. After lunch we looked round Pepys Library at Magdalene and then went to the STC 70th Anniversary Garden Party in the Master's garden at Sidney Sussex College.

Thursday 9 June
Went to the undergraduate rag in support of the Cambridge Fruiting Campaign in the Market Place. 'Joanna Southcott's Box' was opened in the presence of two 'Archbishops' and twenty-four 'Bishops' and 'incumbrances', including the Bishop of Swears and Wells and the Little Bishop of Titchfield. The box contained, amongst other things, bananas, buns, beer and a tip for the Derby.

Saturday 11 June
The first boat, having gone up a place each day so far, rowed over Head easily. There was a big bonfire again for Centenary Year.

Tuesday 12 July
Worked at Anglo-Norman then sculled to Horse Grind, where the river was blocked by a dredger across the stream.

> [Except for the railway bridge there was no bridge across the Cam between Jesus Green and Baitsbite Lock three and a half miles away, so there were numerous ferries known as grinds. The ferry at the Pike and Eel at Old Chesterton was the most important of all to rowing men because it was there that all coaches crossed the river. The grind was for a long time worked by the landlord of the Pike and Eel, named Brown, who except for passing the time of day with his passengers, seldom spoke. D.N. Thorne, an undergraduate who frequently coached the lower boats, was equally taciturn. Thorne was commonly called 'The Dragon', presumably from his initials, for nobody could be less dragon-like then he. One day, however, when coaching a boat from his cycle upstream from Baitsbite, he was roused from his usual quiet meditation by the sound of his eight crashing into Brown's ferry in mid-stream. Spurned to anger by the negligence of his cox, he roared to him, at the top of his voice: "YOU BLOODY FOOL!" The Ferryman, thinking this vote of censure was directed at himself roared back "BLOODY FOOL? WHO'S A BLOODY FOOL? BLOODY FOOL YOURSELF!". Upon this the Dragon, waving his arms deprecatingly, shouted back, "NOT *YOU*, YOU BLOODY FOOL, I MEANT *HIM*, YOU BLOODY FOOL!" Honour was satisfied as Brown realised that it was not he who had been publicly stigmatised as a bloody fool, and both men relapsed into their habitual calm.]

~ 1927 ~

Friday 29 July
Went into town and got instructions from W.T.A. for the Italian tour, which I am leading tomorrow for 25 including myself.

Wednesday 17 August
Barnet. Met Marie at Golders Green and we went to the Waggon and Horses.

Friday 16 September
Cambridge. Left Cambridge by car with A.P. Bryant to stay with him at Coton Grange, Guilsborough.

[A. P. (Buddy) Bryant was an American student at Jesus College. He was a keen oarsman, overflowing with high spirits that sometimes brought him into conflict with authority. After several minor incidents he stood at the entrance to the College Hall one evening while dinner was in progress, levelled a pistol at the high table – probably as the result of a wager – and fired it. It did no harm, apart from making a tremendous noise and causing great consternation. After a tutorial conference it was decided that Buddy Bryant was to go down. Knowing him to be (to use a phrase of Duckworth's,) "not positively evil, don't you know", FB interceded on Bryant's behalf and it was decided that he was to be allowed to stay up provided FB accepted responsibility for him. This meant that he was to live with FB at the Oratory House, attend at least one Chapel there every day, be regular at lectures and supervisions and report to FB every night at 10 p.m. to prove that he was in. At the end of his three years at Cambridge he went back to the United States and during the Second World War distinguished himself in the American Navy. One day soon after the war he reappeared at the College and FB took him to dine at high table. Duckworth, the Master, who happened to be presiding that evening, said to him, when FB introduced him, "I do not recollect, Mr Bryant, having seen you at this table before", to which Bryant replied "No, Sir, I've only shot at it." "Indeed", said Duckworth, "then I conjecture that you must be unique among the members of this College, don't you know." The last time that FB saw Buddy he found that he had become a vestryman of his church in Miami – what we in England term a parochial church councillor.]

Sunday 9 October
Had tea with Mr Edleston who appointed me Fen Reeve of his manor of Chesterton.

Christmas Day, 25 December
South Mymms. Snow falling and Mymms is isolated.

[It became the biggest snowfall in living memory.]

Money received for Academical Year 1926–7.
  March Term 1926 £142.19s. 6d.
  Lent Term 1927   £131.16s. 0d.
  Easter Term   £193. 8s. 6d.
  Long Vac Term   £10. 1s. 0d.
  TOTAL =   £478. 5s. 0d.

[No further entries for December]

~ 1928 ~

[During the annual church meeting at Easter 1928, Allen Hay remarked that there had not been a wedding in the parish for over twelve months. The local weekly newspaper reported him as saying, "It is not that the young women of South Mimms are not comely: I am sure young men would find excellent wives here. Possibly the men are shy, but I would remind the young ladies that it is Leap Year."

The popular dailies, with characteristic exaggeration, came out with such headlines as 'Village where nobody weds' and photographs of 'The Matchless Maidens of Mimms'. Some of the papers, whether intentionally or by accident, stretched the Vicar's "twelve months" to twelve years. He was soon bombarded with letters – some serious, others facetious – from unmarried men all over England and abroad, asking to be put in touch with the matchless maidens. There were so many applicants that he had to announce that there were not nearly enough unmarried women to go round. Upon that, unmarried women from all over the world wrote asking to be put in touch with the unmarried men and he received over a thousand letters in all.]

Tuesday 24 April
Cambridge. Playford and I had an interview with Heffer regarding a history of the Boat Club that we propose to collaborate in writing.

Friday 27 April
The Patriarch, Matriarch and Monica [the Vicar, Mrs Hay and their younger daughter] arrived by car. Took them round the town and, as we came in to tea, Heffer's van was delivering advance copies of my *Saint Giles*. The Patriarch was much surprised when I handed him a copy.

~ 1928 ~

Tuesday 8 May
At 4 p.m. I went to Prior's to read a paper on my Anglo-Saxon researches.

[Oliver Prior, who was the first Professor of French at Cambridge, lectured in the University Arts School in Bene't Street. Undergraduates appeared to give him endless amusement for his face always wore a smile when he was with them. No matter on what hour they called on him, and he apparently never went to bed before one o'clock, they were always welcome, whether they came to discuss linguistic problems or were paying a social call. He was the instigator of the University classes in French translation, for which FB was paid so much a head for over twenty years.]

Tuesday 22 May
Attended the Rustat Audit Feast.

[Tobias Rustat, an official of the Court of Charles II, bequeathed his property to the College, mostly to found scholarships for the education of sons of the clergy. He also founded a feast, still held at the College every year in May. Under the terms of his will every Fellow who attends receives a crown piece at table.]

Monday 11 June
Working on the Jesus College Boat Club book for the next week or so.

Wednesday 27 June
Playford took me in his car to Stowe School, where he is teaching, and which has fine grounds. We discussed the book. Stayed the night in Buckingham, which is a very quiet town.

Sunday 8 September
South Mymms. At Solemn Evensong at St Giles I held forth on "Hymns".

Wednesday 19 September
Travelled to Portsmouth for the Old Egyptonians Reunion. After a delightful evening I stayed the night at George Cockram's.

Saturday 22 September
South Mymms. The first wedding in 18 months took place at St Giles and the church was packed to the doors.

Wednesday 26 September
Cambridge. Started with Steve [Fairbairn] alongside me on the towpath coaching two Light Fours to Baitsbite and back.

~ 1928 ~

Tuesday 9 October
Full term began. Spent the morning interviewing pupils. In the afternoon fix-tubbed freshmen under Steve's instructions, then on the towpath with him and eight of them in a boat, very quick work as this was their first day. At 8.15 p.m. I attended a Boat Club meeting in the Common Room, which was addressed by Steve.

Saturday 13 October
Coached an VIII by myself for the first time to the bridge and back.

Saturday 27 October
As the Book Club sale was taking place in the Combination Room, the rest of us took coffee in Mr Watt's rooms. Dr Duckworth asked me to present his apologies for not coming, to which Tommy (Watt) replied that he knew Dr Duckworth had made a vow never to enter his rooms.

Tuesday 13 November
Out with my VIII to the bridge and back, with Steve coaching them. He made me get in at bow on the way down and keep in till we reached the boathouse. Went a good pace, which nearly cooked me as I was in such poor condition.

Friday 16 November
We had a relay race of all six boats to Clayhithe and back. It was sunny and calm when we started but at about 3 p.m., when we left Clayhithe, a roaring downstream wind rose, such as I have never seen before except at sea. The narrow waters of the Cam were soon a mass of billows and high spray. Frequently we couldn't move our cycles along but had to walk or run. The wind was so terrific that, although the boats were rowing hard, they stood suspended for several seconds, held back by big waves and furious wind. Nevertheless my 5th boat did extraordinarily well. Jimmy Fraser said I ought to be a proud man. I was! Few other clubs seemed to have boats out and most of these sank. On the way home the banks were littered with abandoned VIII's, IV's and sculling boats, with oars and sculls lying everywhere and men swimming here and there. At 5 p.m. Joe Harmsworth called to see me, the first time for three years!

Saturday 24 November
At the Roosters Annual Dinner I opposed the motion "That May week is pernicious". Manning proposed the toast of the Roosters who "glory in the name of Britain" – in fact he was inclined to think the Roosters and Britain synonymous.

~ 1928 ~

Friday 30 November
In view of tomorrow's publication of *The Jesus College Boat Club*, Q [Sir Arthur Quiller-Couch, Professor of English Literature] made me sit in Laurence Sterne's chair in Hall.

Thursday 20 December
Lunched with the Dean at his house, Fen Ditton Hall, a delightful old house with a glorious, carved oak Jacobean staircase.

Friday 21 December
Caught the coach to Mymms. The lighthouse [beacon] is working at the Arterial Road [now the A1/M motorway] for the first time today, I believe. The road is now open to London. The roof is on the new part of the Vicarage and the house now has electric light. The Vicar also has a new dog, a black poodle called Piper.

[No further entries for December]

~ 1929 ~

Saturday 19 January
Cambridge. Okey has retired from the Italian Professorship and tonight in the Combination Room Nairne, Watt and Duckworth said they want me to stand.

Saturday 26 January
After Hall looked in at Lance's and found a Wheatsheaf meeting going on. Had a drink with them and they gave me a certificate saying that I am the first don to drink beer with the members and the first non-member to enter a Wheatsheaf meeting without having his nether garments removed.

> [The Wheatsheafs started in 1922 and faded out in 1933. They existed to drink beer and the gentleman able to drink a pint of pale ale in the shortest time at the last meeting of term became President for the ensuing term. Lots were drawn for the order of drinking and times were taken with a Boat Club stopwatch, the record being three seconds. A member seen to be drinking a glass of water had it thrown in his face. But things got rougher than that. A Mr Grant was seized and deprived of his pants. He was then laid on a table, divested of his remaining garments, and swilled over with beer. Fearing he would catch cold, he was taken to his rooms, powdered all

over and finally rubbed over with face cream. He was then sent to have a bath, put to bed and kissed goodnight by all present. A number of Wheatsheaf members subsequently went on to become parsons and one became a judge.]

Sunday 27 January
House Chapel at 7.45 a.m. Working at *365 Points for Oarsmen* most of the day.

[The book was intended to provide a daily thought for oarsmen, coxswains, and coaches; and in order to avoid monotony and introduce a little light relief, FB fitted a number of quotations to appropriate saints' days, like this:

February 14: (St Valentine).
Orthodoxy is particularly severe on keeping the eyes in the boat. This not only turns the body into cast-iron, but also paralyses the mind.
March 25: (St Dismas, protector against thieves).
Pick the weak point of a crew rather than of an individual.
April 27: (St Zita, patroness of housemaids)
Let the knees rise easily and naturally, just before they feel constrained.
August 16: (St Roch, protector against sores).
Fixed seats are an abomination and should be done away with.
August 25: (St Louis, patron of barbers).
One can tell instinctively by sound and feel whether the blade is being brought through at the right depth.

Although Steve could not tolerate levity in connection with rowing, curiously enough he approved of FB's saints' days, which he may have thought of as useful aids to memory. However, he was indignant when Claude Elliott told him he thought the book funny. The book was called *Slowly Forward* and when Steve asked the reason for this title FB answered that "slowly forward" was one of his favourite admonitions to crews when coaching them. He denied this, asserting that he always said "slow forward!" When FB retorted that in any event an adverb was necessary in that position, he was much amused and somewhat contemptuous. "Adverbs" he burst out. "Adverbs! You're like the rest of the bloody dons – specialised idiots". From that time onward, whenever he introduced FB to anyone he used to add solemnly, "He knows a lot about adverbs" and when he wrote to FB he often ended his letters with "Yoursly everly, Stevely".]

Wednesday 30 January
At 2.15 p.m. I coached the boat to Baitsbite. Rowed a Ditch and a Reach, but not well. In Hall Elliott related that Steve's first remark to him (when

coaching him in a IV years ago) was "You're no more use than a b- - - - sack of s- - -." Q related various anecdotes of train journeys, including a man taking leave of a woman, saying "If I outlive my wife, as I *hope* to do . . ."

> [This remark was always used when he said goodbye to Lady Q in Cornwall on returning to Cambridge, and on one occasion caused two severe looking ladies to leave the carriage in disgust.]

Tommy Watt remarked that Nairne was reading all Q's novels and added (referring to his eyesight), "I couldn't".

Friday 1 February
Coached the boat to the Plough, Percy Bullock substituting at stroke.

> [Percy Bullock was the Jesus College boatman for forty-seven years and had an immense influence for good on generations of Jesus men. An evangelical churchman of the old school, he was for many years Churchwarden of Christ Church, Cambridge. FB said that guests at Bump Suppers usually took Percy to be a don. When he retired in 1972 the Boat Club arranged a party at Skinners' Hall in London where he was presented with a substantial cheque. After his death in 1988 a Memorial Service, held in the College Chapel, was attended by upwards of 400 people.]

Monday 11 February
First lunch in Hall in the history of the College. There was quite a crowd of undergraduates but only Edmonds and I were at High Table. Coached the 5th boat to the Plough but it was so cold that the oars were encased in ice when we got back.

Thursday 14 February
The ice on the river is still harder today. When I walked with the Dean of King's College on Clare Bridge we saw about twenty men skating, I believe this is the first time there has been skating on the Cam since 1895. The first boat was photographed on the ice at Grassy.

Friday 1 March
As the postponed Lent races were due to start today, I went with Lance and found the river frozen right across to Banhams and their heavy barge Nancy II came out and broke the ice; the conservators also flushed the river to clear the floating ice away. Our first boat regained the Headship, my crew were bumped, almost entirely through panic, I think.

~ 1929 ~

Saturday 2 March
The first boat rowed over Head, leaping along with enormous strokes like one man in the glassy water. It looked magnificent from the shore. I don't remember seeing anything to equal it on the Cam.

Tuesday 5 March
At the Bump Supper, Travis was a funny sight with a boiled shirt and sweater on and soon had everything off except trousers and dress collar and tie, naked from neck to waist. At the fire, Barrett had grey trousers, his shirt out fore and aft, dress waistcoat over it and a napkin for a head-dress.

Sunday 10 March
On the Backs the aconites are in their prime and the snowdrops almost so, but the ditches are still full of unmelted ice. I opened the Roosters debate "That it is time the Varsity was run on democratic lines".

Monday 22 April
Coached the Newnham VIII for Lance [for their race against the London School of Medicine at Ely, which they won by 3½ lengths].

Wednesday 8 May
Slowly Forward published. The Master expressed his pleasure with it, and suggested reciting the quotations daily in Chapel and singing them on Saints' days.

Wednesday 15 May
   [From: C A Elliott   To: Steve Fairbairn.
   "It is extraordinarily good of you to send me a copy of *Slowly Forward*, especially after the way you used to talk to me when I was in a boat. The book is most amusing besides being highly instructive – I never knew of the existence of half the saints that Brittain has routed out. Yes, Brittain is a very good fellow and I hope he will stay on here. I am trying to get him into a University job in the Modern Languages School and he is now what they call a 'Recognized Lecturer in French' and we have also given him dining rights . . ."]

Friday 24 May
Caught the coach to Mymms. Took the chair of the Labour Party meeting in the Parish Hall and was surprised at the amount of support. Stayed the night at the Vicarage (now finished), in the new "haunted" room. Found myself wide-awake in the night and it almost immediately struck 3 a.m. as I had often heard the Vicar relate (but not this time).

~ 1929 ~

Tuesday 2 July
Attended the debate on the Speech from the Throne in the House of Lords.

Friday 5 July
At Henley Regatta. At the fair Murray Phelps went behind the Punch and Judy show and kept pinching the performer who could not retaliate because he had Punch on one hand and Judy on the other.

Thursday 11 July
South Mymms. The funeral and Absolutions of the Dead took place for "Old Sweetie". At 5 p.m. I went to a debate in the House of Commons.

Friday 12 July
Went to the woods and watched a squirrel in a tree – the first I have seen there for a long time. The rose bay and campanula were in their prime.

Wednesday 28 August
Looked over Ingham Lodge with Mr Blake.

> [This was probably FB's first visit to the house that became his home on his marriage to Muriel Cunnington in 1959.]

Monday 9 September
Mr White unlocked the big chest in the church. I took out the old vestry minute books, dating back to 1727. I found them engrossing and began copying the entertaining passages. Played tennis with Mark Kirk, Winnie Kirk and Fred Hart.

Wednesday 9 October
Cambridge. After Hall I had to entertain Elliott and Mills with the full story of the Archdeacon's horse. Elliott was indignant when I said I didn't object to mountaineering. He replied that a man might as well say that he "didn't object to the Christian religion".

Saturday 12 October
In the afternoon I took the Light Fours plus Ian Fairbairn, whom I had not met before, to the Red Grind.

> [Ian was Steve's eldest son to whom he (Steve) always referred as "My son, Ian", as opposed to his younger son who was "My boy, Sydney". When FB asked Sydney the reason for this, he replied "I think it's because Ian rows and I don't".]

Sunday 13 October
Dean Inge was at dinner where people were discussing the objects of the war. He said "I always thought it was fought so that we might preserve our civilisation long enough for the Americans to acquire one".

[W. R. Inge was a former Fellow of Jesus College who left to become Dean of St Paul's Cathedral. Known nationally as 'the Gloomy Dean' he was made an Honorary Fellow of the College and he continued to attend feasts until he was about ninety, walking the mile and a half from the railway station and carrying his suitcase. He said little, being afflicted with deafness in his old age, but he would stand by the Combination Room fire after dinner blinking like a great cat and uttering occasional witticisms.]

Wednesday 16 October
Attended the enquiry at the Guildhall about the acquisition of Butts Close by the College.

Sunday 27 October
A Rooster Commission was held to discover whether lectures are a waste of time. I was Mr Justice Boreham-Stiffe and all the witnesses were in costume. It was the most successful Rooster meeting since the "bicentenary".

Thursday 31 October
In the Combination Room after Hall there was a farewell to Foakes-Jackson who returns to America tomorrow. The Master proposed his health. Replying, Foakes-Jackson said he would rather talk than think any time!

[F. J. Foakes-Jackson, a candidate for the eccentric and absent-minded don of popular legend, had been a professor in the United States since 1916 but was a life Fellow of Jesus College and frequently returned to it during his summer vacations. Both Q and Nairne found him more than a little irritating.]

Saturday 2 November
Lively Boat Club dinner in the Hall lecture room, a gas bracket was torn down, glasses hurled about and threats of knife throwing.

Sunday 5 November
Went with Boulay [Lance], as his guest to a meeting of the Natives, which included an oyster feast followed by an impromptu ballad concert. I ate twelve oysters, but Boulay had four dozen and Byron six dozen. (He once ate eight dozen).

~ 1929 ~

[The Natives Club was founded in 1877 by an undergraduate whose mother had sent him a barrel of oysters, which he decided to share with eleven friends. The club celebrated its centenary in 1977, by which time it had acquired a valuable collection of silver. It still flourishes and is still a male stronghold. The Natives Cocktail Party near the Cricket Pavilion is a feature of May Week at Jesus College.]

Wednesday 29 November
I was timekeeper at the Lock to Lock Eights (Fairbairn Cup) this being the first time they are open to all clubs in the University.

[Steve had given Boulay Lance £10 to go and buy the cup.]

Saturday 9 December
Sent my Bibliography of Rowing to the Oxford University Press.

[The Cambridge University Press having turned it down on the grounds that bibliographies never pay.]

[No further entries for December]

~ 1930 ~

[This year marked a turning point in FB's life. He was appointed to a lectureship at Jesus College and granted something he desired more than anything else – rooms in college.]

Saturday 22 February
Cambridge. Last day of the Lent Races. No Bump Supper, as the First and Second boats did badly. I was invited to the Jesus College Boat Club Dinner but declined.

[The dons did not go to the Bump Suppers unless the College was Head of the Lents or the Mays.]

Monday 5 March
Guy Giddins came to dinner, after which we talked of Mymms, his home until a year or so ago. We discovered our common interest only yesterday.

[Guy Hunter Chaffey Giddins had lived at Windmore Hall, South Mimms. He entered the College in 1928, became a schoolmaster, and then a successful horticulturist, judging at the Chelsea Flower Show and being at one time the President of Interflora. Guy and FB made an annual pilgrimage in May to see Mimms Wood in bluebell time and they remained friends all of his life.]

Monday 24 March
Went by train from Euston to Windermere and spent three days in the Lake District visiting the Lattimers at Keswick, also Rosthwaite, Lodor Falls and Crosthwaite.

Thursday 27 March
Mr Lattimer saw me off at Penrith. Arrived at Tebay where Manning and his sister met me with a car and we went on to Ravenstonedale where I stayed at the Black Swan, though I spent most of each day at the Manning's home in the fell country he loves so much.

Tuesday 1 April
Caught the train alone to Carlisle, which has a reddish stone cathedral dating from about AD 1400. It has a fine Norman nave, decorated east window and beautiful silvery-black canopies to the choir stalls. There is a delightful side screen and north choir Perpendicular and Renaissance, the best I have seen in England..

Saturday 12 April
South Mymms. We listened to the Boat Race on the wireless. I stayed the night at the Old Bull (Mrs Reynolds').

[This house, formerly a public house, was demolished when Frowyke Crescent was built.]

Good Friday, 18 April
Delivered the Black Horse sermon.

[In 1698, a benefactor called John Bradshawe left a sum of money for a sermon to be preached on Good Friday. This was given at Evensong in the church until the 1960s when it was transferred to the Black Horse Pub in the Lower Village.]

Saturday 26 April
Cambridge. Q told us a yarn from last term. The new Sidney Sussex building, backing on to King Street, and erected a year or so ago, is very hideous and

like a sausage factory. Next to it in King Street is an underground public convenience labelled 'Gentlemen'. Q met the Master of Sidney Sussex near this point one day and said "Why this invidious distinction? Surely both parts are for gentlemen and it is obvious that both parts are one and the same building." Apparently he insinuated that the convenience is a worthy sort of entrance to the new Sidney building.

Tuesday 13 May
Manning informs me that at yesterday's meeting of the College Council it was decided that I should move into College next term in the new block, designed by Morley Horder.

> [FB was the first to live in it and chose the top floor of Staircase 8 with the Angel Gate just below his windows. Q remarked that he was a little higher than the angels. The Angel Gate is so called because of the angel supporters of the arms of Leonard Jauncey White-Thomson, Bishop of Ely (and consequently Visitor of the College) from 1924 to 1934. His somewhat complicated arms impaled with those of his See were carved by Mr Eric Gill and are displayed on a large shield over the low arch, which faces the east end of the Chapel. On one side FB looked into Chapel Court with the east end of the Chapel facing him and on the other on to Butt Green (soon afterward incorporated in the College Close) and Midsummer Common. It would have mattered little to him where his rooms were situated so long as they were in College, for as he often said, "Bliss was it in that place to be alive and it has been so ever since."]

Thursday 15 May
In translation class a pupil referred to the aspen as "the aspirin tree".

Sunday 25 May
After Hall, the Master entertained us with tales of old Dr W—— and how he got his D.Litt on an unread second or third-hand thesis and Q told the story of the teetotal lunch.

> [The invitation came from an ecclesiastical body and the company was to be a large one. From what he knew of those who were going to be present, Q strongly suspected that, although the lunch was to be at a hotel, it would be a strictly teetotal affair. Before accepting the invitation he asked his retainer, Henry Stubbings – a quaint little bearded man of eighty, who used to run errands for him – if he could discover whether his suspicion was well founded.
>
> "Certainly, Sir Arthur", Henry answered. "I can easily find out about that. You see, the head waiter there is a relation of mine."

An hour or so later Henry came back and said: "Yes, Sir Arthur, the lunch is going to be teetotal, but the head waiter says it will be all right."

"Did he explain what he meant by being 'all right,' Henry?" Q asked.

"Well, Sir Arthur, as far as I could understand he meant it would be all right for you," Henry answered.

So Q accepted the invitation and found himself sitting at a table with several teetotallers. When the lunch began the waiters went round and asked the guests whether they would take ginger beer, lemonade, or water; but they passed Q without saying anything. Q also held his peace and soon afterwards a hand appeared over his shoulder and poured something into his glass. When he tasted it, he found it was lemonade well laced with gin.

After a while his neighbour at table said: "Your lemonade looks a different colour from mine, Sir Arthur."

"Yes", said Q, "it's a special lemonade. Would you like to try it? Good! Waiter, bring this gentleman some of that special lemonade, please."

"My word!" said the other man when he had tasted it. "This is wonderful lemonade. I've never tasted any as good as this before, I wonder if I could get the recipe. Marvellous lemonade Sir Arthur's got here," he said to another luncher at the same table.

"Could I taste it, please?" the third man asked.

"Certainly", said Q. "Waiter, bring this gentleman some of that special lemonade, please."

Before long, everyone at the table was drinking Q's special lemonade. There is nothing more to the story. No one became inebriated, but before the lunch was over there was general recognition that the wittiest remarks and the warmest good feeling in the room came from Q's table. (quoted in *Q – A Biographical Study* by F. Brittain)]

Tuesday 27 May
At the French Principal subjects class we discussed De Vigny's poem on Jephthah's daughter. I pointed out that De Vigny, as usual, makes Jehovah much more terrible than he is in the book of Judges. One of my pupils said, "Oh yes I see that. But who was Jehovah?" Loud laughs came from the rest of the class.

Sunday 1 June
The *Codex Gallorum* was promulgated at the Roosters, the Alcock gown presented and new ceremonies performed. Barrett, dressed as an angel, presented me with a wreath of bay leaves.

Tuesday 3 June
Steve made four changes in the order of the first boat then made them race the second boat again. He muttered several times, "My God, they are good".

~ 1930 ~

Wednesday 4 June
The Dean is full of praise for the *Codex Gallorum*. He read it during a weary two-hour meeting of the Theological Society and said he saw "the hand of Brittain" in every line. Never was such praise received from the Dean! However, he lived up to his reputation for pessimism by saying that Steve must be mad to make changes in the boat so near to the races, that it was fatal, etc. etc.

Saturday 7 June
Q went to the funeral of Wollaston of King's who had been shot by a pupil.

Whit Monday 9 June
Steve still rags me about adverbs.

Wednesday 11 June
Being now an examiner, I gave out papers for the Spanish Principal subjects' exam and, with J. W. Baker, conducted the Spanish oral.

Saturday 14 June
Our first boat was miles ahead but the Bump Supper was remarkably quiet for such an occasion. I went to the bonfire on which an ancient VIII was roasting.

Wednesday 18 June
Visited Pars who was in good form. He is going to keep on staircase 13 of the new building.

Thursday 3 July
Oar, Scull and Rudder was published today. [FB's bibliography of rowing.]

Thursday 21 August
Moved into my new rooms in Chapel Court and by 5 p.m. I had the carpet laid and the keeping room presentable.

> [The Keeping Room is the main room of a set. It originated from the phrase to keep terms. Thus FB would have said that he lived at Barnet and kept at Cambridge.]

Wednesday 27 August
Today is said to be the hottest day for seven years. Read Medieval Latin most of the day.

~ 1930 ~

Thursday 4 September
Barnet. Went to Barnet fair, which is in the top field for the first time this year, and the horse fair is now held in the field next to the county boundary. I'm working on my history of Mymms (and for the next weeks).

Saturday 11 October
Cambridge. The Dean wants me to act as Chapel Sacristan, to appoint servers etc. He says I can do as I like about ceremonial and agreed that in future the server shall go in and out with the celebrant, he shall kneel on the north side till the gospel, and see that the vessels are put out properly.

Wednesday 15 October
Gave my first lecture on Medieval Latin Literature. In the afternoon I went to the river with the boats.

Thursday 16 October
From 5.30 – 6.15 p.m. I was talking with Gittings.

> [Robert W. V. Gittings was elected a Research Fellow of Jesus College after taking his degree. He wrote the words for many items in Rooster revues and was to become the distinguished biographer of Keats and Hardy. The College elected him to an Honorary Fellowship after he proceeded to a doctorate of letters at Cambridge University.]

Friday 28 November
Attended a dinner given by the Master to those chiefly concerned in the recent exchange of New Square and Butt Green, that is the Mayor and Corporation.

Thursday 4 December
Went to the Sung Mass at Oratory House (Nicholas Ferrar) and stayed to breakfast.

> [Nicholas Ferrar was the saintly man who lived at Little Gidding in the seventeenth century, as readers of John Inglesant would remember. He founded a community of families there and is buried just outside the west door of the tiny church, which stands in charming isolation in a remote part of Northamptonshire and its only approach is by a cart track through a farmyard and then across a meadow.]

Thursday 11 December
Read all day as it poured with rain all day. Didn't go outside the College gate but walked a mile round the Cloister, having measured it with string and found that twenty times round (close to the arches) equals one mile.

Friday 12 December
Tea at Fen Ditton (solus) with the Dean who said he would like to see me Chaplain of the College, and if so, he regarded me as his natural successor in the Deanship.

Tuesday 16 December
Elliott told me of a job going at Southampton University but expressed the hope that I would stay and be Chaplain. I made objections, which he tried to demolish.

Friday 19 December
Manning and Elliott came in from a meeting of the College Council and offered me an Assistant Lectureship at £200 a year plus the Librarianship at £43. I accepted.

Christmas Day, Thursday 25 December
Barnet. A small party of Dad, Mum, Frank and I. The Olivers came in at tea-time and later we played whist while Frank played the gramophone.

[No further entries for December]

~ 1931 ~

Thursday 1 January
As the New Year came in I was in the dining room at South Mymms Vicarage with the Vicar. We drank to each other's health and talked till 12.30 a.m.

Monday 5 January
This week I get up early and see the others off so that Mother can rest. Spent the evening at Knightsland. They pressed me to call and to wander round the farm whenever I feel like it.

> [Knightsland is a late medieval or early sixteenth century farmhouse about a mile from FB's home in Barnet. The dining room is lined with linen fold panelling and a spiral staircase leads to the bedrooms, which have wide, oak floorboards. The ill fated Admiral John Byng, who bought the house about 1750, is said to have lived in it while Wrotham Park was being built for him on higher ground half a mile away.]

~ 1931 ~

Saturday 7 February
Cambridge. Elliott looked in during the morning and referring to last Thursday's "blind" after beating Peterhouse at Rugger, said we might as well have a party to celebrate beating one's aunt at draughts!

Friday 13 February
First meeting of the Real Folklore Society in Bernard Manning's rooms. I sang in appropriate costume, male or female, with Bernard as compère and Alan Pars as my accompanist. Songs like 'The Diver' and 'Pansy Faces' cried aloud for burlesque; but I preferred to sing 'Thora' (based on a sentimental novel by Hall Caine) and 'If Those Lips Could Only Speak' quite seriously, as also 'The Man Who Broke The Bank At Monte Carlo'. I believe this to be essentially a pathetic song, and I think I succeeded in getting my audience to accept it as such. My favourite comic items included Fred Earle's 'Seaweed', Billy Williams's 'Save A Little One for Me', Frank Coyne's 'You've Got A Long Way To Go', George Bastow's 'Captain Ginger' and Marie Lloyd's tribute to the marriage of Alphonso XIII of Spain in 1906, 'Tiddley-om-pom', with its tripping tune and rollicking double rhymes:

> Oh the folks they do go on so,
> In the land of King Alphonso

Sunday 22 March
Coached the College Servants VIII. In the Combination Room Duckworth said, "Have you been out into the country lately, Mills?" To which Mills replied, "Yes, today". "Have you noticed a shortage of hares?" asked Duckworth.

Maundy Thursday, 2 April
Went to the Royal Maundy Service at Westminster Abbey at noon and at 3 p.m. to the Washing of Feet at Westminster Cathedral.

Saturday 25 April
Subscribers to my Mymms book reached 224 today and Heffer asked for the MS as soon as possible. Canon Tyndale-Biscoe was in College today in great form. He spoke on Kashmir in the Hall with the Master in the Chair. TB is a very great man.

> [Canon Tyndale-Briscoe was a missionary in India where he ran a school for 1,500 people, mostly adults. He persuaded people who would normally have fought over a disagreement to settle their differences by holding rowing races. A tiny man, he had been a cox in his and Steve Fairbairn's undergraduate days.]

~ 1931 ~

Tuesday 28 April
Edleston called. As usual he dodged the Census last Sunday by spending the night in the train between Gainford and Cambridge.

Friday 15 May
To my great delight the galley proofs of my South Mymms book arrived today.

Monday 8 June
Marking Tripos papers, tea at the Bursary, then to the Boathouse. Dined at Pembroke at 8 p.m. with Comber in his rooms, plus ten pupils after which I sang eight items – some in female and one in episcopal dress.

Saturday 20 June
My first presentation in the Senate House [as Praelector of the College.]

Saturday 19 July

> The Haven
> Fowey
> Cornwall
> Telephone 53 Fowey

Dear Brittain:
   I want you to do me a favour.
   E. M. Forster – the writer – is instituting some kind of article on Cambridge and wants to know something more than is generally known about STC and Jesus College. I don't think there is much to know. But he will be in Cambridge this week and I have made bold to tell him that he might call on you and on the Master. [STC = Samuel Taylor Coleridge]
   Your job, if you will do it for me, is first to lead him around for an hour – show him the few memorials we have of STC (prints etc): bust open my rooms on C Staircase, show him the prints in my dining room, search my gyp room and exhibit whisky from lower cupboard or wine from long one. If he wants a quiet spot for writing, he can find it there (I don't mean the gyp room), and use any of my books in either room.
   Can you do this for me? "You can, and will?" ... Thank you – that's what I call real kindness.
      Yours,
         (signed) Q

[E. M. Forster (1879-1970) examined pre-1914 middle-class attitudes in his novels and the institutions that nurtured them, i.e. the Civil Service, the Church and the public schools. *A Passage to India* (1924), considered

~ 1931 ~

to be his masterpiece, puts his finest scrutiny to work in examining English values and Indian susceptibilities and the spiritual tensions produced by these two clashing civilizations. Forster, who was educated at Tonbridge School and King's College, Cambridge was elected a Fellow of King's in 1946.]

Saturday 26 July
E. M. Forster came to tea and I showed him the Coleridgiana etc. in the Old Library.

Saturday 8 August
Went to see a silly American film (my first talkie), followed by Charles Chaplin's first class *City Lights*.

Friday 28 August
Conducted a strenuous two weeks tour of Southern Spain for the Workers' Travel Association.

Thursday 26 November
Q and I gave a lunch in the Guest Rooms in honour of Old Sebley; the Master was in the Chair.

[F. J. Sebley was retiring after forty years service with Heffers, the Cambridge booksellers. After the lunch, Arthur Gray rose to propose the health of the guest of honour. He knew both Mr Heffer and Mr Sebley well but was apt to be absent-minded. Accordingly, throwing (as he always did) great emphasis on every third or fourth word, he said: "It gives us great pleasure gentlemen, to have with us to*day* our *good* friend, Mr *Heffer*". (Here Q plucked his sleeve and spoke to him in stage whispers.) "What's that, Q? *Not* Mr Heffer? Very *well* then. As I was saying, it gives us *great* pleasure to be here to*day* to do honour to our *good* friend, Mr *Heffer*." (More sleeve plucking.) "What did you say, Q? *Not* Mr Heffer?. *Quite* so. How stupid of me! Definitely *not* Mr Heffer. Very well then. It gives us all *great* pleasure to have with us today our good friend Mr . . ., our good friend who has done so *much* for us for *many* years. We are very glad to have with us to*day* our friend Mr Heffer. (Here Q gave up the sleeve-plucking as hopeless.). "I ask you to rise with me and drink his health. Gentlemen, Mr *Heffer*." And the company rose and drank to the health of Mr Sebley who was as much amused as anyone.]

~ 1931 ~

Friday 27 November
In Hall Barnes asserted that Steve [Fairbairn] had done more harm to the College than anyone else and ought to be drowned in the Cam. Steve has been up more this term than I have ever known.

Tuesday 22 December
Wrote a ghost story *To Encourage the Rest* – my first effort in this line.

[No further entries for December]

~ 1932 ~

Monday 11 January
Cambridge. Coaching on the Cam with Steve and the first three boats. At 9.30 p.m. went to see Comber to fix the Pembroke times. Bush and Gross came in to my rooms from 11.30 p.m. – 12.30 a.m.

> [Lambert Shepherd, called Bush by all Jesus men who knew him, had eyes that went "goo-goo" as his friends termed it, when in his cups. He rowed in the 1st May Boat and in the crew which won the Ladies' Plate at Henley. During the evacuation of the hard-pressed British forces from Dunkirk in 1940, Bush completed a remarkable feat by twice rowing a small boat alone across the English Channel from Dover, bringing back with him several soldiers each time. He joined the Navy soon afterwards and in 1941 was killed in action in HMS Hood.]

Sunday 28 February
The Roosters Debate on Women's rowing drew an attendance of about seventy. Many stayed on in my rooms until 12.30 a.m.

Sunday 6 March
Second performance of the Rooster Revue in East House. It was packed and received a great reception. Most of the High Table was present. Afterwards went to Q's rooms where O. V. Guy congratulated me on a "marvellous show" and Elliott said "I didn't know you had all this histrionic ability". Abbott added "I never cease to admire your versatility."

~ 1932 ~

Sunday 13th March
L. C. Harmer (Fitzwilliam) came to tea. He is paid 4/- (four shillings) per "Briggs" hours by the Cambridge University Correspondence College, which equals one and an eighth hours.

Saturday 19 March
London. Took Monica Hay to see the Boat Race from the roof of the London Rowing Club. Lunched at the Piccadilly Restaurant and then went to see the Head of the River Race from the LRC. Had tea at the Criterion and returned home by coach.

Tuesday 22 March
Barnet. Looked over 5 The Avenue with Mother.

[This was to become the Brittains' new home. It cost £95.]

Wednesday 22 April
Lunched in Hall with the Pundit [J. M. Edmonds] who related how he resuscitated an "almost moribund" boat club at The King's School, Canterbury.

Wednesday 11 May
Conrad Skinner came to Lunch with me in Hall, then I took him to see Q.

[The Revd Conrad Skinner was an assistant master at the Leys School, Cambridge, and a truly remarkable man. Being a Methodist minister, he was a lifelong teetotaller. Q detested teetotalism and strongly disliked non-conformity, so when Q invited Skinner to help himself to port he replied that he did not drink it and made the same reply to offers of sherry, Madeira and whisky. Q looked more and more puzzled and when Conrad finally confessed that he was a teetotaller, a look of horror spread over Q's face. When they left, FB advised Conrad that next time he should tinkle with the glasses and take some soda water. The result was that Q was soon telling everyone that Conrad Skinner was an excellent man.]

Tuesday 14 June
The Patriarch and Monica arrived for the May Ball.

Wednesday 15 June
We had an interesting discussion in the Combination Room about the Ball.

> Nairne: Do you mean to say that some of the ladies took more drink than was ladylike?

~ 1932 ~

Sinker: Yes, and more than was gentlemanly.
Elliott: The sexes really ought to get drunk separately.
FB: It's surprising how gloves have gone out of fashion at dances.
Sinker: Yes, it's all clammy hands and clammy backs.
Nairne: Oh! I think gloves should be worn. I wouldn't like to put my hand on a clammy back.
Abbot: Were you disturbed during the night, Nairne?
Nairne: Yes, I heard a man asking someone whether Dr Nairne might lend him some glasses, so I thought I would sport my oak [i.e. shut his outer door.] Apart from that, I didn't hear the noise much, in fact I thought of several new points about Saint Patrick as I lay awake.

(Here Elliott went over to the Victorian sideboard, or chiffonier, or whatnot, which Nairne and others have denounced for so long and urged its removal.)

Elliott: This thing's not badly made, you know. The doors open and shut. It's a good bit of mahogany, too.
Nairne: (Eagerly) Mahogany? Oh! Did you say mahogany? A beautiful wood. Oh! It's mahogany, is it? Oh! Well, that alters things. If it's mahogany I don't think I shall want it thrown away after all.

Monday 27 June
Barnet. We moved into 5 The Avenue.

Saturday 27 July
Our crew won the Visitors' Cup [at Henley Regatta]. I'm staying with them at Longlands. There was noise until 4 a.m. but not so much as usual this year.

Thursday 7 July
Went to the Odeon at Golders Green and saw *Emma*, my second talkie!

Tuesday 2 August
Barnet. Moving day and housework. At 3.30 p.m. walked to Kitts End Lane and across the big field – delightful views of Wrotham House, of Dyrham gates between two trees, of Knightsland, and of the new Grammar School at Barnet between two other trees. Had tea at Knightsland. At 8 p.m. attended a meeting of the Church Council at the Vicarage.

Monday 8 August
Wrote 'Route 84' for the Barnet Press.

~ 1932 ~

Wednesday 10 August
Cambridge. Lord North came in with Elliott and brought some ancient deeds for me to translate.

Saturday 20 August
Worked on Lord North's documents all day. A storm during the night ended the hottest long spell we've had for many years

Monday 22 August
I received a letter from the Arthur Gray who is staying in Harrogate.

> My dear Brittain,
> Your charming letter is the best of birthday presents – though as you justly note I am far from being 80 yet, in fact not till next week, but I hope to begin a new decade before I return on August 30. My rheumatic son Philip has brought me to Harrogate but – *Laus Deo* – I have no ailments of my own to cure and today have taken a woodland walk of 6 – 7 miles. All you write goes to my heart except always that I least deserve your most kind remarks about my Masterhood. I think it is in the air of Jesus, and for 20 happy years I have particularly to thank the Fellows and you and the wise guidance of Abbott, Elliott, Manning in especial. I have not felt old because they don't let me, and I don't like to be thought old and out of date. I like to take freshmen about the Lodge and show them the portrait of old Dr Ashton, Master for 51 years, a very learned man whose learning was buried in his grave. When I tell them that by precedent I should have 31 years more of tenure I rather think they are dispirited – at least they don't say *ad multros annos*. With advancing years I hope to make new friends and harbour some new ideas. In our society I don't care for unanimity but very much for animinity. I wish that I could know undergrads as you do and so I hope when I entertain lunch parties I may count on you to come and talk undergrad talk and bridge the gulf between me and them.
> I go tomorrow for a week to Goathland, Whitby.
> With very much gratitude for your loyalty to the College.
> Yours ever
> (signed) Arthur Gray.

Saturday 1 October
Began to move out of my rooms at the top of 8 Chapel Court into a set on the top floor of C staircase in First Court, immediately over Q. Slept in my new rooms.

~ 1932 ~

Saturday 8 October
Had just finished lunch in my rooms when in came "Chippy" Prior (whom I hadn't seen for ten years) and his sister home on leave from Bombay. We talked much and I showed them round.

Wednesday 26 October
Lunched in Hall with Q and Edmonds. I hadn't intended going but Q called to tell me there was liver and bacon *and* sultana roll. In the afternoon I went to Baitsbite with the Fours and after Hall to the Dean's rooms with H. Playford for wine with the Fours.

Wednesday 2 November
Q talked about parsons in Roseland, all of whom he says are "as mad as sheep". The Rev. Epaphraditus Dunn who rises at 6 p.m. starts visiting about 10 p.m. Once he showed Q's daughter and a friend round his church by torch. A figure rose from the pews, "That's my sister", he said. "She sleeps here, she likes it." A parson named Bond of St Just-in-Roseland had a wife who couldn't stand him any longer and left him, so he put up a tombstone in the churchyard, which read "To the memory of —— wife of —— Bond, BA Oxon, who departed on —— This man used to give a kettle to every woman at church on Christmas Day and a top hat to each man. He retired recently but still lives there, and is "as happy as a duck".

Friday 4 November
A. J. W. Hill, who keeps on the bottom of my staircase, came to breakfast.

> [Alan Hill, CBE, became FB's lifelong friend and publisher. Chairman and Managing Director of Heinemann's, his experiences round the world *In Pursuit of Publishing* are excellently described in his autobiography of that name.]

Saturday 19 November
At The Roosters Annual Dinner I acted as Orator at the Orderization of William Nicholson who is painting Q's portrait for us.

> [This portrait is one of the three Nicolsons at Jesus, the others being of the Master, Arthur Gray, and of Tommy Watt. The Q portrait remains the property of the Roosters but was handed over to the College on permanent loan in the sum of one and chickspence – denaris XVIII – when FB died. This fact is recorded in Latin below the title.]

~ 1932 ~

> 11 Apple Tree Yard, St James's, SW1
> Monday night.

Dear Brittain
    Can I trouble you? I don't know the pet name of Q's gyp and I left a silk MA gown in a parcel (you and I know why I bought it) in the cupboard in the bedroom where I slept off my excesses. If you can have it sent to me here I shall be so much obliged
        Yours ever sincerely
        (signed) William Nicholson.

Saturday 3 December
Translating Lord North's deeds, then to London to the Florence Restaurant in Rupert Street for the first reunion of the old Second London Hospital Unit – about 50 present.

Sunday 4 December
Lunched at the Lodge. Douglas Timins and Miss Mahy were also there. The Master held forth about Charles Whibley's iniquity in leaving nothing to the College. "We expected him to do WELL by the College but he didn't leave us a PENNY! All he left was a monstrous relict".

Monday 5 December
Worked on Lord North's deeds. Went to Hall, Edmonds dined. When I left the Combination Room, Nairne rushed to come out with me and expressed his dread lest Edmonds come and bore him. "Really, he is too dreadful", he said. However, when I went to Thorpe's I found the Pundit there. I sang some Italian songs. The Pundit fairly thrashed the piano (but not while I was singing).

Christmas Day, Sunday 25 December
Barnet. After a long wait for a bus I was late for church so sat in the nave. Frank's engagement to Elsie Lawrence was announced. We drank their health.

Wednesday 28 November
Helped Dad to put in posts for a new fence.

Thursday 29 December
Creosoted the new fence.

[No further entries for December]

~ 1933 ~

[This was the year in which Adolph Hitler came to power in Germany and the Japanese were over-running Manchuria, but life at Cambridge continued in its usual, pleasant way.]

Tuesday 17 January
Cambridge. Saw Mrs Mitchley working with her hat off.

[At this time all bedmakers were required to wear a hat when they were working. Mrs Mitchley was the bedmaker on C staircase. She was admirable in every way and Q called her the best bedmaker in Cambridge, which became abbreviated to 'the BBC'. Once someone asked FB when Q was likely to come up, to which he replied, "The BBC says he's coming tomorrow". "What?" said the enquirer, "Do they broadcast it now?"]

Tuesday 7 February
Went to the training breakfast in Hall and in the afternoon to the boathouse. After dinner I was in the Combination Room alone with Duckworth. He told me of a Chinaman, Mr Wu, who, on leaving Cambridge today gave him "a packet of tea; as a gratuity, don't you know?"

Friday 17 February
Watched the rugger at St John's Rugger ground where we beat them 8–6 in the Cup.

Sunday 5 March
We presented the Rooster Revue *Sweet and Low*. It was packed out and received great applause. Thorpe said I was on the stage for three or four minutes as Lady Houston before he recognised me. William Nicholson, who has given us a silk gown designed by himself for the Grand Marshall of the Red Herrings, said he thought the Revue was first rate.

[The Nicholson gown was still being worn by "Trusty and Well-Beloved Mr Grand Marshall, Old Fish in 1992. The second 'l' in Grand Marshall was decreed to be correct after that spelling appeared in the fillets (minutes) of a Shoal.]

Monday 6 March
Received a note to say that I am elected to the Footlights Club. Went to see the crocuses in Trinity College, a glorious sight.

Friday 7 April
Barnet. Walked to Kitts End, Sawyers Lane and Bridgefoot. The limes are gradually opening, the larches are wonderful and the celandines brilliant. Had tea at Knightsland, then went to Evensong and Stations of the Cross.

Good Friday, 14 April
I attended Presanctified Mass at 8 a.m. followed at 10 a.m. by Mattins and Litany. The Rev. C. B. Mortlock preached the Three Hours Service from 12 noon to 3 p.m.

Friday 5 May
Cambridge. Spent the afternoon with the boats. Steve, being in a trailer pedalled by Claude Elliott said, "I've got the dons where I want them". Simon Bonham-Carter translated "screws" by "scroux", which he alleged he had found in the French and English dictionary, as indeed he had as the French pronunciation of the English word.

Wednesday 17 May
Took Paul Sinker to lunch at the Footlights to convince him that there is such a place.

Thursday 18 May
At the Rustat Feast Q carefully avoided Bullough, so as not to have to congratulate him on his election to the Professorship of Italian.

Friday 2 June
Elliott has been elected Headmaster of Eton. He stood us champagne in Hall.

Monday 5 June
It is very hot. Tonight was the first performance of the Footlights May Week Revue *No More Women*. Bill Nichols and I were encored for our Policewomen's turn.

> [FB helped to write the script of this revue. It got its name because in the previous year women had been included in the cast for the first time and the revue was not a success. Women were not introduced again for another twenty years or so.]

Tuesday 13 June
The Master's Lodge
Emmanuel College
Cambridge

My dear Brittain,
   Of one thing I can assure you, you have removed the filth entirely from the show – it is the only Footlight's show I have seen, to which not the slightest exception can be taken on these grounds . . .
       (signed) E. Welbourne

Friday 16 June
The Coleridge "quasi-centenary" celebration, Foakes-Jackson having persuaded the College to celebrate the centenary of S. T. Coleridge's death a year in advance because he is in England this summer. There was tea in the Fellows' Garden and a small exhibition of Coleridge relics in the Shield Library. Sixty-six were present at the dinner in Hall, including E. V. Knox, with whom I went to Q's rooms afterwards until 12.30 a.m.

Saturday 3 July
Barnet. Attended Frank's marriage at the Register Office, Marriott Road.

Friday 14 July
The Centenary of the Oxford Movement was celebrated at St Giles, South Mymms.

Wednesday 19 July
Cambridge. Lunched at Magdalene with Killanin, after which we went to the Oratory House and I introduced him to Wilfred.

[Lord Killanin was an undergraduate at Magdalene College and they had become friendly through the Footlights Club. One afternoon FB came off the river wearing a ragged raincoat, ancient battered hat and with his shoes and trousers covered in mud. Being in need of a haircut, he went straight to the nearest barber's shop. He realised at once that he had gone to the wrong shop because the walls were decorated with posters advertising race meetings and hunt balls and were hung with antlers, foxes masks, riding whips and binoculars. It was clearly the daily resort of the nobility and gentry of the hunting, shooting and fishing fraternity. There were no customers when FB entered, but there were four assistants on view who ignored him, which was not surprising considering his tramp-like appearance. He took off his battered hat and muddy raincoat, hung them up and sat in one of the vacant chairs. After a few minutes one of the assistants turned to him and, raising his eyebrows, said "Haircut?" and got slowly to work with an air of "it irks me, but I suppose I must do it". A minute or two later, there was a commotion as the two assistants who had been sitting down sprang up, rushed to the swing doors, pulled them open, bowed as a customer walked in, and said "Good afternoon my Lord", remaining respectfully standing while he took a chair. FB recognised him at once as Michael Killanin, a youthful peer of the realm, who obviously came to this shop every day for a shave. Killanin did not notice FB until one of the assistants changed his position. "Well I'm dashed! It's you Freddie, is it?" he said. FB was conscious immediately of a more delicate touch on his hair than before, as the hairdresser got on with his work. Killanin and FB chatted until his shave was finished, when he said "See you at lunch at the club tomorrow" and left. Even after Killanin had gone, no one ventured to sit down. When FB's haircut was finished one of the assistants fetched and helped him on with his filthy raincoat while another respectfully presented his battered hat. When FB felt in his numerous pockets for money to pay his bill he found he hadn't a farthing on him! Explaining the situation and offering to bring it along later he was told "That's all right, Sir. There's no hurry. Any Friend of his Lordship..." FB felt almost inclined to add "Need never bother to pay" but he didn't. Instead he walked grandly out, with a bowing assistant holding a swing door on each side of him. When he told Michael Killanin about his adventure at lunch next day they both agreed it would make an admirable sketch for a May Week Revue, without any touching up, adding only a song, with the refrain *The British nation dearly loves a Lord*.]

Sunday 13 August
Dined at the Oratory House. I found a passage in a history of English Romanism from which I saw that they didn't use Italian pronunciation of Latin until about 1850. This made me write an article, which I called *Cheese and Chaws*.

Tuesday 22 August
Cycled home from Cambridge via Ashwell, Baldock, Stevenage, Lemsford and South Mymms. There was wind on my starboard bow most of the way when not straight ahead, but I dismounted for only three hills.

Sunday 27 August
Barnet. It is very hot today. Held forth at Evensong on St Augustine of Hippo.

~ 1933 ~

Monday 4 September
I was woken by droves of horses coming along the Avenue to the fair. Watered the garden, then went to the pleasure fair. Worked at *Cheese and Chaws* – G. G. Coulton has pronounced it "excellent".

Sunday 1 October
There were 35 men and boys in the Chancel besides the Vicar [at St Giles].

Tuesday 21 November
Cambridge. Today is Q's 70th birthday. Lunched in Hall with him and Manning and Barnes, who held forth about the great superfluity of damned secondary school and other "low class people" now admitted to the University. Q says Barnes hadn't washed for a week. He certainly hadn't shaved for three days. After lunch I went to Q's rooms with eight or nine undergraduates and drank his health.

Thursday 30 November
The Roosters Annual Dinner was held in Hall for the first time. There were about sixty present and it was very orderly.

Friday 8 December
A. J. W. Hill came to breakfast. Mrs Mitchley tells me she is going tonight to an "Activity Play". Had tea with Michael Brown and heard the following story: A man said to his friend "When I got home last night I found my wife in bed with gout". The friend replied, "Do you know if he's one of the Lincolnshire Gouts?"

Saturday 16 December
Barnet. It's very cold. Walked with Abbott (now retired to Barnet) and Miss Abbott to Dyrham Park, where the lake was covered with skaters. At 7 p.m. I went to the Grammar School, my first time in the new building (in King's Road Barnet).

> [Edwin Abbot, the Senior Tutor who had admitted FB to Jesus College in 1919, was now living with his sister in Barnet. Trains were his hobby and he spent many happy hours sitting on a fence beside the railway line at Hadley Wood, watch in hand, timing the flying Scotsman or some other express.]

Wednesday 20 December
Cambridge. Had a meeting at the Cambridge University Press with S. C. Roberts about *Cheese and Chaws*. He says that with a change of title the CUP

will publish it. After Hall the Master came into the Combination Room and fell asleep in his chair, which we had never seen him do before.

[No further entries for December]

~ 1934 ~

Friday 12 January
Barnet. The thrushes are singing loudly in our cherry tree.

Saturday 13 January
Travelled by coach to Cambridge and arrived at 12.45 p.m. In Hall Nairne said, "I admire the beautiful platform at York station more than I do the Cathedral". Duckworth talked about a pond with "a herbaceous growth whereby the navigation of the children's craft was impeded".

Friday 19 January
Proofs of *Latin in Church* arrived today. In Hall I had a conversation with the Dean, P. Gardner-Smith, as follows:

The Dean:	"How long is that book of yours on Latin pronunciation?"
FB:	"Oh, quite short – about seventy pages."
The Dean:	"Seventy pages? Do you call that short? I should have thought that was more than enough for a subject like that."
FB:	"I consider myself squashed flat."
The Dean:	"Not at all but it is a dull subject, isn't it, to write about at such length? Of course you may have made it less dull but I should have thought seventy pages too much."

[FB received the following letter on the subject from the Dean, dated 16th March:

Many thanks for *Latin in Church*. You will have some interesting reviews.
I'm afraid you will be a voice in the wilderness for the pronunciation you commend is nobody's child. It would sound almost heretical to Romans, and it would be almost equally strange to Classics and anti-Classics like me. Still you have had your fling and smitten the enemy.

*Ah*braham is not a very "scholarly introduction", for the Hebrew is Abraham.

    Congratulations,
    Yours, P. G-S.

Then in Hall conversation between them continued as follows -

The Dean: "Greenhalgh has gone to hospital with mumps. J. N. Duckworth will be the next no doubt, as they were sitting at the same table."
FB: "Were they the only two?"
The Dean: "Oh! No, but you see Duckworth is coxing the Varsity boat and it would be most unfortunate if he were to get mumps as it would mean missing his Blue. I feel sorry for him. He is practically certain to get mumps as he has not had it before. Very hard lines indeed to miss his Blue like that."
FB: "But he hasn't actually got mumps has he?"
The Dean: "No, but there's plenty of time yet."
FB: "But I suppose it's just possible he won't get mumps?"
The Dean: You're very captious tonight. You see if he gets mumps it will mean missing his Blue and that'll be very hard lines. Fancy missing a Blue through mumps" ... (and so on, ad infinitum.)

Tuesday 30 January
In the Combination Room Edmonds asked me if I thought that most dons were faithful to their wives. "I can assure you that I am and always have been, absolutely", he said.

Saturday 3 February
Pars took me home in his car. The first time I have been home in February since 1914.

[He picked him up again next morning.]

Saturday 10 February
Sir Herbert Richmond, Professor of Naval History, was elected a Professorial Fellow of the College today and Tillyard was re-elected a Fellow.

[E. M. W. Tillyard, a Jesus Man, and an authority on Milton and Shakespeare, later became Master of Jesus College.]

~ 1934 ~

Monday 12 February
Okey and I went to tea with Q. Okey told us that he goes once a month to teach Italian to Ian R. Maxwell-Stuart who is serving fourteen years for burglary, having previously been tried for murder and later robbery with violence but acquitted.

Friday 16 February
Went to see the aconites at St John's College, which are more numerous than ever – there are sheets of them.

Thursday 22 February
I was in bed all day with a chill. Jepson brought me news of the Lent Races. We unexpectedly bumped Pembroke and went Head.

Saturday 25 February
Still in bed and my voice has gone entirely. We finished Head easily.

Thursday 1 March
Out for the first time [since 21 February]. The lesser-spotted woodpecker in the tree by Bin Brook was making a terrific noise, like two trees grating against each other.

Saturday 10 March
Went to a tea dance and cabaret at the Footlights. I performed as the Professoress of Domestic Economy teaching knitting etc. to undergraduates.

Wednesday 14 March
[FB sent the following letter to S. C. Roberts at The Cambridge University Press:]

Jesus College
Cambridge

Dear Roberts,
　I received the complimentary copies of Latin in Church yesterday, and am writing to thank you for publishing it at all and particularly in such attractive form. If the reviewers are as pleased with the contents of the book as I am with its appearance I shall be very happy indeed.
　Comber seems pleased with my dedicating it to him.
　I have been hustling Q about that portrait. After he had ejaculated several times: "My God! I'll beat up that devil Nicholson", and after promising to write to him that evening, he eventually did so. Result – Nicholson is in Scotland. ("My God! You simply *can't* get hold of the

devil. Why in God's name is he always running off somewhere?") However, I understand that sittings really will be resumed and finished at the beginning of next term.

Q goes down tomorrow, leaving the College about noon. I am giving instructions this evening about the Going-down Ceremony, and hope to marshal the procession tomorrow as usual.

Yours sincerely
(signed) F. Brittain.

[Q's Going Down Ceremony came about one day at the end of term when FB chanced to call on Q just as he was about to leave for home, so he walked with him to the gate and saw him into his car. There he handed him the spare bowler hat with which, for some unknown reason, he generally travelled. (He possessed black, grey and brown bowlers for particular occasions). Q was obviously pleased with this send-off. FB therefore made a point of calling on him the following term at the time when he knew he was going down. On this occasion FB went with him all the way to the station where he saw him into his train. Within a year or two this had developed into a grand ceremony in which the chief officers of the Roost all took part and sometimes a car-load went to the station with Q.]

Monday 23 April
After lunch the Pundit said, "I have got twenty-seven at my lectures but certainly no more than eleven will continue, probably only five, perhaps only three". Arthur Fraser came in to my rooms after Hall and stayed until 1 a.m.

[Arthur Fraser was Captain of Boats 1933-34. During his term of office the Captain's rooms were moved from next to the Combination Room to the present Captain's set in the Carpenter tower in Chapel Court. He expressed his pleasure at the move, saying that he did not like his quiet Boat Club parties disturbed by the noise of the dons drinking their port.]

Monday 30 April
On my way through the Cloisters I heard a woman say to her companion, "They are all parsons at this College, aren't they?" "Yes", came the reply!

Wednesday 2 May
Cycled the Madingley round then watched cricket on the Close. Edleston, who is up for the Newmarket Races, called and introduced "my friend, Mr Greenan", i.e. his under-gardener.

Tuesday 22 May
Heard the following conversation about Cambridge street names:

> Edmonds   "Is it true that Senate House Passage used to be called Fornication Lane?"
> Mills: "I don't know but Comberton Lane, judging by what I have seen there, well deserves the name".
> Edmonds: "Is that so? I don't get as far out as that myself."

Saturday 26 May
Attended the training breakfast. F. M. G. Stammers was elected Captain of Boats for next year and the Yak Secretary. W. L. H. Duckworth is feeding a mole with long narrow strips of meat cut up to look like worms. "It consumes them with the greatest avidity, don't you know", he said.

Wednesday 6 June
May Races and all our six boats made a bump – a record for Cambridge.

Thursday 21 June
Barnet. Turned out two bedrooms and painted the inside of the big front bedroom.

Monday 25 June
Went to Abbott's and sat in the garden while he told me how he had been swindled by a confidence trickster.

Saturday 7 July
At Henley Regatta staying with the crews at Cowfield Farm. It is very hot. We won the Ladies' Plate and broke the record. A most enjoyable regatta, I think I enjoyed it more than ever, chiefly because there were no gramophones or wireless at the farm.

Saturday 14 July
Barnet. Went to the Abbey of Christ the King at New Barnet; queer people there.

> [Mr J. S. M. Ward founded the Abbey (as the outcome of visions vouchsafed to him at Golders Green) and assumed for himself the title of Father Superior of the Kingdom of Christ (Orthodox Catholic Church of England). Not content with this he soon raised himself to the episcopal purple and styled himself Archbishop Ward. He was often seen shopping in Barnet in scarlet cassock, cape, biretta and pectoral cross, accompanied by the Reverend Mother Superior of the Abbey (Mrs Ward) in white

robes. They also directed the much-publicized Abbey Folk Park – "the only open-air park in the British Empire: admission 1s 3d" – to which schoolchildren were taken in large parties.]

Sunday 22 July
Cambridge. Went with J. N. Duckworth to Linton, Hadstock and Radwinter and back by Saffron Walden. No noise in the streets there, no cars in sight as we drove along the streets of old houses along which people were going to church. The bells were ringing – sweet, silvery bells. The sound of them and the beauty of the scene smote me to the heart and gave me a physical pain.

Monday 30 July
Bonham-Carter was sent down today for climbing in on Sunday at 1.30 a.m.

Thursday 11 October
Had tea with Professor Okey who was 82 on 30 September. He gave me two waste-paper baskets of his own make: one finished only a few days ago, the other made to illustrate his article on basket-making in the 1910–11 *Encyclopaedia Britanica*.

Thursday 18 October
Paid my first visit to the new University Library.

Tuesday 30 October
Lunched at the Footlights. Q says Ezra Pound is merely impudent.

Wednesday 31 October
Attended a meeting of the Cambridge University Coxswains Club, Conrad Skinner was in the Chair. I was elected Vice-President.

Saturday 4 November
The Roosters Village Fair was opened by Q. I conducted the auction sale (Clawktion) and did palmistry blindfold.

Wednesday 21 November
Took Michael Killanin to Q's – he expected someone terrifying.

Wednesday 12 December
Read Grace in Hall for the first time.

> [Oculi omnium in te aspiciunt et in te sperant, Deus: tu das illis escam tempore opportuno.
> Asperis tu manus et imples omne benedictione tua.

Benedic nobis, Domine, et omnibus tuis donis quae ex larga liberalitate tua sumpturi sumus, per Jesum Christum Dominum nostrum.
Deus est caritas.
Que manet in caritate manet in Deo et Deus in illo.
Sic Deus in nobis et nos maneamus in illo.]

[No further entries for December]

~ 1935 ~

Monday 11 January
Left Euston for Chester with E. V. Knox to attend the dinner of the Mid-Cheshire Pitt Club where EV spoke on parody.

Saturday 12 January
We arrived back at Euston soon after 3 p.m. and had tea at EV's house at Clarence Terrace.

Wednesday 16 January
Cambridge. Took Thorpe to lunch at the Footlights, then he showed me over the Zoology labs. Went to the Boat House with Conrad Skinner. I took him to Hall and to my rooms where I had visitors until 12 midnight.

Friday 8 February
Went by car with R. Gittings to the aconite wood near Abington – a glorious sight – then to the snowdrops in the wood near Fulbourn.

Monday 11 February
St Radegund's Day dinner in the Q-bicle.

> [The Q-bicle was the Fellows' Guest Room opposite Q's rooms. He annexed it and called it his dining room and was quite offended if a Fellow had a guest staying there for more than a day or two.]

Saturday 23 February
Last year we broke the Cam record for the Lents and this year we broke our own record. The first boat started and finished Head, the second boat went up three places, the third boat went up four, the fourth, fifth and sixth up three each, a total equivalent to twenty bumps.

Sunday 24 February
Took Sir Herbert Richmond to the Roost to get him emperched.

Wednesday 13 March
Went to Q's rooms for the 'Going-Down Ceremony'. [See 14 March, 1934]

Tuesday 26 March
Arrived at Dieppe with the Dean and Mrs Gardner-Smith.

> [FB was going with them to France and Spain as, in the words of
> P. Gardner-Smith, their guide, philosopher and friend.]

Wednesday 27 March
We drove to Poitiers and went to St Radegund's Abbey where the Abbe was saying Mass. The sacrist who was serving him left the altar to sell us postcards in the vestry and then ran back to the altar to ring the sanctuary bell. We left Poitiers and lunched by the roadside after a very fast run of 100 miles. We travelled on through Bordeaux and put up at Biarritz, having driven 265 miles today.

Friday 29 March
Attended High Mass at Burgos Cathedral. The retable was veiled in violet except for the middle strip. The clergy in the stalls were censed by two thurifers who were preceded by a mace bearer in a red silk mantle with a flat hood of white fur.

Sunday 31 March
Went to the Mozarabic Mass at Toledo Cathedral [surviving here only in Christendom] with the celebrant in a voluminous Gothic violet chasuble; there were no silent prayers. After the offertory he knelt, holding the veiled vessels, on the lowest step and prayed. We went next to the Roman Mass at the high altar. As at Burgos, only six of the eight candles were lit, none of the retable was veiled, all the vestments were dark violet, not the reddish tint worn in England. The mace bearer was in a sort of long violet tunicle with a big white cravat and an eighteenth century type wig. The MC was in a cassock and black mantle only with no cotta at all.

Monday 1 April
We left Toledo for Cordova where we visited the Mosque and the Cathedral.

~ 1935 ~

Wednesday 3 April
We left Seville, then went off the main road among the hills. We had a grand view of the mountains and Malaga where we stayed at the Hotel Regina and had fresh broad beans for dinner.

Thursday 4 April
Left Malaga and ran along the coast through sugar cane etc., then over the mountains on a new first-class road to Granada. Walked in the Alhambra gardens with wisteria in full bloom, which was a glorious sight.

Monday 8 April
Left Alicante and had a fine run by the sea to Valencia passing miles of orange groves, blossom and fruit.

Palm Sunday, 14 April
Attended High Mass at Rouen Cathedral where the choirboys wore long white albs with red capes attached to which were little red riding-hoods, which they pulled over their heads as soon as they came out of the choir. In the procession (numbering quite two hundred including a number of seminarists), the Archbishop and Canons carried both palm and box branches, but all the others box only.

Thursday 2 May
Cambridge. Dined at St Catharine's College with the Master after which we set the Medieval Latin paper for the Tripos.

Monday 6 May
King George V's Silver Jubilee. Went to Midsummer Common to see the procession of vehicles start and then to Jesus Green and mixed with the big crowd. After Hall watched the fireworks from the Close. Entertained men in my rooms until 3 a.m.

Thursday 9 May
Ann Steinbrecher from Chicago (a peach), and Edith Johnson, a lecturer at Wellesley, USA, came to tea.

Thursday 16 May
Attended the Memorial Service for Professor Okey at Caius College.

Friday 24 May
Empire Day. Q said he detested Empire on account of the awful people and ideas with which it is associated. The mention of Empire Day, he said, makes him vomit.

~ 1935 ~

Tuesday 4 June
Nairne (as quoted by Barnes in the baths this morning) said "Some of the finest views in the world are those you get from lavatory windows".

Saturday 15 June
We finished Head of the River. At the Bump Supper the Master made an excellent speech and old Hutch also spoke. He said the difference between 'Fairbairnism' and orthodoxy was like getting to a particular destination by consulting the ABC instead of Bradshaw.

[A. M. Hutchinson was a close friend of Steve Fairbairn. He had a long drooping moustache, a sorrowful countenance, and a quiet voice. He was as taciturn as Steve was loquacious. Nevertheless Steve always consulted him before settling any matter saying, "That's right, Hutch, ain't it?" Hutch would say, "Yes, Steve", to which he would reply, "There you are, Hutch says it's right so it must be".]

Friday 23 August
Barnet. Worked on my *Medieval Latin and Romance Lyric* most of the day, then went to Knightsland and examined the sixteenth century wall paintings which were revealed on Wednesday.

[These depict the story of the Prodigal Son and are as colourful today (1990's) as when they were first uncovered.]

27 November
Cambridge. Played the title role in *The Silver King* and so had the pleasure of declaiming the magnificently hyperbolic line "O God put back thy universe and give me yesterday!"

[The part of the Silver King's little daughter Cissie, was played by J. N. Duckworth. He was as plump and rosy-cheeked as a Della Robbia cherub but had to say "I'm starving, Jakes. I've had nothing to eat for three days" – an assertion that brought down the house. Vivian Cox, afterwards a well known playwright, theatre director and manager of the Mermaid Theatre in London, acted the part of the Silver King's wife, Nellie and the part of FB's faithful henchman Jakes, was played by his pupil, afterwards Sir David Trench, Governor of Hong Kong.]

[No further entries for November or December]

~ 1936 ~

Friday 10 January
Cambridge. Dined at 12 Clarence Terrace with E. V. Knox.

Monday 20 January
King George V died just before midnight.

Thursday 23 January
Went with Q and Richmond to the Senate House to hear the Vice-Chancellor read the proclamation of the new King, Edward VIII.

Tuesday 28 January
King George V's funeral. We had a service in Chapel at 10 a.m. and it was very well done.

Wednesday 12 February
Training breakfast with the crews. In Q's rooms from 10 – 11 p.m. concocting songs for the Rooster Review.

Tuesday 18 February
With the Varsity Boat, which contains David Burnford, Tom Cree and Noel Duckworth, to Baitsbite and back. Took G. G. Coulton to the Guest Night, saw him off, then went to Q's rooms with Richmond and S. C. Roberts, Secretary of the Syndics University Press.

Saturday 22 February
Went to the Lents by taxi in pouring rain. We finished Head so went to the Bump Supper and bonfire on the Close. Frank Stammers was in my rooms until 1 a.m.

Sunday 1 March
Produced the Rooster Review *The Twerp's Progress* in East House.

Sunday 15 March
I hear that Nairne died this morning. The crocuses at Trinity are very fine today.

[During the Easter vacation FB worked solidly on the *Medieval Latin and Romance Lyric*, interspersed with going to see the Mossmans at Knightsland, walking with Abbot, usually through Hadley Wood to the Railway and back, and the usual Holy Week and Easter celebrations at St Giles. Visits to London theatres included the non-stop revue at the Windmill theatre and a matinee at Daly's, called *St Helena*.]

Friday 29 May
Cambridge. Q had a poisoned foot. I applied hot fomentations every few hours.

Saturday 13 June
Went to Q's rooms. Richmond looked in to say goodbye. Q, knowing that Richmond was going to be elected Master of Downing College said, "I'm not going to say goodbye, you devil".

Tuesday 16 June
Marvellous weather. Had supper in Hall with Paul and Ruth Sinker and R. & K. Gittings. Went to the May Week Ball and danced most of the night. We had a photograph taken about 6 a.m. next morning then had breakfast at the Gittings's house at Harston.

Sunday 12 July
South Mymms. Attended the Dedication Festival at St Giles. Met Gillie Potter in the Vicarage.

[Gillie Potter was a radio comedian who broadcast the goings-on at his mythical Hertfordshire village of Hogsnorton.]

Tuesday 28 July
Made up a game for teaching French genders.

Saturday 15 August
Went with the Paveys by car to Weston-super-mare.

[They toured the area and returned via Bristol – where FB noted seven altars in the Cathedral, - and the Cotswolds where he liked Burford and its church best of the villages.]

Wednesday 2 September
Working on the *Medieval Latin and Romance Lyric*, then to Knightsland working in the hayfields.

~ 1936 ~

[Haymaking was a long job in those days. After it was turned it was made into smallish heaps called "cocks" for ease of carting. The cocks were then pitched by hand with a hay-fork onto a horse-drawn cart carrying a man who spread it evenly. At the rick another horse was going round in circles to drive the elevator into which the hay was thrown and carried to the top of the rectangular rick until it was thought to be the right height to be "topped off". Later, when it had settled, it was thatched with straw to keep out the rain.]

Friday 11 September
Returned to Cambridge and began moving my things across the landing into my new rooms.

[These were Dr Nairne's old rooms - the top left-hand set on C staircase.]

Thursday 29 October
Lunched at the Pitt Club with Michael Killanin. At 8.30 p.m. I appeared as the porter in *Macbeth* at the ADC Theatre.

Monday 7 December
Attended to Q who had cut his finger, and went to the station with him. There I found four or five Roosters meeting a train and I roped them in to the 'Going Down Party'. It was a great sight on the platform, eight of us plus porter with a truck of luggage plus guard etc. finding a place. The porter started to pile the luggage into a 1st class compartment but Q made him take it out as there were other people in the compartment and he apparently didn't like the look of them. This happened twice. Then he said he would travel 3rd class in order to be alone. Again the porter started putting the luggage in but took it out when an official came running up to say there was an empty 1st class carriage lower down so we all moved along to this. Q was quite unperturbed though the train was being delayed and people were putting their heads out of windows wondering why. At last Q and the entire luggage was safely stowed and I handed him the spare bowler which he put on the rack. We all raised our hats, or rather Q and I did as no one else was wearing a hat, and off the train went.

Thursday 10 December
My pupil Shamsher Singh came in. Then I went to the Union and heard the broadcast of King Edward VIII's abdication.

Thursday 24 December
Barnet. The Vicar was taken to the Wellhouse Hospital, Barnet General this morning so I conducted Evensong, delivered the Bradshawe Sermon and

distributed the bread. The Bishop of the Arctic, A. L. Fleming, celebrated at midnight.

[His episcopal signature was 'Archibald The Arctic'.]

Monday 28 December
Visited the Vicar in hospital. He is seriously ill with pneumonia.

[No further entries for December]

~ 1937 ~

Friday 12 February
Cambridge. At my morning lecture I called on a man to translate. He raised the ingenious excuse, "I am writing down all your jokes and I haven't got them all down yet".

Sunday 28 February
As usual on Sundays I made tea for about nine at about 4.15 p.m.

Tuesday 9 March
Dined at the Varsity Arms [University Arms Hotel] as one of about seventy guests of Tikka Shamsher Singh to celebrate the Golden Jubilee of the reign of his father-in-law, the Maharajah of Jind. Lord Birdwood in proposing the chief toast kept on introducing Indian terms and translating them, e.g. "We had japati (or pancakes) for chota hazri (or breakfast)" and so on ad infinitum. Will Spens, the Master of Corpus Christi College, had himself announced as "The Master of Corpus", which I thought was all wrong. When I told Q he said, "Of course he should have had himself announced as the Master of Caucus".

Monday 15 March
Went to Oxford and stayed a night with A L Rowse at All Souls'.

[Alfred Lesley Rowse, the English Historian born in St Austell and a protégé of Q's, was educated at Oxford and became a fellow of All Souls' College.]

~ 1937 ~

Wednesday 17 March
Barnet. The Vicar is not yet able to officiate but is looking his old self.

Wednesday 12 May
The Coronation of King George VI. Went to Chapel at 7.45 a.m., lunched in Hall and Joe Harmsworth called afterwards.

Monday 31 May
At 5.22 p.m., just as I was having tea, Q came in and, holding out his hand said "Hail, Fellow of Jesus", this being my first intimation. Then the Master came to congratulate the College, himself and myself, as he put it. Soon after Duckworth came and left the Statutes, "The honour has been delayed far too long", he said.

Tuesday 1 June
At 1 p.m. I was admitted to my Fellowship in Chapel. Richmond paid me the greatest compliment by coming from Downing for it. In the Combination Room after Hall the Master proposed my health in a long and entertaining speech.

Sunday 6 June
[**The Sunday Times.**
"Mr Fred Brittain, Librarian at Jesus College, Cambridge, who has been elected a Fellow, is one of the most popular dons in the University . . . His annual chef d'eouvre in the Boat Club is carrying out the arrangements for the Fairbairn Cup Race. It is he who works out with mathematical precision the finishing times of the crews whereby, on paper, boats starting at an interval of, say, 15 minutes, appear to have rowed a dead heat."]

Sunday 13 June
'Bush', Shepherd and Jack Crawford called: they had dossed the night in the Common Room. At the Roosters Annual Breakfast-at-Lunchtime [it being Hangover Sunday, i.e. the day after the Bump Supper] Tom Langton was installed on the Grainsack.

[Tom Langton was the hero of an epical escape from Tobruk across the African desert to El Alamein in the Second World War. An account of his most superhuman endurance is to be found in Gordon Lansborough's *Tobruk Commando*. It tells how Tom helped, cajoled and bullied his men 400 miles without food and little water on a journey which lasted two months, and for which he received the Military Cross. Twice a rowing Blue, Tom's voice on the radio was familiar every spring when he broadcast the commentary on the Boat Race.]

~ 1937 ~

Tuesday 17 June
Being awake at 3 a.m. I sat at my window. At dawn without a sound, First Court was a wonderful sight and I was much moved as I looked at it and thought of its past and my amazing good fortune in sitting at this window as a Fellow of Jesus College.

Saturday 31 July
Cycled to Fen Ditton Hall for the College Servants' Garden Party.

[The Dean and Mrs Gardner-Smith had chartered a boat, invited the staff to tea and arranged entertainment afterwards. They were therefore disappointed when, soon after tea, the boat arrived to collect them and the party left. The following year they issued the same invitation saying that they hoped the guests might stay a little longer than before. The spokesman said they would be glad to, adding, "You see, sir, last year we didn't know as how we were going to *enjoy* ourselves".]

Thursday 19 August
Started writing *A Short History of Jesus College*.

Monday 23 August
Left Euston for Stranraer. On the ship the steward told me there was no cold meat but there was some cold ham if that would do instead. Major and Mrs Rowland met me and took me by car to their house in Lismenary, Ballyclare, Co. Antrim. Everywhere the gate posts are of stone or brick, sloped like pillar boxes and white-washed like the houses. Barn doors are red and carts are orange-coloured; there are "pikes" of hay. Time doesn't count, when one leaves a shop the assistant says "goodbye", when one *enters* a shop at any time after about 4 p.m. he says "goodnight".

[No further entries for 1937]

~ 1938 ~

Tuesday 4 January
London. Had lunch with Pars and his mother at Acton, afterwards went to see Steve Fairbairn at the Mostyn Hotel, Portman Square, and thence alone to tea with Iris and Gerda Morgan at 12 Cheyne Gardens.

~ 1938 ~

[Iris and Gerda Morgan were two of H. A. Morgan's four daughters; the other two rejoiced in the names of Coral and Blenda. Henry Arthur Morgan had been Master of Jesus College from 1885 until 1912, i.e. just before Arthur Gray. He was known as Black Morgan to distinguish him from the Dean at the time, Red Morgan, the colours relating to their hair; they were unrelated. Black Morgan became extremely deaf and could only hear with the help of a hearing aid, a cup-shaped appliance attached to a flexible tube which he inserted in his ear. The story is told that one night at a feast at another college, the waiter having asked if he would take burgundy or claret and not getting a reply, was offered the cup in which to speak. Not realising its function he poured the wine into it.]

Wednesday 19 January
Spent the afternoon with the boats. In the Combination Room Barnes said that when he was about eighteen, he and three other men organized the smuggling of arms from various Cuban ports to Tampico in Mexico. They made three such expeditions and did very well indeed financially. Finally someone dropped a lighted cigarette at the place where the ammunition was stored. It blew up a large part of Tampico and two hundred people were killed. He afterwards went to the "trench" where they were buried and "said a prayer", and that was why he had never been to Mexico since. Until this moment, he said, he had never told anyone about it and no one had known the cause of the explosion. Mills, Duckworth and others were present at this discussion. Mills said nothing.

[FB, who was a pacifist, having enlisted in the Royal Army Medical Corps almost at the outbreak of World War I, where he served on the hospital ship *Egypt* helping to save lives, would have been horrified by this confession.]

Sunday 20 February
The Roosters Annual Lunch was held at the Lion Hotel followed by elections and the installation of David Fairbairn as President. Afterwards went to my rooms and worked on the libretto of the Rooster Revue *Words to that Effect*.

[David Fairbairn, Steve's great-nephew, returned to Australia and became a politician and a diplomat. Among his appointments were Minister of Development in Australia and Ambassador to the Netherlands. He was made KBE in 1977.]

Thursday 12 May
Left Cambridge with Robert Gittings, and had sandwiches in the car near Stevenage, and then went to North Mymms Wood where we saw millions of

bluebells in staggering beauty. We were back in College by five, both feeling we had seen a vision, indeed a miracle.

Monday 16 May
Received a telephone message from Ian Fairbairn to say that Steve died at 5 a.m. At the College Council meeting later the Master brought up the subject of the burial of Steve's ashes in the Lodge garden.

Tuesday 17 May
The Master announced that, though he agreed to a service in Chapel, he would have no one whatever trampling over his garden at the burial of the ashes. No one was to be present except the family and myself. Duckworth called on him to parley with him but was rebuffed. There was deadlock till evening. At one point we thought of holding a service over the ashes somewhere in the College unknown to the Master but this idea was ultimately rejected. It was finally decided that I should go and plead with him. I went, with my knees knocking, but came away with permission for the Dean to conduct a service at the burial in the Master's garden and for the Fellows and the Boat Club to be present. He nearly wept saying, "You understand me, Brittain, the other Fellows don't".

Wednesday 18 May
Had a very busy day, being besieged even before 8 a.m. about wreaths, etc. After the Memorial Service I went to the railway station and met the train bearing Steve's ashes accompanied by Mrs Fairbairn, Sydney and his wife, and Ian. We drove to the Master's garden and formed up a procession with Sydney (carrying the ashes) and Ian, Mrs Fairbairn and Sydney's wife, David Fairbairn and Brian Coulton, Manning and myself. Alan Burrough, Tom Langton and Jo Savill all emerged from the Chapel carrying wreaths. Duckworth and Q were already at the grave [in the angle between the south transept and the choir of the chapel]. No others were present except the Master who had gone into the Lodge to get his gown when he saw that we were wearing ours; he reached the grave just before the end. The Dean officiated. David Fairbairn and Brian Coulton lowered the urn into the grave and I sprinkled earth over it. Scarcely was the Blessing over when the Master said, "You will come in and have a cup of *tea, won't* you, Mrs Fairbairn?" and we all went into the Lodge for a while.

Saturday 22 May
Spent most of the day writing an obituary of Steve.

Friday 27 May
Didn't go to Q's after lunch as I was annoyed with him.

~ 1938 ~

Saturday 28 May
Tonight we dined in the Guest Room. Afterwards the Master came in followed by a porter carrying a bust of Charles Whibley for which the Master found what he called a good place in the Guest Room, to the annoyance of Q who was not pleased at having it in what he calls "my dining room". The Master was wearing shoes (I have only seen him in boots before). I noticed that his right ear is ? an inch higher than his left.

Monday 20 June
We broke off the Council meeting a few minutes for the admission of C. H. Wilson to his Fellowship.

> [Charles Wilson became Professor of Modern History and a distinguished author, especially of the histories of business houses, e.g. of Unilever and W. H. Smith, etc. He was elected a Fellow of the British Academy and created CBE. He died in Australia in 1991 and his ashes were scattered where emigrants from his native town, Market Rasen in Lincolnshire, had settled in the eighteenth century.]

Tuesday 21 June
A. L. Percival was admitted to his Fellowship. I could see Ingulphus (the Master) looking at first sadly resigned, then increasingly pleased as ALP read his Declaration and at the end he said, "You're a better scholar than I thought. You read that better than anyone – not a single false quantity". This caused general amusement because it is known that Percival, (an engineer) had been carefully coached by me in all the quantities, phrases, slight pauses, longer pauses, etc. which were clearly marked in his copy of the Declaration.

Thursday 23 June
Called the American University Union in Gordon Square to enquire about the "Intercollegiate University" of which Bernard Manning and I were suspicious. We were told the AUU had been fighting it for years. The executive secretary said that from time to time she received visits from people (mostly elderly clerics) who had paid fees to the IU and received "degrees" from them. The recipients, on being told by friends that these degrees were worthless, had called at the office of the AUU and had the same assurance. The secretary said that the IU did not actually function in the USA and that it was run mostly by Englishmen. She produced a handbook of it in which the name of the Registrar was Churchill Sibley. I then remembered that a man calling himself Archbishop Sibley had lately performed episcopal functions at the so-called Abbey of Christ the King, New Barnet.

~ 1938 ~

Tuesday 28 June
Went to Twyford to stay with Mr and Mrs F. G. Mitchell in a cottage attached to the White Hart at Sonning-on-Thames for the Henley Regatta.

> [The Mitchells became FB's close friends; their younger son 'Bud' was a pupil of his. 'Tiny' Mitchell was about the biggest man to be seen in a very long day's march; his wife had been called 'Blackie' since her girlhood. They entertained in the generous style, for which they were famous, at their beautiful old Essex home called Albyns (this was destroyed by bombs just before the end of the Second World War) and later at Norman Cross and finally at Clopton Manor. They shared FB's devotion to the Church of England, to Jesus College and his interest in theatricals. He gave many performances (mostly of music hall turns) in the spacious hall at Albyns or in the drawing room at Clopton in which the whole parish would sometimes assemble. Blackie would be his accompanist and Tiny would make him up with equal skill for a male or female part. It was like stepping back three centuries in English rural life, the whole life of the village centred on the Mitchells as it had done on Sir Roger de Coverley but the Mitchells had none of Sir Roger's autocratic ways.]

Thursday 30 June
Lunched in the Enclosure tent with Bernard Manning. After dinner we held a Shoal of the Red Herrings at White Hart Cottage. We elevated Alan Burrough as Grand Marshall and made Mrs Mitchell the first Dame of the Order of the Red Herring.

Wednesday 6 July
Staying at Albyns I watched television for the first time.

Tuesday 9 August
Cambridge. In the cloisters a girl attending Summer School asked me the way to the Hall and I showed her round the College.

Tuesday 16 August
Caught the Cornish Riviera express to Lostwithiel and went by car to the Fowey Hotel, which is the nearest house to Q's house, The Haven.

Wednesday 17 August
Went with Q to the barber's, then to the Town Clerk's office and the Yacht Club. After lunch Q rowed me by dinghy across the harbour to his garden which he calls "the farm". We walked into the village of Bodinnick and returned to Q's for tea.

Thursday 18 August
To the barber's with Q again then he and his deaf man Joe Welch rowed me up Pont Creek from which Q and I climbed up the hill and into the beautiful church of Lanteglos.

Friday 19 August
Went shopping with Q then by train to Lostwithiel and walked to Restormel Castle. Back to the Haven for dinner.

Saturday 20 August
We were joined by Anna Hanson and a governess car ("jugle") and set out for Polperro, stopping at Maple Burrow to inspect the tomb of Jonathan Couch and his wife Jane Quiller (Q's grandparents) in the cemetery adjoining the Non-conformist chapel. On the way back we examined Lansallo church where eight bells were pealing – it was most beautiful.

Sunday 21 August
Attended Sung Mass at Polruan: not one word was audible between the sermon and the "Our Father" before the Agnus. At 2.15 p.m. went with Guy Symondson [Q's young cousin] by motor boat to Polperro with its delightful harbour. There at the house of Jonathan Couch we saw, hung up on a rafter, the key on which Q's novel *Dead Man's Rock* is founded.

Saturday 27 August
At Albyns. The Dame drove me to Burnham-on-Crouch where we stayed the weekend on board the 'Girl Nancy' out in the stream. Dined at the Royal Corinthian Yacht Club of which Tiny is Commodore.

Monday 29 August
Five hours work with Bud and Alan Burrough. [FB was coaching them daily this week.]

Thursday 1 September
Played squash racquets with the Dame. C. B. Mortlock and two friends came to tea.

> [C. B. Mortlock was an ecclesiastical journalist in charge of a city church in London. His column in the *Church Times* appeared for many years over the pseudonym "Urbanus".]

Tuesday 13 September
Tiny and the Dame's twenty-eighth wedding anniversary dinner at Quaglino's, then we went to a musical comedy *The Fleet's Lit Up* (with Stanley Lupino and Doris Day) at the Hippodrome.

Friday 28 October
Cambridge. Read a paper on the Troubadors to the Jesuits, the Jesus English Society, and the Jesus Musical Society in the Master's Lodge and sang several songs. Ingulphus took the chair and talked nearly twenty minutes introducing me – all about Fortunatus and the bad state of the College Chapel in the 1870s. I found later that he thought I was going to talk about Latin hymns.

Saturday 5 November
Went to the final of the IV's races on the river, which we won for the third year running. It was a wonderfully hot sunny day, like JUNE.

Tuesday 22 November
A lunch for The Old Psalts was held in my rooms.

> [This society campaigned to keep the old psalter in Chapel; each meeting ended with a chorus of "Pshaw".]

Saturday 26 November
Practised songs in the Old Hall of the Master's Lodge. [Now used by Fellows and others and called the Prioress's Room.] He was above in the Conference Room and told a man with him that he could hear me singing Latin hymns below, but this man says that at that moment I was singing 'A little bit off the top'!

Wednesday 30 November
Dined at the Fountain with Tiny, the Dame, Bud and Alan. When we came out Bud and Alan were progged for being without gowns.

> [In those days undergraduates had to wear gowns after dark. If caught by the Proctor without one a fine of 6s. 8d., the equivalent of ⅓rd of a pound, was imposed. This was quite a hefty fine in 1938).]

[No entries for December]

~ 1939 ~

Friday 3 February
Cambridge. Lunched at 47 New Square with Alan, Bud and Jo Savill etc. Went to the Lodge with Duckworth to do sealings.

> [Two Fellows had to be present when the College seal was placed on legal documents.]

Wednesday 8 February
Training breakfast. Went to Q's rooms after lunch, he was surprised and pleased to hear that I have a copy of Robert Bloomfield's poems. He read passages aloud to me and expressed his pleasure at them.

Friday 10 February
Took Trevor Jones to lunch in Hall. Went to Chapel at 7 p.m. with F. J. E. Raby who is spending the weekend in the Q-bicle.

> [Trevor Jones, the Germanist lexicographer and F. J. E. Raby became two of FB's closest friends after they were elected Fellows of Jesus College. Trevor, having a wife and family and home in Cambridge, taught in FB's rooms until the latter's death. After the death of his wife Frederic Raby lunched with FB every day. The three would always meet for sherry before dinner and go into Hall together. It is strange that the first mention of both the friends occurs in the diary on the same day.]

21 March
Albyns. Travelled to town by car with the Dame and with her to Buckingham Palace where she signed the book. Then we lunched at Clariges with Tiny, Bud and Cherry and Rosemary Bruce.

> [Cherry and Rosemary Bruce were Lord Trent's granddaughters. Cherry married Bud and Rosemary married Alan Burrough.]

Easter Sunday 9 April
South Mymms. The font cover designed by Ninian Comper was dedicated before the morning service as a memorial to John Gerken [who had been Churchwarden at St Giles for many years.]

Saturday 13 May
Cambridge. English Tripos examiners meeting at Tillyard's house, then to the Boathouse. Men came to my rooms later, including the Yak who has just changed his name to Seeley.

> [E. A. Szilagyi, always known as the Yak, was of Hungarian extraction. Whenever he met Dr Duckworth the latter would always enquire about the Hungarian wheat crop and when he went with the Boat Club to row in Hungary he was fêted as a local hero. In fact he was the most English of men and had never visited Hungary before in his life.]

Monday 15 May
London. Gave a broadcast talk on the Sequence at the BBC.

Friday 9 June
Training breakfast followed by election of Boat Club officers. The Dean kept Chapel waiting for them until 8.45 when there were thirty present.

Monday 19 June
Attended a Council Meeting at which it was decided to terminate Barnes's Fellowship and R. Y. Jennings was pre-elected in his place.

> [R. Y. Jennings became Wherwell Professor of International Law and, after his retirement, a Judge of the International Court at The Hague. He was knighted and made an Honorary Fellow of the College in 1982, and was later President of the International Court at The Hague.]

Saturday 24 June
Went to Marlow Regatta with Tiny and the Dame. Our 1st VIII won the Grand.

Wednesday 12 July
Cambridge. I am writing the Jesus College Cambridge Society Report. Broad beans and bacon for lunch with Bernard Manning, Chas Wilson and J. S. Whale.

> [This was known as the Bean Feast and was a regular feature with the four friends. It consisted of three courses: (1) broad beans and bacon, (2) bacon and beans, (3) beans and bacon.]

~ 1939 ~

Thursday 27 July
London. Attended the Lambeth Conference committee on *Episcopi Vagantes* at Grand Building, Trafalgar Square. Met H. R. T. Brandreth, Amplett-Mickelthwaite, etc.

[In August Bernard Manning and FB took advantage of the leisure of the Long Vacation to carry out a plan on which they had been meditating for some time. They visited every parish church and chapel in Cambridge and wrote a report on them, calling themselves the William Dowsing Society after the Puritan iconoclast who had visited the churches of Cambridgeshire and Suffolk in 1643 under the orders of the Long Parliament, to deface or remove objects of reputed superstition. Dowsing had kept a journal of his tour with entries such as this:

At Little Mary's we brake down LX superstitious Pictures, some Popes and Crucyfixes, & God the Father sitting in a chayer & holding a glasse in his hand.
    At Peterhouse we pulled down ii mighty great Angells with wings, and divers other Angells, & the IV Evangelists & Peter with his Keies over the Chappell Dore, & about a hundred Chirubims and Angells.

The William Dowsing Society in its report employed similar language and spelling like this:

Saint John's College hathe a most decente & statlie Chapel, though divers in their folly mislike it. Yet it seemede bare in ye middes, by reason y^t they cherisshe here a beggarlie superstition concernynge Vistas & hadde hid awaye ye brave & comelie Lecterne. We did sette it back in his proper place.
Holie Trinitie Chirche ... We espied nigh on .ccc copies of a Booke of rhymes & ditties entituled *Songes of Prayse*. When we hadde made a fyre in Markett Street, we caste thereon ye saide bookes & made a myghtie greate blaze of ye same.
At *Saint John's Churche* in ye Hills Road we digged up all ye tiles before ye Altar & did out divers foolishe Banners. Item, we brake downe & utterlie destroied .i superstition called a Children's Corner.
In ye chapel at *Ridley Hall* we turned ye lecterne straight. We tooke away thereforme .i superstitiouse booke called ye Revised Version and did put ye Bible in place thereof.
From ye Chapell of *Westcott House* we took out ye Revised Version and destroied .xLvj. tip-up Seates. Item, at ye gate of ye House we utterlie destroied & abolishede .i foolish Coney & .i superstitiouse Pigge.

In short they expressed their dislike of various ecclesiastical usages that were popular at the time. Although one of the two members of the society described himself as a "believer in east worshippe and dropping worship" and the other as a "painfull and fanatical upholder of Master Calvin", only one very brief passage had to be omitted from the report through any disagreement between them. It was published as a pamphlet with the title *Babylon Bruis'd & Mount Moriah Mended* and reached its eighth impression.]

Saturday 2 September
Spent the weekend lazing on board the 'Girl Nancy' with Tiny and the Dame at Burnham-on-Crouch, fishing by trawl in the 'Red Herring' and sailing in the 'Nauta' on the Crouch and the Roach.

Sunday 3 September
At 11.15 a.m. we sat in the saloon and heard the Prime Minister say that we had been at war with Germany since 11 a.m.

Thursday 7 September
Cambridge. RAF cadets arrived and were quartered in College. After Hall we entertained the officers and cadets to beer and smokes in Hall. Speeches were made by Duckworth, the Master and Wing-Commander Mason.

Friday 8 September
A Roost was held in my rooms attended as well by about sixteen cadets, six of whom we examined and passed for emperchment.

Sunday 10 September
Attended the Parade Service in Chapel but didn't like it. We had a few verses of Isaiah VI, Psalm 52 and hymns instead of canticles. One cadet called it "completely anti-Christian".

Thursday 28 September
L. A. Pars and I called on the Master to congratulate him on his eighty-seventh birthday.

Friday 20 October
Lectured at the Pitt Club as all our usual rooms have been taken over by the RAF.

Tuesday 24 October
Took the train to Broxbourne and thence by car to Albyns. Epping Forest is lovely with autumn colours and we saw three deer. All the Mitchell family were at dinner (it was the Dame's birthday as well as mine). Then I gave a talk to about forty-five people on "The Use and Abuse of the English Language".

~ 1939 ~

Monday 30 October
Cambridge. Lunched at the Pitt Club, which the College has taken over temporarily. Today's lunch (to take the place of Hall lunch) was the first meal there.

Thursday 9 November
Breakfast with Snow White and seven or eight others. He leaves today, having been called up. Lunched at the Pitt Club with Q, Bernard Manning, Jennings, Dodd and Conrad Skinner. Went to the river and back with the 4th boat then back to Post Reach and up with the 1st, 2nd and 3rd boats.

> [Snow White, alias Geoffrey Gilbertson, was so called because he was well over 6 ft tall and made the rest of the crew of his boat look like seven dwarfs. He later contracted polio and was confined to a wheel-chair, but this did not prevent him from becoming Company General Manager, Personnel of ICI and being knighted for his services to the disabled in 1981.]

Sunday 12 November
There was a meeting at 8.15 p.m. in my rooms to consider entertaining evacuees.

> [The official evacuation of children from major urban areas had begun on 1 September]

Monday 20 November – Saturday 25 November
I was very busy with rehearsals for the evacuees' pantomime at various times.

Friday 1 December
Showed Miss Murray and about twelve Girtonians over the College. Had two rehearsals for the pantomime. Some Medieval Latinists came to tea (as is usual on Fridays). Went to Hall and then had another rehearsal.

Saturday 2 December
Went to Morley's Holt to see the start of the December Clinker VIII's (substitute for the Fairbairn Cup). C. H. Dodd came to tea.

> [Professor C. H. Dodd, a Congregationalist, was the first non-conformist to hold a Cambridge Chair in Theology. He was a Professorial Fellow of Jesus and became an Honorary Fellow in 1949. A prolific writer, he was responsible for the production of the New English Bible and did much of the translation himself.]

Sunday 3 December
The Master came into the Combination Room and soon got on to E. H. Morgan who "did more harm to the College than anyone else ever did".

> [E. H. or 'Red' Morgan, Dean-cum-Senior Tutor of the College in the last part of the 19th century, was very lax with the result that the College fell into disrepute. Arthur Gray, as Junior Tutor, tried to administer an antidote to 'Red Morganism' and so became very unpopular with undergraduates. To the end of his life Gray could always be roused to wrath by any mention of the repugnant name. In his last days when he became lethargic, he could be awakened immediately by such a remark as "but surely Master, there must have been something to be said for Red Morgan". There is a story, which must have been unknown to Arthur Gray or he would surely have repeated it many times. It alleges that when Red Morgan was a schoolmaster one of his colleagues died, leaving a widow totally unprovided for. Red Morgan thereupon stepped gallantly forward, started a subscription list on the lady's behalf and did not relax until he had collected a considerable sum. He then married the widow.]

Thursday 7 December
The pantomime was performed at the Guildhall to a huge audience of evacuee children. Afterwards I had a party in my rooms.

Christmas Eve, Sunday 24 December
South Mymms. No Midnight Mass this year as the church is not blacked out.

> [Blackout regulations, requiring concealment of all artificial light, had come into force on 1 September 1939.]

[No further entries for December]

~ 1940 ~

Friday 5 January
Dick [the Mitchells chauffeur] called with the car and took me to Albyns where there was a fancy dress dance in the hall for the staff and I sang a few songs.

~ 1940 ~

Saturday 6 January
Frozen roads stopped me from getting home to attend the Christ Church Boys' School Reunion.

Saturday 27 January
Cambridge. A thick fall of snow continued for 24 hours.

Thursday 8 February
After Hall I went to Clare College and addressed the Dilettanti on Troubadors and sang songs. The Finns are still holding their own in spite of the Russians doing their utmost to break the Mannerheim Line. Atrocities in Poland continue.

Saturday 17 February
There was a special meeting of the College Council at which we gave Paul Sinker leave of absence for special service at the Admiralty. There has been a hard frost all week. Canada as well as the whole Empire is mourning Lord Tweedsmuir, its Governor General – a brilliant author who wrote *The Thirty-nine Steps* under the name of John Buchan.

Thursday 22 February
Stayed in my rooms as I have a cold but kept on working. Went to bed about 8 p.m. and then a meeting of the Boat Club was held in my rooms.

Monday 26 February
Attended a Council Meeting at the Lodge. A letter was read from the Bishop of Ely asking us to appoint a representative on a commission, which (at the Vicar's request) is to consider the future of All Saints' church [opposite the College entrance]. We suggested the Dean. The Master objected saying the commission should have a predominantly lay element and not (here he glared at the Dean) a "pack of parsons". He suggested that if we must have a Fellow, that it should be Duckworth. "The Commission will be all the better", he said, "if our representative is a bit of a heretic". Duckworth declined and the Dean was elected. "I don't congratulate you", the Master said.

Saturday 2 March
Went with Tiny and the Dame by car to Abington where we lunched at Jeremiah's Cottage and looked at the millions of aconites in the wood nearby. Back in Cambridge we looked at the aconites at St John's College. Geoff Gilbertson, on leave from Sandhurst, called later.

Thursday 7 March
Went to the training breakfast and Chapel. At 1 p.m. Balme was admitted to

~ 1940 ~

his Fellowship in Chapel. Went to the March VIII's [the wartime equivalent of the Lent Races.] After Hall the Master came into the Combination Room and proposed Balme's health. He said "I was admitted to my Fellowship by the Bishop of Ely in his drawing room in town. I thought there might be some work attached to my Fellowship so I went to the College but was told to get out of it quickly".

> [David Mowbray Balme became the founding Principal of what was to become the University of Ghana. Once it was well established he returned home and later became Professor and Head of the Department of Classics at Queen Mary College, London. Always unconventional but never eccentric, he cycled from his home in Beckenham through the Blackwell Tunnel to Queen Mary College wearing a flat cap, gauntlets and a mask against petrol fumes. He moved later to Leicestershire where he could indulge his passion for horses and fox-hunting and where he died in 1989.]

Friday 8 March
After Hall attended a meeting of the Jesuits [the Jesus College Historical Society] in Manning's rooms and as he was away I presided. Pettoello read a paper on Dante.

Saturday 9 March
Last day of the March VIII's. Went to the training breakfast and then Chapel – about twenty-seven present, which was good as they had come from the Pitt Club after breakfast. Bernard Manning and I went to the races and saw Jesus finish Head; the second boat bumped Trinity Hall I, and the third boat bumped 3rd Trinity. Went to the Bump supper, after which I entertained men in my rooms until 1.30 a.m.

Tuesday 9 April
Germany invaded Denmark and Norway – they called it protection!

Saturday 13 April
Barnet. Telegram from Duckworth to say the Master died last night.

Monday 15 April
Cambridge. While I was having a late tea with Bernard Manning the Dean came in and made a true and typically Decanal remark, "This is the first funeral we've had for years without any unpleasantness".

Tuesday 16 April
The Master's funeral took place at 2.30 p.m. and I acted as usher. The Chapel was full. Afterwards the coffin was wheeled on a bier into every Court with

the family and Fellows following, then back through the Chapel into the Master's garden and to Comberton for burial.

> [The custom of wheeling the Master's coffin round the College was carried out at Dr Corrie's funeral in 1885 'according to custom', but no one knows when the custom originated.]

Tuesday 23 April
The Society met to consider the election of a new Master. Went to Hall and then to a Red Herring Shoal in the Q-bicle. "Weathercock" Peacock [later Sir Geoffrey Peacock, CVO, sometime Remembrancer of the City of London] was very entertaining about his first very brief encounter with the Reverend P. Gardner-Smith. "The first time I called on the Dean he asked me my name. 'Peacock, Sir', I said. 'Oh! Peacock' he replied. "I knew your brother. Good Morning." End of interview! Our airmen continue bombing Stavanger, Oslo and Alborg in Denmark, but the Germans are thrusting out from Oslo.

Saturday 4 May
Watched the Incogniti cricket match on the Close. Took the train with Charles Wilson to Stortford and bus to Much Hadham to stay at the Red Lion. Walked along the beautiful river Ash, round the back lane following the river to the ford. It was delightful in the twilight.

Sunday 5 May
Went to church at 8 a.m., walked along the Ash, then attended Sung Eucharist and walked along the Ash again. As Charles Wilson said, "Much Hadham's beauty can't be exaggerated, it is like turning over several pages of a picture book of Beautiful Britain".

> [On the 10th of May the Germans invaded Belgium and Holland, on the 14th the Dutch Army surrendered, and on Tuesday 28th the Belgians did likewise. Mr Chamberlain resigned as Prime Minister and was replaced by Winston Churchill.]

Tuesday 28 May
We elected W. L. H. Duckworth Master and he was duly installed.

> [W. L. H. Duckworth was the first scientist to become Master. He had been a Fellow since 1893 and his modesty, scholarship and unfailing courtesy won him the affection and respect of both senior and junior members of the College.]

~ 1940 ~

Sunday 2 June
I was elected Lord Protector of the Roost [for the duration of the war]. Afterwards we tried the Rev P. Garden-Scythe (the Dean) for Anti-Roost propaganda. Our men are evacuated from Flanders day by day via Dunkirk, where they are bombed and machine-gunned with no cover.

Friday 14 June
We heard today that Paris has fallen and that Mussolini has decided to come into the war so Italy is now definitely our enemy.

Saturday 27 July
Caught the train to Harlow and thence by car to Albyns. Went to Epping cinema where we saw Mae West and W. C. Fields in *My Little Chickadee.*

Monday 5 August
Cambridge. After Hall and the Combination Room Mills, Pars, Tillyard, Thorpe and myself went into the Fellows' Garden and discussed how the Master is apparently using the Lodge without waiting for the Council to decide (after a report from a committee) to what use it is to be put.

Friday 16 August
Went to Tedburn St Mary via Salisbury, Ilchester and Exeter to stay a fortnight with the Dame, Cherry Mitchell and Joe.

> [The Mitchells had taken Colley House, Tedburn, in Devon to get away from the bombing.]

Sunday 8 September
Barnet. The great bombing raids on London are taking place every night this week.

Tuesday 8 October
Cambridge – full term begins. Took the MS of my *Short History of Jesus College* to Heffers.

> [Rev F. J. Foakes Jackson, DD, D.Litt. D.Theol.
> 86 Dana Place
> Englewood, New Jersey
> 12 December, 1940

My dear Brittain,
    Your letter and above all your book pleased me immensely. Of the book Mrs Jackson says it is the most interesting and the best recent account of

the College. When I remember what the place was before the last Master was elected I wish you had known it and done justice to Morgan's rule, which began in 1885. I was the first Fellow to be elected in his Mastership. The only member of the society there who attained any eminence beyond a good degree, was Arthur Gray who at his death was recognised as a true antiquarian and a master of English prose. Its classical eminence began with Abbott. Just think of the men we have produced since in other fields!

Slowly and with much thought, I have decided that you have proved one of the greatest assets we have chosen as Fellows, both because of your influence with the men, and your intense interest in our College. May you continue long to exercise both to our benefit.

    Ever your friend
    (signed) F. J. F. Jackson

Yes. I got the report of the Society. I have had no letter I can remember from you. It may have been lost.]

Wednesday 6 November
5 The Avenue was damaged today. [FB's home in Barnet was hit by enemy action.]

Wednesday 18 December
The Commemoration of Benefactors was held in the Chapel nave this year. Attended the Audit Feast, attenuated fare and the RAF officers were the only guests. Paul Sinker and Charles Wilson had come from the Admiralty for it.

Thursday 19 December
Took the bus via Huntingdon to Norman Cross and stayed the night.

> [The Mitchells had moved from Albyns to Norman Cross on the outskirts of Peterborough.]

Saturday 21 December
Travelled by car via Bristol, where we saw the results of air raids, to Tedburn St Mary and spent Christmas there with the Mitchells.

[No further entries for December]

~ 1941 ~

Friday 3 January
Clothall. Aunt D. being ill and mother unwell I did a good deal of housework until I went back to Cambridge on the 11th.

Sunday 19 January
Cambridge. I presided over the Roost in my rooms. S. M. Hilton was elected President.

> [Sidney Hilton, cock-nomen Stilton, qualified as a doctor and became Professor of Physiology at Birmingham University. He and his wife Mary came to Breakfast-at-Lunchtime in June 1989, his first time for 40 years. He was pleased to find the same absurd ritual going on. Mary replied to the toast 'The Guests' in a most gallinaceous speech.]

Thursday 23 January
In Hall tonight the Dean, commenting on the recent victories over the Italians in North Africa, said, "The tragedy of it is we're conquering countries which we don't want and which are utterly useless". Again in Hall one night after a second air raid on Bristol, he said, "What on earth the authorities are doing I can't imagine, to allow stocks of food to be kept together as they did. The streets of Bristol are running knee deep with butter and margarine. Enough food was destroyed to feed the whole country for a month".

> [He had probably been listening to the defeatist propaganda of the traitor "Lord Haw-Haw", who broadcast from Germany every night.]

Friday 7 February
Lunched at the Pitt Club with men up to collect their MA's, including C. W. J. Bowles [later Bishop of Derby] and Vivian Cox.

Friday 25 April
Went to the Backs to see the daffodils, which are still in their prime. Had tea at St Francis House, my first visit.

> [The Franciscans had taken over the Oratory House and renamed it accordingly.]

~ 1941 ~

Saturday 3 May
Went by car, with Dick driving, to Norman Cross and lunched with Tiny and the Dame at the Grand Hotel, Peterborough. Afterwards we went on to Spalding, Holbeach and Long Sutton where we viewed all three magnificent churches. We saw fields of tulips in full vivid flower, including a white one which, from a distance we thought to be chalk.

Sunday 4 May
Tiny and the Dame took me to Walpole St Peter to Sung Mass in the gorgeous church. Lunched at Norman Cross where the tulips are out and the gardens are open today to the general public at 6d. a head in aid of the Red Cross.

Wednesday 7 May
Q arrived back late, today. In the Combination Room someone said, "I see we've brought down thirteen German planes". The Dean replied, "But we've lost eleven". Someone else said, "Apparently there were no bombs dropped on——", to which the Dean replied, "Probably saving them for Cambridge", and later "What's that? We've taken Sollum? Well, it's only a heap of ruins".

Thursday 29 May
Had tea with the Judo Club at a café opposite Sidney Sussex College, and was elected Treasurer. At 8.30 p.m. drank port with the boats in Pars's rooms and sang about twelve songs. I was fire watching on the Chapel tower from 10.30 to midnight.

> [On 4 June the ex-Kaiser Wilhelm, German Emperor 1888–1918, died in Holland. On 26 June Hitler declared war on Russia.]

Monday 23 June
It is very hot. Took the train to Welwyn Garden City and thence by bus to Barnet. It seemed strange but pleasant to be home again.

> [The family had returned from Clothall, his mother's Hertfordshire village, where they had spent the early days of the war.]

Sunday 6 July
Mymms. Attended the Dedication Festival at St Giles. The church looked most beautiful with pink and blue Canterbury Bells. Read the first lesson and held forth at Evensong. It was delightful to be there again.

Wednesday 16 July
Cambridge. Jam roly-poly in Hall at which Raby, Alan Percival and I expressed pleasure. The Dean said, "It would be better if it wasn't made with mouldy flour". The Master dined as it was Raby's first time since his election as a Fellow, and proposed his health.

> [Palace Hotel
> Rhyl
> Flintshire
> 5 March 1941
>
> My dear Brittain,
>   I can't describe my gratified astonishment when I read the Master's letter this morning, telling me that the Society of Jesus College invited me to become an Honorary Fellow. This is truly an honour beyond all my hopes, and one which in especial measure I must attribute to your kindness. I can truly say that the College has always had a high place in my affections, and that as an undergraduate I rarely passed along Jesus Lane without turning aside to walk round the Cloisters, and, if the door was unlocked (in those days it was sometimes locked) to go into the Chapel which, more than any other in Cambridge, spoke of the 'last enchantments of the Middle Ages'. I cannot help mentioning a thought which is uppermost in my mind, the gratification which the news will give to my wife.
>   I was glad to see the appreciative notice of your History of the College in *The Times Literary Supplement*.
>   I had a very nice letter from Miss Boseli the other day. She told me of Gaselee's recent visit to Newnham and of the costume which he wore.
>   I was very sorry to read of the death of my old friend Randel Harris. Glover wrote a fine appreciation of him in the *Manchester Guardian*.
>   Needless to say, I look forward to my next visit to Cambridge, but I seem literally to be chained to my desk at Rhyl for some time.
>   Yours ever,
>   (signed) F. J. E. Raby]

Sunday 20 July
The Dean said, "Did you hear Lord Haw-Haw last night? He scored a number of bulls-eyes against our ridiculous news service. The Americans are not going to do anything which leads to getting hurt." Then, "Why do they call this stuff strawberry fool? There isn't a drop of cream in it."

Friday 25 July
Went to Westminster Abbey with Tiny and the Dame for the consecration of

Edward Wynn as Bishop of Ely and of B. Robin as Bishop of Adelaide, by the Archbishop of Canterbury [Cosmo Gordon Lang] and a dozen more bishops.

Monday 28 July
Cambridge. It is very hot again. Worked at Castilliard's brief *Advertissment touchant la pronunciation Latine*. At 2 p.m. met the South Mymms Mothers' Union, thirty-two of them including two children, and took them over the College. We had tea at the Dorothy Café and then took them round the Backs.

Thursday 7 August
Pars, the Dean, Charles and Angela Wilson and I went to Ely for the enthronement of Edward Wynn as Bishop. He carried Bishop Wren's crozier and looked very fine. We had tea in the Deanery garden.

Wednesday 1 October
Venn was installed as Vice-Chancellor.

> [Venn's name is in constant use among archivists as the compiler of *Alumni Cantibrigiensis*, his record of Cambridge graduates from the earliest times to 1900.]

Monday 7 November
At 7 a.m. went by car with Charles and Angela Wilson via Sawston and Stortford to Audley End. Day broke soon after we left. There was a fine sunrise later and a grand view of Audley End and the trees along the road and the yellowing leaves of Epping Forest. From there I went on by bus etc. to Barnet and spent the rest of the day indoors, except in the evening I went to the Abbotts' and to Mrs Saines's for a while.

Wednesday 19 November
Cambridge. Accompanied Bernard Manning to County Hall where he was X-rayed. He was admitted to the Evelyn Nursing Home [now a hospital] at 4.30 p.m.

Thursday 27 November
Tillyard said he had a curious dream last night. He went into a church and was surprised to see Q pushing faggots under the font in which he was making a big stew.

Saturday 29 November
Went to visit Bernard Manning at the Evelyn, then to a Scholarship Examiners' meeting in Dr Stewart's rooms at Trinity College. At the Roosters Dinner about fifty-four were present, all guests of J. H. Lockwood

who fed us on pheasants and hares from his shoot in Yorkshire and paid for all the drink as well.

[H. F. Stewart, Dean of Trinity, lectured on French writers of the seventeenth century laying special emphasis on St Francis de Sales and Pascal. The more FB knew him the more he admired him.

J. H. Lockwood entered the College when he was fifty-three years old. His son, Peter, came up in 1941 and Horace was so attracted by the College and its life that he asked if he might become an undergraduate. This was readily agreed to but he was never matriculated and so was, in fact, not a member of the University. He was made an Honorary Cockerel in recognition of his generosity to the Roosters.]

Tuesday 2 December
The Master received a cable saying that Foakes-Jackson had died.

Monday 8 December
Returning from the weekend at Norman Cross I was alarmed to see the College flag at half-mast. The porter told me that Bernard Manning died at 5.30 this morning. RIP.

Wednesday 10 December
The first part of Bernard Manning's funeral service was held in Chapel, after which the coffin left for burial at Ravensdale [his Westmorland home].

Thursday 11 December
Attended the Requiem for Bernard Manning at St Clement's at 8.45 a.m. and Vespers for the Dead there at 2 p.m.

[FB's memoir of his friend, Bernard Manning, which he wrote later was considered by many to be one of his best books. He received many letters about it including the following from Lord Quickswood:]

The Lodge
Eton College
Windsor
8 June 1943

Dear Mr Brittain,

I read with the deepest interest your memoir of the late Mr Bernard Manning who must have been a most attractive and remarkable man. As to the future of the Church of England I doubt whether it will split, it is very tough; but if it did I should be, I suppose, in the same communion as the

Church of South Africa and the episcopal Church of Scotland. Was it Pusey or Keble who said the Catholic Church was once included in one upper chamber? I should not lose faith in it if that happened again.

I am,
>Yours sincerely
>(signed) Quickswood

[No further entries for December]

~ 1942 ~

Saturday 10 January
At Norman Cross. Went to a pantomime in Yaxley Village Hall. During the interval I sang 'Captain Ginger', 'Seaweed' and a 'Little Bit off the Top'. Tiny made me up magnificently.

Saturday 17 January
There was a Memorial Service for Bernard Manning in the College Chapel. The congregation was large and about thirty stayed to tea in my rooms afterwards.

Sunday 15 February
The news arrived that Singapore had fallen. In Hall the Dean said, "Can't say I think much of Churchill as a strategist". Pars replied, "At any rate he's a good speaker and keeps people cheerful. He's speaking on the wireless at 9". "He'll be a great man if he can keep people cheerful tonight; how much longer do you think we can hold out", said the Dean. After dinner a Roost was held in my rooms.

Friday 20 February
At dinner Q cursed the carrots in the soup and said, "Everything we get is infected with carrots".

Saturday 21 February
Chas Smyth and his wife came to lunch.

>[The Revd Charles Hugh Egerton Smyth read a paper on 'Nationality' the following week to the Jesuits in FB's rooms. He was a member and sometime Dean of Corpus Christi College, Cambridge and became a Proctor in

Convocation at Westminster, and later an Honorary Canon of Lincoln Cathedral.]

Friday 27 February
Took A. F. Pegler and P. G. Ward, plus Q , to lunch in Hall. Lunch restarted there today as the Pitt Club has been taken from us for a British Restaurant. This inspired Q to write on the spur of the moment:

> Though our club has had notice to quit
> Yet as Britons we still claim admittance,
> So our last one and eight-pence we'll split
> And we'll feast at the Pitt for a pittance.

Saturday 28 February
Not one day this term without frost so far and not one game possible on the Close, we could easily skate on the ice in First Court. Yet curiously it is the best weather for my health for twenty years or more. Normally I have continuous colds from November to May with flu and bronchitis on top and use about eight handkerchiefs a day. This winter I needed to change my handkerchief only when it looked too dirty to carry about.

Thursday 5 March
Snow everywhere, having fallen during the night. The March VIII's began today – we rowed over Head.

Friday 13 March
Took P. G. Ward and J. McMullen to lunch in Hall and we resolved to found a John Mason Neale Society.

[Its objects were to perpetuate the life, works and chief interests of the cleric (1818-1866) who was responsible for so many hymns, both original and translations from ancient Greek and Latin hymns. Described by Peter Anson as perhaps the most brilliant and versatile priest of the Church of England in the nineteenth century, Neale founded the Camden Society with his friend Benjamin Webb while he was still an undergraduate at Cambridge. After ordination and a short period as Chaplain of Downing College, he accepted the benefice of Crawley but had to give up parish work owing to ill health. In 1846 he was appointed Warden of Sackville College, East Grinstead, a seventeenth century almshouse. He was instrumental in the revival of the religious life and founded the Society of St Margaret in 1855. This caused trouble with the Bishop of Chichester who was under pressure from the Brighton Protestant Association, and ended with the hideous episode of the Lewes Riots after the funeral of one of the East Grinstead Sisters.]

~ 1942 ~

Sunday 22 March
South Mymms. Worked at a memoir of Bernard Manning all this week.

Palm Sunday, 29 March
At 11 a.m. I was MC at St Giles but the Patriarch messed things up with silly last minute changes. Had supper at the Vicarage; Katharine is home on leave from the WAAF at Cirencester.

Saturday 4 April
We are few in number but have managed all the Holy Week ceremonies. The clocks go forward another hour tonight.

> [Double Summer Time was instituted to save an hour of blackout and to help land workers to produce more food.]

Easter Sunday, 5 April
At the Sung Mass we had a procession – the church was full of troops.

Friday 24 April
Cambridge. Q arrived about 5 p.m. and at 6 p.m. we left by car with the Bishop of Ely to Godmanchester for the institution and induction of Ralph Gardner. The Bishop dropped a brick in his sermon by referring to the ancient borough of Godmanchester as "the beautiful village".

Sunday 12 May
Caught the bus to the White Hart (South Mimms) and then to the woods, left-handed to Bluebell Corner. Unfortunately found the trees (beech and larch) had been cut down and the fence set back so that the slope and the little gullies are now wide open to the sky. Nevertheless the bluebells in the open were a wonderful sight with bright sun streaming on them. When I first saw them at a distance through the trees they were such an intense, unearthly blue that I wondered at first if I was dreaming.

Tuesday 19 May
Cambridge. The first meeting of the John Mason Neale Society was held in my rooms. P. G. Ward [the Rector of Harston] was elected President, J. McMullen Secretary and myself Treasurer. Ward read a paper on some of the less known works of Neale.

> [In 1992 the Society celebrated its golden jubilee with a dinner at Jesus College, though after FB's death in 1969 it met at Corpus Christi College with the Revd Dr William Horbury as secretary and then at Magdalene College as the guest of the Chaplain, the Revd David Hoyle. It returned to

~ 1942 ~

Jesus College in the late 1990s, when FB's widow, Muriel Brittain was made a Fellow Commoner there.]

Monday 22 June
At the College Council the Master [Dr Duckworth, who never said anything in one word if he could say it in ten,] recorded in the Minutes that an undergraduate had been given permission to his "entering the matrimonial state whilst still in *statu pupillari*".

Monday 27 June
Went to Peterborough and lunched at the Grand, then to Evensong at the Cathedral with an excellent sermon by Edward Ely and procession. The Dean (Simpson) in his cope, red skull cap, spectacles and wrathful face looked like a misericord seat or a gargoyle.

Sunday 12 July
South Mymms. I was MC at church at 11 a.m. The new Bishop of London [the Rt Revd Geoffrey Fisher, later Archbishop of Canterbury] pontificated and preached.

[Many years afterwards Geoffrey Fisher recalled his visits to Mimms, "Strange things went on at South Mimms" he said, "when I used to go there as Bishop of London I never knew what was going to happen next".]

Friday 17 July
Attended a meeting at Heffers about taking over the editorship of the *Cambridge Review*.

[The *Cambridge Review* founded in 1879 and reputed to be the oldest University weekly in existence, was printed and published by the well-known firm of William Heffer and Sons of which Ernest Heffer was, at the time, managing director. FB held this post for six years. It was impossible for him to get secretarial help during the war years except for the voluntary help of his old friend Vincent Robinson. Robinson used to write out FB's letters in a copperplate hand from his shorthand notes and return them to him the next day for signature. FB was proud of the galaxy of talent he had in his contributors, which included G. M. Trevelyan, Sir Herbert Richmond, David Knowles, Charles Smyth, Charles Raven, Muriel Bradbrook, Q, S. C. Roberts, G. G. Coulton, Edmund Blunden, Mary Ellen Chase, C. H. Dodd, and Sir Harold Spencer-Jones, among others. P. F. Radcliffe was his never-failing music critic, and Denys Wilkinson and Claude Harvard were his indefatigable sports editors.]

~ 1942 ~

Monday 20 July
The Dean, Alan Percival and I were appointed Assistant Tutors.

Monday 27 July
An air raid caused a fire at the Union at 2 a.m.

Friday 30 October
Talking about J. M. Barrie, Q described him as "a genius but a queer man".

Sunday 1 November
Something that the Dean said in Hall made Pars remind him that it is All Saints' Day. "But all the saints are dead" said the Dean, to which Q replied, "Well I know a few at any rate".

Tuesday 22 December
Attended a sherry party for about twenty-five at Norman Cross. I sang 'Sarah in our Sector', which I had just written. Nothing seems to happen now except in this or that "sector", so I brought Henry Cary's 'Sally in Our Alley' up to date.

>Of all the girls whose speech was plain,
>   There wasn't one like Sally:
>She wasn't uppish, or too vain
>   To live down in our alley.
>But since the war reports she's read,
>   Our Sarah is corrector:
>She hasn't moved her board or bed,
>   But she dwells in our sector.
>Until she read communiques
>   My pretty little Sally
>Lived in the East End all her days:
>   She hung out in our alley.
>But Sarah now such words derides;
>   She'll bluster and she'll hector
>Till I agree that she resides
>   In London's Eastern Sector.
>When pretty Sal I used to chase,
>   Her speech, though plain, was pleasing.
>She'd sometimes say: "I'll smack your face
>   If you don't stop your teasing."
>But Sarah now without a doubt
>   Speaks English that's selecter
>She says: "I'll fetch you such a clout

>   Right in your facial sector."
> If Sal at supper used to take
>   Too much, when she had eaten
> She'd say: "I've such a belly-ache:
>   Lord Woolton's got me beaten."
> Now Sarah often ends a feast
>   By saying, sweet as nectar;
> "Oh, what a pain in the middle east
>   Of my abdominal sector!"
> Oh! We hope we'll soon be married by the rector;
>   In our sector there's a house on which we're keen.
>   With tele-lens projector
>   You could see the Western Sector,
> If it wasn't for the sectors in between.

[No further entries for December]

~ 1943 ~

Monday 11 January
Cambridge. Dined at the University Arms with Luxmoore.

[Lord Justice Luxmoore was an Honorary Fellow of the College. During his undergraduate years in the 1880s he had been less distinguished for work than for Rugby Football and his practical jokes, one of which became famous. He and a friend had climbed to the College roof one quiet Sunday afternoon to pour a bucket of water down another man's chimney, but poured it down Luxmoore's chimney by mistake. Not surprisingly he went down with only a pass degree but he made good by his native ability and hard work.]

Wednesday 13 January
Cambridge *Review* work and to tea with Ernest Heffer.

[Ernest Heffer, the managing director of W. H. Heffer & Sons, was a big breezy man with his own special type of humour, which often took the form of pretending to be a bully. It was sheer pretence, for he was a most kind-hearted and generous man and nothing delighted him more than if someone saw through his pretence quickly and paid him back in his own coin. He could, however, be very obstinate, particularly if FB asked him to approve of some *Review* expenditure, which he considered unnecessary. On one occasion on receiving a refusal, FB raised his voice in protest and thumped the table. Heffer reacted by ringing the bell for his private secretary and when she appeared he said in a solemn voice, "Miss Southwick, send out at once for a soap-box". "A soap-box, Mr Heffer?" "Yes, a soap box. The Editor of the Review wants to address a public meeting." To this the embarrassed Miss Southwick replied, "Oh, Mr Heffer!" and retired to her own office.]

Thursday 21 January
The Dean, handing an evening paper to Alan Percival said, "There's a very depressing paragraph about our shipping losses. Lord Haw-Haw will have a good deal to tell us about it tonight, I expect".

Friday 22 January
Q returned from Cornwall after lunch. He said that the chambermaid at the Great Western Hotel at Paddington last night was "as drunk as Chloe". He recalled that when he was an undergraduate at Oxford, he ran a paper called *The Rattle* each day during the Torpids one year. On the last day of the races he wrote the whole issue between 7.30 p.m. and midnight.

Saturday 30 January
Took Wilson Harris, editor of the *Spectator*, to Hall. We sat a long time in the Combination Room with Q.

Sunday 31 January
Addressed the Cambridge University Congregational Society on "The Case for Anglican Worship".

Thursday 11 February
The Dean (with the recent Russian successes in mind) said, "I don't suppose you people will agree with me, but I think the time has now come to make a negotiated peace with the Germans, otherwise we shall have Bolshevism spreading all over Europe".

Wednesday 17 February
James Wood arrived to stay in the Q-bicle while painting the Master's portrait.

[James Wood, a highly individual painter, was a member of Jesus College. He was under the impression that Duckworth was a botanist so he included a large plant in the painting. On learning that the Master was an anatomist, he inserted a skull, but said that he could not remove the plant, so it remained.]

Thursday 25 February
Joan Emmett, President of the Cambridge University Women's Boat Club came to lunch.

Saturday 6 March
Last of the March VIII's. Our boat was very close to Pembroke but just failed to catch them and finished third. There was a Rooster party in my rooms at which I was created Archdean and presented with an elaborate grant of Rooster Arms. At about 10.45 p.m. I went to the police station (on receipt of a telephone message from the porter) and bailed out B. H. Coleman.

Sunday 7 March
Went to King's with Tiny and the Dame and we walked to the bridge. Clare Bridge looked like a piece of stage scenery with the mist (unusual at this time of year) giving a theatrical backcloth effect. It was a lovely sight in the sun. We walked through the King's crocuses and back through the Trinity crocuses.

Monday 8 March
Attended a meeting at the University Press with C. H. Dodd, T. Knox-Shaw and S. C. Roberts to revise the list of Black-Letter Saints in the University Calendar. At the College Council meeting it was agreed to nominate me as Pro-Proctor* for the next academical year. In Hall the Dean said, "Ugh! This nasty rhubarb sends a cold shiver down my spine. Rhubarb isn't fit for human consumption at any time but this is only fit for the dustbin. Still, we must bear our cross".

> [*The Pro-Proctor is a mere upstart, dating only from the year 1818, but the office of Proctor is one of the most ancient in the University, dating back to the thirteenth century. There are always two Proctors at a time; they are the representatives of the Masters of Arts of the whole University and originally had charge of the finances. They were no doubt elected to keep an eye on the Chancellor and other more or less permanent officers who might be tempted to misappropriate the common funds or override the rights of Masters.]

Wednesday 5 May
Showed Gilbey and three Benedictines over the College. [Mgr Gilbey was Chaplain to the Roman Catholics at the University.] James Wood let me see the Master's portrait, which is nearly finished.

~ 1943 ~

Monday 17 May
Bishop Edward Wynn came to tea. At the Roost later he was emperched (with special privileges) and then created Doctor of Rooster Lore *jure dignitatis*. The correct Rooster pronunciation is - you're a-diggin' taters! Went with the Bishop to Sidney Sussex Chapel for the annual chapter of STC and Solemn Evensong with a sermon by the Bishop, and then a Te Deum.

Thursday 20 May
R. R. Pennyfather [a shipmate from FB's First World War days] walked in, quite unexpectedly. We talked for an hour then I had pupils, so he went and looked round the town and lunched out. He came back to tea and I took him to Hall and he stayed the night in the Q-bicle.

Thursday 17 June
At Norman Cross. Stopped smoking after dinner today.

> [FB was at this time smoking more than sixty cigarettes a day, and decided it was time to quit. He succeeded in breaking so strong a habit only because he remembered Dryden's line, "Men are but children of a larger growth" and applied it to himself. He made no resolution to give up smoking permanently but merely to try it for a day. During that day (which he found difficult enough) he kept telling himself that he would be able to smoke all day next day. Having got through the first day, he decided to make it two days, then three, then a week, then a fortnight, a month, three months, six months and finally a year. All the time he was telling himself that he would be able to smoke as usual next week, next month, and so on. Within six months he was cured and found life much simpler without cigarettes. During the first six months, however, his output of work halved. He had associated smoking so closely with his work that when he stopped smoking the work wanted to stop too. In June Wilson Harris had commissioned FB to write an article for *The Spectator* in commemoration of Q's eightieth birthday, which was to fall on the following 21 November. He intended to write it in July but could not write a word. He knew that if he smoked ideas would come, but he did not want to give in. When the last possible day for submitting the article had almost arrived he became desperate. He consulted his friend and colleague, Eustace Tillyard, and told him he would take whatever advice he suggested. Tillyard advised FB to write to Wilson Harris saying he could not write the article after all. That broke the spell. He went back to his rooms to write the letter to Wilson Harris but wrote the article instead, straight off and without difficulty.]

Friday 25 June
Barnet. Had tea at Knightsland where the grass is being cut. Home by the road – beautifully free from the noise and smell of traffic. [The wartime petrol rationing was responsible for this.]

Saturday 26 June
Met the Bishop of Ely and we went by train to Swindon to spend a week with the Mitchells at Furze Coppice, Savernake.

Monday 28 June
Walked through the Forest with the Dame to Marlborough to do some shopping. From 5 p.m. to 10.30 p.m. I watched them fishing for trout at Dunsford Mill.

Friday 16 July
Cambridge. Attended a scholarship examiners' meeting at Downing. Prince Obelensky walked back with me and came in for some time. Frank and Elsie [his brother and sister-in-law, staying the week in Jesus Lane] came to lunch and in the afternoon we looked round Christ's, Emmanuel and Sidney Sussex Colleges before going to Heffers. After Hall C. H. Dodd said he was surprised to hear from somebody that Frank was my *younger* brother.

Sunday 18 July
I presided over a largely-attended Roost in my rooms. S. G. Harries read his B.Cy [Bachelor of Cockellty] thesis on 'The Origin and Development of the Twerpometer!'

Thursday 22 July
Went to King's College Chapel for the Sung Requiem for Sir Stephen Gaselee. I sat between Dodd and Wilfred Knox.

> [Sir Stephen Gaselee, a kindly gourmet, was a past editor of the *Cambridge Review*, a Medieval Latin anthologist and Keeper of the Papers at the Foreign Office.]

Sunday 1 August
Went to St Giles [Cambridge] for the 11 a.m. service. Sat in the Fellows' Garden a good deal of the day. S. G. Harries and A. R. B. Fuller joined me later and we picked mulberries.

> [The mulberry tree in the Fellows' Garden at Jesus College dates back to King James I's time. The King decreed that a number were to be planted to help the silkworm industry.]

~ 1943 ~

Wednesday 4 August
The Rev Owen Chadwick of St John's, now at Wellington College, called and stayed to Lunch.

[Owen Chadwick became Master of Selwyn College and was knighted.]

Wednesday 8 September
Barnet. Walked to 63 Lancaster Avenue, Beech Hill, Cockfosters, a pleasant house with a cornfield adjoining the garden, into which Charles and Angela Wilson moved today. I was their first caller. At 6 p.m. we heard on the wireless that Italy had surrendered.

Friday 24 September
In the morning I did not go to Abbotts as planned, as he had taken out his lunch with him to watch trains at Hadley Wood. At 2.30 p.m Mr Stanbridge and I went for a walk. We had just got to the corner of Marriott Road when we saw a working man and a woman. He said, "Have you got 20 minutes to spare, Guv". I didn't quite grasp the situation at first, and said no. Then I remembered the Register Office was on the corner. "How long did you say". "Twenty minutes, not more." "Yes", I said, "I have, have you Mr Stanbridge?" "Yes." "Then let us do what he wants", I said. "What's that?" "He wants us to witness his marriage." "That's right, Guv", said the man, "my witnesses haven't turned up and it's past 2.30 now." So we went and witnessed the marriage of Brian and Beatrice Griffin.

Friday 1 October
Cambridge. Went to the Senate House. Heard the speech by the retiring Vice-Chancellor, witnessed the enthronement of the new one (Hale, Master of Emmanuel), and the installation of B. C. Saunders of Magdalene and W. Lowther Clarke (deputy for Sutherland of Pembroke) as Proctors; and Edward Raven (nominated by Christ's), and myself as Pro-Proctors. At 10.30 a.m. we all went in procession along King's Parade and Downing Street to Emmanuel College, followed by forty or fifty members of the Senate.

[E. E. Raven, affectionately called Dave, was a brother of Charles Raven, Master of Christ's. He shared the Pro-Proctorship and the Proctorship with FB and they became great friends. On one occasion he said to Freddy, "I had an unusual experience last week". "Oh yes, what was that?" FB replied. "I met a Bishop and he didn't know you!" Both of the Proctors, or their approved deputies, must be present at every Congregation of the Senate before any University legislation can be passed or a degree conferred. The Senior Proctor reads out the proposals, which are called Graces. If there is no opposition the Junior Proctor calls out "placet" and the Grace has become an Ordinance. The Proctors preside over the formal election of a Vice-Chancellor in June and install him on the first weekday in October, first jointly occupying the throne during the brief interregnum after the previous Vice-Chancellor has vacated office. The election of the Vice-Chancellor is a farce. The Council of the Senate is required by statute to nominate two heads of colleges for the office. One of these two is to be elected by members of the Regent House, voting by secret ballot. By law, either of the two could be successful but it is always understood that the first on the list is to be elected and that the second will become Vice-Chancellor after him. There would be pandemonium if the second on the list were chosen!]

Tuesday 5 October
Took the train to Oxford and spent the afternoon in Blackwell's Bookshop. Dined in Hall at Jesus and slept the night at the college.

[Jesus Oxford and Jesus Cambridge have a reciprocal arrangement whereby Fellows are entertained at either place.]

Friday 8 October
On the train to Cambridge from Oxford I had the company of Whetstone (head verger at Ely Cathedral) from Verney onwards. The American airmen in the compartment were so impressed by his manner and conversation and his black suit with a stiff, tight-fitting collar and broad black tie, that in the blackout, they assumed him to be the Bishop of Ely and I basked in reflected glory. In Hall the Dean said, "When the war is over Hitler should be appointed Commissar over the Jews in this country".

Wednesday 13 October
Went out on a Proctorial "walk" for the first time with Constables Johnson and Childerley. Nothing much doing. Several men were rebuked for smoking while wearing a gown and one for carrying his gown. We ran into one smoker in Rose Crescent – obviously a freshman – terrified at finding himself face to face with a Proctor.

Sunday 17 October
Q came to tea. I showed him the letter from the editor of the *Spectator* asking me to write an article for his 80th birthday, as "a lot of people forget he still exists he dates back so far and it would be useful to remind them he is still here and still active". Q said, "Shush! He's dead but he doesn't want it generally known".

Monday 25 October
Went to Q's rooms after Hall and we talked of Conan Doyle who stayed with him at Fowey. "He wasn't first rate as a writer of detective fiction", said Q, "but he was the pioneer of it." Q also talked about people he had known, e.g. Thomas Hardy. The first Mrs Hardy was a great trial to TH, she considered she had married beneath her, being an archdeacon's niece. She thought she had never had justice done to her. When she died Hardy built up a great romance in his mind about her and wrote this down in *A Pair of Blue Eyes*.

Friday 29 October
Took Professor Dobie (USA and Emmanuel) to Hall, after which he talked to the Jesuits in my rooms on "The History of Ranching" – most interesting and entertaining.

Wednesday 3 November
Q told me he intends to send his resignation to the Vice-Chancellor after Christmas. I said it wasn't for me to contest his decision, which I could quite understand but his going would be a sad day for me.

Sunday 21 November
Reading the menu in Hall, which consisted of tomato soup, game pie and pineapple trifle, Dodd pronounced it excellent! The Dean said, "I hate them all. It's a good thing Q isn't here *or we should have some grumbling*".

Wednesday 24 November
Professor A. E. Richardson, RA, addressed the Neale Society on "English Church Architecture in the nineteenth century".

Thursday 25 November
At 9 p.m. I was out on Proctorial duty. Caught a gownless Selwyn man in the Chimney [the entrance passage to Jesus College from Jesus Lane] only a yard outside the porters' lodge – probably the first man ever to be "progged" in the Chimney. He said he was afraid of getting his gown torn.

Sunday 28 November
A Rooster Concert was held in my rooms. There were fifty or more present including several girls. I sang various songs including, as Sister Betsy Co-ed of the Order of St Radegund, 'We nuns of St Radegund down Jesus Lane'.

[No entries for December]

~ 1944 ~

Saturday 15 January
Cycled with Frank Stammers and S. G. Harries and the first boat to Baitsbite in lovely sun with narrow bands of dense fog here and there.

Monday 17 January
The STC met in my rooms for a social gathering. C. D. Waddams, D. Marsh, SSF, Partridge of St Luke's, Telfer of Clare, B. de Winton of Trinity and about two dozen male and female undergraduates were present. I told them the saga of the Archdeacon's Horse and stories of Arthur Gray, Nairne, Foakes-Jackson, etc.

Friday 21 January
South Mymms. Katharine Hay's wedding to Victor Ross took place. I acted as assistant to the celebrant and the Vicar gave her away. Later he paid me the greatest compliment one man could pay another, by saying earnestly "I would rather have had you for a son-in-law than all the other men in the world".

Sunday 23 January
Cambridge. Katharine and Victor arrived from Kingston. I opened a bottle of champagne and Q , S. G. Harries, and I drank their health. We all went to Evensong at King's then to tea in my rooms, after which Katharine and Victor left by cycle. At the Roost in the evening we elected J. D. J. Havard (Claude) to the Grainsack.

> [Claude Havard qualified both as a doctor and as a barrister and became Secretary of the British Medical Association.]

Thursday 27 January
Attended the College Council meeting at which the Master referred to "timber in the form of trees". This reminded us of a meeting last term when he said of some WAAF officers' billeted in the College, "The conduct of these ladies in regard to conveniences in the form of gas rings was unbelievably dishonest".

~ 1944 ~

Friday 4 February
Attended the Westcott House Council. The Principal-elect was there and came to tea with me afterwards.

> [William Greer, the Principal-elect, became Bishop of Manchester three years later.]

Thursday 18 February
Q came to tea in his bright brown knicker suit with shooting spats. He says two lectures a week are quite enough for the ordinary man.

Ash Wednesday 23 February
Went to the litany at Great St Mary's. The Senior Proctor sat in the north west stall of the chancel, the Junior Proctor next to him and he recited up to "O God, Merciful Father", the Vice-Chancellor doing that and the rest. The Proctors walked immediately after the Vice-Chancellor. When the others had gone after Hall, Q and I sat and talked quite an hour. He did most of the talking. England in his early manhood was a very good place, he said. He pictured a peaceful England and a peaceful world during his time until the Jameson Raid, which was the turning point. He saw then that many of this country are out for an expanding empire, which we hadn't the power to run. The Kaiser's telegram to Kruger made our government demonstrate with the fleet. This resolved Germany to become a naval power and so on. He chiefly blamed Cecil Rhodes whom he execrated: "…and to think that there is a statue of him outside Oriel [College, Oxford] facing the statue of the Virgin Mary".

> [Prompted by disillusionment with gold mining prospects within Rhodesia, Cecil Rhodes conceived the Jameson Raid to protect his own and other British Capitalists' gold mining interests in Witwatersrand. Being within the Transvaal republic, Witwatersrand was subject to the laws of Kruger's government and their heavy mining industry taxes that favoured the interests of rural Afrikaners. By the 1890s there were thousands of British and other *uitlanders* (outsiders) living, in Johannesburg. Fearing that they might outnumber the Afrikaner electorate, and that giving them the vote might lead to the overthrow of his government, Kruger had passed a law giving only white males with a minimum of fourteen years residence the right to vote, which effectively deprived British adults of the franchise. Peaceful agitation had produced no tangible results and as Rhodes distrusted German overtures to the Kruger government he devised a plan to stage a coup in the Transvaal. It was to start with a spontaneous uprising of the *uitlanders* in Johannesburg supported by members of Rhodes' own police force under the command of the Administrator of Rhodesia, Dr Jameson. Rhodes failed to realise that not many *uitlanders* were concerned

enough about the vote to risk their lives in an act of treason and the uprising was poorly organised and supported in Johannesburg. Claiming that he was going to the aid of British women and children, Jameson decided to go ahead with his side of the operation. When he crossed the Bechuanaland border on 29 December 1895 he found himself surrounded by the forewarned Transvaalers and was forced to surrender on 2 January 1896. (Shillington K., *An African Adventure*, Rhodes Memorial Museum, p.47-49).]

Saturday 11 March
At 2 p.m. attended a Congregation of the Regent House. A Grace was non-placeted by 45 to 43. At 6.45 p.m. Laurence Picken was admitted to his Fellowship in Chapel. The Master dined and afterwards we drank Picken's health.

[L. E. R. Picken is a zoologist, biologist and musicologist, especially of the music of the Tang Dynasty of China. In 1975 the Society for Asian Music published a special volume of his essays in his honour, which prompted the following tribute in the College Annual Report:
"Among the scholarly Chinese there is a charming custom of bestowing a special name of honour upon a colleague who has earned their highest esteem. This volume reveals that they know Laurence by the name of Loren, meaning 'delighting in human heartedness'. All Jesus men will agree that the name is the perfect picture of the man."]

Sunday 12 March
Attended the Litany and Sung Eucharist at King's. The Vice-Chancellor and General Montgomery came out with the Provost.

Friday 14 April
Barnet. Walked to Kitts End and the Wash. Saw a glorious array of daffodils at Trenchard's, plenty of furze bloom at Kitts End and golden palm still in its prime; hornbeam catkins are just beginning to appear, the poplars are in full catkin everywhere, looking from a distance like the burning bush.

Monday 17 April
From the Cock and Bull News Agency, i.e. the Dean and Dodd: "Trinity College is going to be the Second Front headquarters". Also, "The German miners are getting more than twice as much food as the British, so Haw-Haw says and if that's true it's very interesting".

Thursday 20 April
More Cock and Bull: "Have you heard any more about HQ being at Trinity, Dodd?" "No".

Tuesday 2 May
Out on Proctorial duty and caught two men without gowns. They walked through us and the Constables would have let them go but I realized who they were.

Wednesday 3 May
The meeting of the Cambridge University Church of England Council was held in the Parlour at Caius College and addressed by the Provost of Coventry on the projected new Cathedral there.

[German bombing raids had destroyed Coventry Cathedral.]

Saturday 6 May
General Ironside was dining as the Master's guest and in the Combination Room he talked about the events of 1940 when he was Chief of the Imperial General Staff. He said that when he asked the French Commander what his plan was just before Dunkirk he answered, "Je n'ai pas de plan". He said that thirty thousand of our men in France hadn't been in the Army six weeks.

Tuesday 9 May
Professor A. E. Richardson called at 9 p.m. We strolled round the Fellows' Garden and the Close and then went to Compline at Westcott House. Peter May [Vice-Principal of Westcott House] came back for a cup of tea.

Friday 12 May
The porter 'phoned after tea and said the Master would like to speak to me. I went down to meet him and as we walked round he said, "Have you had any reply from Q since you wrote?" – "No." – "I have heard from his daughter." – "Oh yes." – "He won't be coming up this term." – "No?" – "In fact he won't be coming up again at all". – "How is that?" – "He died today."

Saturday 13 May
Cycled with the third, fourth and fifth boats to Baitsbite and back in glorious weather with the hedges white with May and heavy with the scent of it.

Wednesday 17 May
Went to see S. C. Roberts of the Cambridge University Press about writing a book on Q. After the Rustat Feast Charles Wilson brought his guest, A. Clifton-Taylor, to my rooms, with others who stayed until 3 a.m.

[Alec Clifton-Taylor became well known later on as the presenter of several television series, including *Six English Towns*.]

Friday 19 May
Tiny and the Dame came to lunch after which (with me wearing my silk gown for the first time), we went to the Senate House for conferring honorary degrees on the Prime Ministers of Australia and New Zealand.

Monday 5 June
Went to a meeting of the Languages Faculty Board at the Old Schools. On the agenda was the appointment of a Reader in Romance Philology. The Chairman (E. K. Bennett) said that a meeting of Heads of Departments had nominated myself. I was astonished! Bennett said that I had better leave the room while they discussed it. I replied that I was much flattered but I simply couldn't do the job. Loud laughter followed and nothing more was done.

Monday 24 July
We elected Denys Wilkinson to a Research Fellowship.

[He became the youngest Professor of Nuclear Physics at Oxford and then Vice-Chancellor of Sussex University. During his time at Oxford he in turn became High Steward of the Roost but agreed to stand down on moving to Sussex, saying that he was willing to give way to an older man, i.e. Sir Alan Cottrell who was Master of Jesus at the time and a brilliant Rooster.]

Saturday 5 August
Took men round the Fellows' Garden after Hall; they ate mulberries and played bowls.

Friday 11 August
Took Gilbert Coleridge to Hall, after which we sat in the Fellows' Garden.

[Gilbert Coleridge was a descendant of Samuel Taylor Coleridge; he executed the bronze memorial to his ancestor, which is on the east wall of the south transept in Jesus Chapel. It depicts the poet with the albatross of the *Ancient Mariner* flying over his head.]

Sunday 20 August
A wet day, the first we've had for months.

Saturday 26 August
Furze Coppice, Savernake. Went with Tiny and the Dame by Mr Penny's taxi

~ 1944 ~

to Chiseldon church where Richard Jefferies was married) and up to the top of Liddington Down. Lunched inside the earthwork by the Jefferies monument.

[FB read a number of Q's novels during this vacation, interspersed with potato picking on his father's allotment at Barnet.]

Monday 2 October
Cambridge. Went to the Senate House where E. E. Raven and I were elected and installed as Proctors. After conducting the Vice-Chancellor to Emmanuel Lodge, I returned to the College for a group photograph in the Fellows' Garden, then a reception in my rooms. The Master proposed my health and Tiny proposed Mother's. The family lunched with me in the Q-bicle.

[FB received the following letter from his mother dated 6 October, 1944.

Dear Fred
  I arrived home about 7 on Monday terribly tired, in fact I have not got over it yet. But it was an unforgettable day and I would not have missed it for anything. I hope I did the right thing when Mr Mitchell proposed my health. I was so taken by surprise and never dreamed of such a thing.]

Sunday 15 October
B. T. Wicks and two other freshmen arrived for a Roost at 8.15 a.m., having been told the meeting would be at cockcrow!

Monday 16 October
In pouring rain I went to the Senate House, thence with the Vice-Chancellor to Trinity Lodge, where we were presented to the Assize Judge (Mr Justice Singleton), who wore a red cassock open down the front, a fur-edged red cape, black ecclesiastical scarf, full wig, bands, and a hood of white fur, Cambridge pattern, with tippet forming a full cape. He explained that the hood is worn only in Cathedral cities and University churches. The Sheriff stood by in velvet breeches and sword; the Chaplain and the Under Sheriff were in morning dress. Went to Great St Mary's where the Judge arrived at 12.30 p.m. and the preacher gave an excellent, short sermon. We broke away at the church door. Attended the Proctorial tea at St John's at 4–5.30 p.m [Edward Raven, the Senior Proctor, being Dean of St John's.]

Saturday 21 October
On my Proctorial walk a man engaged in a "treasure hunt" got me to give him a "Proctor's note".

~ 1944 ~

Sunday 29 October
Went to Evensong at All Saints'. A new window was dedicated and the Bishop of Ely gave the sermon.

Tuesday 31 October
Received a visit from the usual three – George Giri, Claude Havard and David Perrins.

> [All three were reading medicine and liked to work together in FB's rooms. George Giri became Surgeon-Captain, RN, and on retirement second in command to Claude (John) Havard at the British Medical Association. David Perrins received awards for contributions to hyperbaric medicine and was medical adviser to Action for Research into Multiple Sclerosis.]

Sunday 5 November
Guy Fawkes night. Dined with E. E. Raven at St John's. We were nicely settled in the Combination Room when the police rang and asked us to deal with a rag on Market Hill where a car had been turned over, the petrol run out and a match put to it. We stayed till 11 p.m., moving crowds on and taking names.

Tuesday 7 November
Took tea at Westcott House with S. C. Neill, Bishop of Tinevelly. A. W. Lawrence was admitted to his Fellowship at 7.10 p.m.

> [Arnold Lawrence was Professor of Classical Archaeology at Cambridge. He later followed D. W. Balme to the new University of Ghana.]

Tuesday 14 November
A Roost Extraordinary was held in my rooms and I presided. An undergraduate who came late and whom I provided with a chair and a Codex [Gallorum = Rules of the Roost] thinking he was a candidate for Roostership, proved to be an Emmanuel man who had come to be "progged" for wearing his overcoat over his gown the other night.

Tuesday 5 December
Three Homertonians came to look round and stayed to tea. One, whose father was Q's doctor at Fowey, said Lady Q was the daughter of a publican who kept the Ferry Inn at Bodinnick, nevertheless the girl has a great respect and affection for her - as she should have.

~ 1944 ~

Sunday 10 December
South Mymms. An air raid "alert" sounded just after the third collect at Evensong.

[No further entries for December]

~ 1945 ~

[During the years of the Second World War the diaries note endless lists of names of men who called on FB when visiting the College on leave.]

Sunday 11 March
Cambridge. Percy Merriman of the Roosters Concert Party was made an Extraordinary Cockerel.

[The Concert Party, a well-known company of professional entertainers, had been founded by Percy Merriman in France during the First World War. They first got in touch with the College through reading about the Jesus Roosters in a newspaper. When the company came later to give a performance in the town FB invited them all to supper and took them round the Fellows' Garden by twilight. It was July and the still air was perfumed with half visible roses, night-scented stocks and lime blossom. To them, visiting for the first time, it was fairyland. One of the company was seen pinching his arm and heard murmuring, "It can't be real, I must be dreaming".]

Saturday 24 March
Went with the bulldogs to the Provost's Lodge at King's and there took chocolate, before going to the Sermon in King's Chapel. E. E. Raven and I sat in the returned stalls on the north side next to the Vice-Provost. The choir met us at the west door and sang a processional hymn, then followed the Bidding Prayer, Sermon and Benediction and motet and we went out in silence. The Provost conducted us to the outer gate.

Wednesday 18 April
After Hall we sat in the Fellows' Garden. Mills says it has never before been possible on the first day of Full Term. This is a very advanced spring; the chestnuts, lilacs and wisteria are in full bloom, the laburnums half open, the cherries over.

Saturday 21 April
Went as Proctor to the Memorial Service for President Roosevelt at King's.

Monday 23 April
The blackout ceased today. We seemed dazzled by light in Hall and in our rooms.

Monday 30 April
Awoke to find two inches of snow lying on the ground this morning.

Tuesday 1 May
B. N. Bebbington was my guest for lunch in Hall.

> [Bebbington was the Chief Constable of Cambridgeshire. He was made an ordinary undergraduate at the College, the Proctors gladly granting him dispensation from wearing academic dress after dark. He went on to become one of Her Majesty's Inspectors of Constabulary and the Home Office Adviser on Police Management Services. He broadcast frequently on police matters and also wrote several children's books.]

Tuesday 8 May
VE Day [Victory over Europe]. At 11 a.m. I attended High Mass at St Giles, Cambridge.

> [FB recalls this momentous day, the end of the war in Europe, in his autobiography *It's A Don's Life*. My memory of the day is a welter of many sights and sounds, he wrote. I remember the music of the bells in Great St Mary's in full peal after the long silence; peripatetic music provided by the Home Guard, the Cadet Corps, and a band of girl pipers; the summoning of the Proctors to the Guildhall at 4 o'clock to appear on the balcony with the Vice-Chancellor and the Lord Lieutenant while the Mayor addressed the vast crowd which had gathered on Market Hill. After the Mayor's proclamation we made the Guildhall our Proctorial headquarters for the rest of the day. I remember some scores of service men and civilians who danced for the whole of the hottest hour of a hot afternoon; the Master proposing a toast in Hall that evening; Market Hill packed again to its utmost capacity to hear a broadcast of the King's speech; the torchlight procession which drew most of the crowd away afterwards to a huge bonfire on Midsummer Common; the delight and cheers of those who stayed behind and watched a dozen airmen, commando men and American soldiers climb up from the front of the Guildhall to the balcony with the greatest ease and disappear into the building; the undergraduate who climbed up after them and the astonishment on his face a few moments

later when he found that he had walked into the very room where the two Proctors and the Chief Constable were in consultation; and the walk back to Jesus College in the small hours through streets where lights were still shining from many uncurtained windows and through college courts where friendly searchlights were playing on flowering chestnuts and laburnums.]

Monday 2 June
Went to the Senate House to receive nominations of candidates for Parliament.

[The Universities of Oxford and Cambridge still sent their own members to Parliament. The following week FB was at the Regent House for some days sorting voting papers as part of his Proctorial duty.]

Friday 13 June
Truro, Cornwall. Tiny and the Dame took me to Lis Escop [the official residence of the Bishop of Truro] where I am staying with Bishop J. W. Hunkin for the unveiling of the Q memorial in Truro Cathedral tomorrow.

Saturday 14 June
The Bishop dedicated the memorial at Evensong and I gave an address. A number of people went back to tea at Lis Escop, including Tiny and the Dame.

> [Lis Escop
> Truro
> 27 July 1945
>
> My dear Brittain,
>   We all thoroughly enjoyed having you here and hope very much it will not be long before you come again. Your natural persuasiveness brought the East Wind of my natural Protestantism back several points. Reasonable Catholicism is a beautiful thing but one sees so little of it in these parts.
>   Thank you so much for the invitation to review these C.U. Sermons, which I gratefully accept. I will take the book with me to the Isles of Scilly in August.
>   Again our warmest thanks.
>   Ever Yours sincerely,
>   (signed) J. W. Truron]

~ 1945 ~

Monday 16 July
Staying with Lady Quiller-Couch and her daughter (Foy Felicia) at the Haven, Fowey. In the afternoon I went to St Austell where A. L. Rowse showed me round and I had tea at his house afterwards.

> [Later that week FB spoke at the unveiling of the memorial to Q, which stands on the headland at the north end of Fowey Harbour.]

Thursday 26 July
Most of the General Election results were declared today and it's a great Labour Party victory.

Friday 27 July
Took Major A. L. Symonds (the new University MP) to Hall.

Bank Holiday Monday 6 August
I was elected Steward of the College today.

> [The duties of the Steward vary in details from college to college. At Jesus they are very wide, including as they do the security of the College, the supervision of the kitchen, buttery, wine cellars, Combination Room and other common rooms, the planning of feasts, the maintenance of courts and gardens, and the housing and feeding of vacation conference attendees. The Steward, being responsible for the catering (albeit through the medium of a Manciple), has the most thankless of all College Offices; for even dons are known to grumble about the food and there are undergraduates at every one of the colleges in the University who are firmly convinced that the food provided at their own college is the worst in Cambridge.]

Wednesday 15 August
I had just gone to bed when, about 12.15 a.m., men came in to say the war [with Japan] was over and we had a glass of sherry, which I had kept since 1939. After dinner went to the Guildhall on Proctorial duty but things were quite quiet.

Friday 17 August
As there was a very big late crop of peaches hanging on the wall of the Fellows' Garden and the head gardener was away, Tillyard, Thorpe, Wilkinson, Lawrence and myself went there and helped ourselves after dinner.

~ 1945 ~

Sunday 19 August
Attended the Thanksgiving Service at Great St Mary's. We took all the Proctorial insignia: halberd, linstock, partizan (short pike) and a metal tube about a yard long called 'the butter measure'.

[The linstock used to be used to hold lighted tow for the firing of cannon. The constables carry these ceremonial weapons on special occasions only.]

Friday 24 August
Started writing my book about Q.

[FB worked on the Q biography sometimes twelve hours a day for the whole of the rest of the vacation, apart from a short holiday with the Mitchells at Furze Coppice.]

Friday 28 September
Hall was at 7.30 p.m. again. Captain Austin is back and rang the bell.

[Captain Austin had a distinguished career in the Royal Marines during the First World War, having taken a leading part in the famous raid on the German U-boat base at Zeebrugge. After retiring he saw an advertisement for a Head Porter at Jesus College. He applied for the job and was called for interview not having the faintest idea what to expect. As Alan Hill told the story during his speech at the JCCS Dinner in 1984, Austin was taken into a room with three men sitting behind a table. The man in the middle (Arthur Gray, the Master) seemed very old and obviously needed a haircut. The old gentleman said to Austin, "I see you were on the Mole at Zeebrugge". "Yes", he replied. "Good! Then you know what it's like when things are getting rough." Austin got the job.]

Monday 1 October
Raven and I installed Thirkill as Vice-Chancellor at the Senate House and we retired from office as Proctors and I was re-admitted to the office of Senior Proctor (with James Stephenson of St John's as my junior). At noon Eustace Tillyard was admitted as Master in Jesus College Chapel by the President W. H. Mills.

[E. M. W. Tillyard had entered the College in 1908 and had been Senior Tutor throughout the greater part of the Second World War. A Doctor of Letters and a specialist on Shakespeare and Milton, he enjoyed an international reputation for scholarship. Like Arthur Gray he was a Liberal in politics, whereas Duckworth was a strong Tory.]

~ 1945 ~

Wednesday 10 October
The Gumcestrians [inhabitants of Godmanchester, Hunts, pronounced Gumster in the Roost], Ralph Gardner [the Vicar], Mrs Gardner, 'And', 'Reen', Dora, Joan, Jean and the German friend arrived. Took them round the College and we had tea in my rooms with Alan Percival, Kenneth Lindsay, David Balme, C. A. B. Bernstein, David Perrins, Claude Havard and numerous other people who kept popping in and out on Proctorial and other business.

Sunday 14 October
The Roost was the biggest I have ever seen. There was a queue two deep all the way from my door [on the second floor of C staircase in First Court] to the ground so we had to hold it in the Common Room.

Wednesday 24 October
A joint birthday party for the Dame and me was held at the Angel in Peterborough with thirteen friends. Came back to Cambridge by car, arriving at 1.15 a.m., and then read *Cambridge Review* proofs for an hour.

[No further entries for 1945]

~ 1946 ~

Tuesday 1 January
Barnet. I had bronchitis and didn't go out for several days.

Saturday 2 March
Cambridge. We finished Head of the Lents and lit a bonfire on the Close - in the snow.

Monday 4 March
Meeting at 2.30 p.m. with the Languages Board. Later went to Ely with the Bishop to give a talk to the Ely Literary Society on Q. Stayed the night with the Bishop.

Friday 2 April
Barnet. Caught the bus to Bignells Corner and walked back via the Wash. The blackthorn is in full flower where it is sheltered from the east wind, otherwise not open at all. The daffodils at Trenchards have suddenly become

a mass of yellow, ten thousand tossing their heads. The ash leaves are just beginning to show.

Friday 5 April
Perfect day (it's a heatwave now). Dad and I moved my books upstairs where I now have my study.

Maundy Thursday 18 April
Went with Tiny and the Dame to the Royal Maundy Service at Westminster Abbey, distributed by the King in person.

> [In England the Maundy, from Mandatum, our Lord's command to his followers to love one another, is referred to by St Augustine about AD 600. King John is known to have taken part in the ceremony in 1213 at Rochester, but no reigning monarch participated from 1685 until King George V restored the custom in 1932 and attended the Abbey in person to hand out purses to the number of poor men and women corresponding to the Sovereign's age.]

Holy Saturday 20 April
I was MC and sang the whole of the Exsultet at the Blessing of the Paschal Candle and Evensong at St Giles.

Tuesday 7 May
Cambridge. The Annual Meeting of the Cambridge University Church of England Council at Caius College. Stead (King's) said he "much enjoyed" my financial statement.

Thursday 23 May
Went to the printing works to make up the *Cambridge Review* [as every Thursday during term.]

Friday 7 June
Met Mr Phelp of Watford on King's Parade.

> [Some of FB's guests were complete strangers to him when he first entertained them and Mr Phelp was one of these. He had stopped FB to ask him to explain something in his guidebook. On discovering that it was his first visit to Cambridge, FB invited him to tea at the College. He was so interested in everything he saw that FB invited him to stay to dinner in Hall. Finding that he had not made a hotel reservation for the night, FB invited him to stay in College. He enjoyed his visit so much that next morning FB felt he must invite him to stay for a week and he did. FB had seldom known

a guest to be so enraptured with the place as Mr Phelp was, or one whom it had given him so much pleasure to entertain.]

Friday 21 June
South Mymms. Served the Vicar in church at 8 a.m. It was his 80th birthday. Had breakfast with him, then home and back to College in the afternoon.

Wednesday 31 July
Cambridge. A meeting was held in my rooms to form the "Friends of Little Gidding".

[Its objectives were to maintain the parish church of Little Gidding and to perpetuate the memory of the saintly Nicholas Ferrar who lived at Gidding early in the seventeenth century, as readers of John Inglesant will remember. The Bishop of Ely leads the Friends' annual pilgrimage in July. The tiny church stands in charming isolation in a remote part of what used to be Huntingdonshire, miles from any town. The only approach to it is by a cart track, through a farmyard and then across a meadow. Corn grows up to the very walls of the church and its diminutive graveyard, where Nicholas Ferrar is buried just outside the west door. The nave, with its seats arranged as in a college chapel, holds only thirty people so the rest of the pilgrims have to stand outside. Even so the church has enough seats to accommodate the whole parish on ordinary occasions. In later years the annual service was a Eucharist celebrated on Nicholas Ferrar's table tomb, with the community cat often 'assisting' the celebrant and the birds in the surrounding trees supplying the music.]

Thursday 15 August
Audited the College silver.

[The College's extensive stock of silver is the responsibility of the Steward.]

Sunday 8 September
South Mymms. At church there were twenty-four of us in the chancel, mostly grown men as few boys were present.

Monday 16 September
Went to Lichfield Theological College to serve on a board of selection of ordination candidates (26 of them).

Thursday 19 September
The candidates left after lunch. I had tea at the Palace.

~ 1946 ~

Friday 27 September

The Provost of Wakefield
The Cathedral Vicarage
Wakefield

Dear Mr Brittain,

In spite of your kindly prohibition I feel I must send you this line to thank you for your most welcome letter.

The Conference last week was well worth while and there appeared to be general agreement that it struck the right note. For that not a little credit must go to yourself for your sage counsel and, may I say, for both your humour and your discernment. I was truly thankful that you were on our panel and, incidentally deeply appreciative of the opportunity of getting to know you…

It seems to me that these conferences fulfil a wholesome and useful purpose, – especially in this transitional period; perhaps they might well be continued indefinitely; it will be interesting to see what happens.

With all kind wishes.

    Ever yours sincerely
    (signed) Noel Hopkins

Tuesday 1 October
Gillie Potter, Raby and I went to the Senate House where I was installed as Senior Proctor. After conducting the Vice-Chancellor to Clare, I went back to College and held a reception in Hall for a hundred and twenty or more persons, including Mother. We had coffee, sandwiches, etc. and a photo was taken. Alan Percival told Ernest Heffer that Gillie Potter was a medieval scholar who is a comedian by profession and that I am a comedian who is a medieval scholar by profession! Most of the rest of the day I was showing parties round the College.

Friday 11 October
Honorary degrees were conferred on the Generals Eisenhower and Montgomery.

Tuesday 15 October
Four girls from Homerton College came to look round and stayed for tea. Dined at the Union with the President and Herbert Morrison as it was the reopening of their dining room.

Thursday 24 October
J. M. Edmonds was admitted to his Fellowship in Chapel.

~ 1946 ~

[J. M. Edmonds, who had come up to Jesus in 1894 and taken a first class in Classics, was a member of the High Table at Jesus for many years. Refer also to the note following Thursday 2 December 1920.]

Wednesday 30 October
Attended the Forrester Sermon at All Saints' church and distribution of pensions, and then on to the Susanna Forrester lunch at the Lion at which I had to read her Will.

Saturday 9 November
Professor A. E. Richardson came to lunch and tea, between which he painted the view from my windows.

Thursday 19 November
Dined at the Union with Lord Mountbatten and Gillie Potter. I took a small part in the frivolous debate between them. Admiral Lord Mountbatten has recently been created a peer and appointed Viceroy of India by the Labour Government. I reminded him that the last time I heard him speak at the Union was in 1920 when he opposed a motion "That the time is now ripe for a Labour Government"!

Tuesday 26 November
We had a discussion in the Regent House on the admission of women.

Tuesday 3 December
Lunched at the Dorothy with the Caius crowd then, plus the Mayor and Chief Constable, kicked off one of the three balls in the Foot-the-Ball match on Parker's Piece.

[There were three balls, three goals and three teams playing against each other simultaneously on a single pitch. The novelty of the game, coupled perhaps with the announcement that the three balls would be kicked off by the Mayor, the Senior Proctor and the Chief Constable, attracted a large crowd of spectators. When FB was asked to take part in the kick-off he readily agreed, particularly as he was told that the Mayor and Chief Constable would be doing the same. When FB arrived at the ground the Chief Constable came up to him and said, "I knew it would be quite in order for me to take part in this, because the organizers told me that you and the Mayor were doing so!" FB came away from the match with the Mayor, who remarked thoughtfully, "I wondered at first whether to take part in the kick-off or not, but agreed to do so when they told me that the Chief Constable and you were going to be in it!"]

Tuesday 24 December
South Mymms. Attended the Bread Service at St Giles (small rolls this year).

Christmas Day, Wednesday 25 December
I was cantor at St Giles at 11 a.m., then home indoors for the rest of the day – a quiet and happy time.

Tuesday 31 December
Walked to the Wash, which is in full stream, it would have been fine to float down it in a canoe. Went to the Cambridge Theatre, London to see Puccini's opera *La Boheme*, sung in English.

~ 1947 ~

Sunday 26 January
Cambridge. Charles Smyth preached the University Sermon and made some people laugh aloud.

Tuesday 4 February
We had a Rooster expedition to Grantchester where we gave a concert and danced.

Wednesday 12 February
Donald Attwater addressed the Neale Society on Father Ignatius.

> [Joseph Leycester Lyne, known afterwards as Father Ignatius, was born in 1837. He claimed to have re-established the Benedictine Rule in the Church of England by restoring the ruins of Llanthony Abbey in the Vale of Ewyas, Herefordshire, and establishing a monastery there.]

Friday 7 March
Took my Proctorial walk and looked in at St Francis House for Stations of the Cross and later looked in at the United Hunts Ball at the Dorothy.

Monday 10 March
At Home to my pupils at 9 p.m.

Tuesday 11 March
At Home to High Anglicans at 9 p.m.

~ 1947 ~

Tuesday 18 March
Went by car to Little Gidding with Kitson Clark. The country is as black as mid-January with so much snow lying about and great floods. The ash buds are as they were in mid-winter and everything else the same with the exception of the lilac buds, which show a little green

Saturday 17 May
After Hall I went with Norman Hoyte and Rachel Attwater to the bluebell wood at Eversden. We heard and watched a nightingale singing.

Tuesday 3 June
Took part in the procession from the Senate House to Trinity College where I was presented to the King and Queen and the Duke and Duchess of Gloucester

Wednesday 5 June
Went with the Vice-Chancellor, Registrar, Treasurer, etc. to Oxford for the periodical consultation and lunched at Corpus.

Saturday 5 July
Henley Regatta. The Master came to lunch. We won the Grand.

> [The year 1946-47, under the captaincy of F. L. (Larry) Whalley, was *annus mirabilis* for the Jesus College Boat Club. The Club won the Coxwainless Fours in the autumn and in the spring held the Headship of the Lents and won the Tideway Head of the River race. In the Easter Term the first boat finished Head of the River and, after winning the Marlow Grand, went on to Henley and won the Grand Challenge Cup for the third time in the history of the College. The boat was brilliantly coached by D. A. Mays-Smith and brilliantly stroked by C. B. R. (Chris) Barton. The cox was Desmond Harriss who steered no fewer than eleven victorious first boats during his three years' residence.]

Saturday 13 September
Barnet. Picked peas – a huge crop.

Wednesday 10 October
Cambridge. Congregation and Installation of C. E. Raven, Master of Christ's as Vice-Chancellor. I retired from office as Senior Proctor though continuing as Additional Pro-Proctor.

~ 1947 ~

Tuesday 28 October
Dined at Girton as the guest of the Mistress, after which she consulted me about academical dress for women and when and how it should be worn. I recommended stiff squares (instead of the Oxford floppy one) to be worn whenever men wear them, (e.g. by Praelectors), also in Great St Mary's, if they prefer. She said her Fellows all agree. Also, as they won't use surplices, hoods with their gowns in Chapel on Sundays and festivals, also distinctive marks on Girton and Newnham gowns – a roundel ermine for Girton and a star for Newnham.

Monday 3 November
Lord Killanin came to lunch. Gillie Potter called (between trains to Norfolk) and I introduced them to each other.

Tuesday 4 November
We had a discussion in the Senate House on the admission of women to the University. Only one man spoke at all – Bruce Dickins, against.

> [Bruce Dickins was Professor of Anglo-Saxon and a Fellow of Corpus Christi College.]

Tuesday 11 November
The Jesus Tractarians came in for a chat at 1.30 p.m.

Friday 14 November
Took a party of undergraduates by train to Ely. The Bishop conducted a service for us in John Alcock's chapel, then we all had tea together in the town and caught the 5.15 p.m. train back.

Thursday 20 November
Attended Princess Elizabeth's wedding in Westminster Abbey. Spent a little time with the Smyths afterwards. Walked over Lambeth Bridge and met C. Havard and C. Bernstein, who took me to Waterloo. Back to Cambridge and went straight to the printing works. At 5 p.m. I had a potato meeting of Stewards at Pembroke.

Friday 5 December
> [Having sent the Bishop of Peterborough a copy of his biography of Q, FB received the following reply.]

[The Palace
Peterborough

... First my wife and then I read your life of Q and both of us sat entranced by it. I don't know which I admire more – the man whom you set out to paint or the skill with which you did it; and all the while, as I thought of Q's rooms and yours above them, and all the intimacies of College life, which hardly anything else can equal, I was saying to myself, "All this is written by one who has seen his subject from within and yet has never for a moment obtruded his own person on the page".

Thank you very much. It is a model of what a biography should be and your Press has indeed collaborated with you.

Yours, with great gratitude.
(signed) Claude Petriburg]

[No further entries for December.]

~ 1948 ~

Thursday 8 January
Attended the Alcuin Club committee at 3 Dean's Yard, Westminster.

[Alcuin was a celebrated ecclesiastic and a man of learning in the eighth century. He wrote several theological treatises, commentaries on the Bible, etc.]

Monday 26 January
Cambridge. Beveridge was admitted to his Fellowship in Chapel.

[Dr W. I. B. Beveridge was Professor of Animal Pathology at the University. After his retirement he returned to live in Australia where he was born.]

Tuesday 17 February
At 7.10 p.m. Pars rang me up with the private news that I had been approved for Litt.D [Doctor of Letters].

~ 1948 ~

Saturday 28 February
Took the degree of Litt.D, followed by a big gathering for tea in the Prioress's Room.

Tuesday 2 March
[Allan Bank, Graham Road
Malvern

Dear Brittain,
May I join in the chorus of congratulations and pleasure? I doubt if the Doctorate has ever been conferred with such sincere applause ... You have, apart from your main work, supported and befriended the University in many important paths and I should like to say how much I have admired your conduct and control of the *Cambridge Review*. It has always seemed to me most vital that this should be in the right hands and in former days I have blushed for shame at its outrageous lack of principle. You put this all right and may your fine work be an example to later generations. I hope the University realizes what it owes you in this matter ...
With kindest remembrances and best wishes.
Yours sincerely,
(signed) A.B. Ramsay]

Ascension Day, Thursday 6 May
With Eric Yates in his BA gown and John Upton in his undergraduate gown, I set out in scarlet (my first public appearance in it) for the Sung Eucharist at King's. We went in Legge's Rolls Royce. The service was sung to Stanford in B flat. On coming out, as I'd forgotten to ask Legge to pick us up and I funked coming back in scarlet through the crowds of early closing day shoppers, I took off my gown and put it on my arm to cries of "shame" from the Chaplain and choral scholars outside the Chapel door. "Yes, I know" I said, "I'm a coward". Eric offered to carry it and did so. Then he said, "I don't see why I should carry everything. You carry mine", which I did. Even so the scarlet was very conspicuous and Eric got admiring looks and remarks about "what a young Dr!" We each put on our own gowns again in Whewells Court, and so back to College. Went to the University Sermon: walked there with Dodd who was, of course in black. I was warmly greeted by the Vice-Chancellor at the Senate House and walked in the procession. Gave Dodd a lift in my taxi as far as his turning and I went on to Heffers printing works to make up the *Cambridge Review*. Had to show my scarlet gown and bonnet to everybody there. Eric Yates, Donald Witney and other undergraduates had said they would stand me tea at the Milk Bar on Market Hill. At 4 p.m. I rang up for Legge's man. "Back to College, Sir?" - "No, to the Milk Bar on Market Hill" – he thought he hadn't heard properly and I

~ 1948 ~

had to repeat it. "I'm having tea there", I said. He obviously didn't believe me but reluctantly drove me to the Milk Bar in his Rolls Royce. When I stalked in the wretched undergraduates hadn't come and I found myself facing a group of curious bus-drivers etc., so I beat a hasty retreat and went to the Copper Kettle on King's Parade. There was only one vacant seat, at the end of a table for three, pushed against the wall, with an elderly cleric (whom I knew slightly) on one side and an attractive girl of about twenty-five on the other. She kept looking at me and at the gown folded across my knees. I talked a little to the cleric who went soon after. I wanted to break the ice so that at last I said, "Excuse me, can you tell me the time, please?" – "Yes, it's just on 5; and what's that you've got there?" – "It's a Litt.D gown. I'm going to the service at King's at 5.15 and the Dean, who is a friend of mine, says he will throw me out if I go in black as this is a scarlet day" – "Quite right too." - "I don't know whether you feel like coming? I shall be happy to escort you there if you don't mind walking with me in this fancy costume." – "That's an idea", she said with a laugh and came with me. I laid my bonnet on top of the pillar-box outside while I put on my gown, and we went in and sat next to the Dean (my usual place). On coming out I asked if she would like to come and see the College and have a drink. She said she would and told me she was an Old Girtonian, Pamela Maguire, now teaching at St Neots. I should think that (quite by coincidence) fifteen men came in for a drink between then and Hall time; also a Swedish Professor whom I had offered to take to dine at high table on behalf of Stanley Thomas. I got some food sent up for Pamela and told her I would be back as soon as I could after Hall. After making various unsuccessful attempts in the Combination Room, I managed to get Dodd to talk with the Professor, as they are both interested in Archaeology. I then slipped out without a word, picked up Pamela and took her to John McKeown's 21st birthday party in Chapel Court. "Will it be alright if I come", she had asked. "It will indeed", I said, "they will be delighted to see you"; - as of course they were. After staying there about an hour I took her to the end of Jesus Lane, so that she could get a lift to St Neots – she had served in the ATS for four years, she said. When I crept back to the Combination Room they had all gone; however, I tracked the Swede down to S. Thomas's rooms and found them engrossed in archaeological talk and the Swede said he had had a *most* enjoyable evening.

Saturday 15 May
Barnet. Home for Mother's 80th birthday. Frank and Elsie and the Tyrwhitts came to tea and stayed till 8 p.m.

Sunday 16 May
My first Whitsunday at home since 1919. Sang in the choir at 11 a.m., afterwards at the Vicarage and the White Hart.

~ 1948 ~

Friday 28 May
Lunched at the Dot [the Dorothy Café in Sidney Street] in honour of several Lambeth Conference Bishops who were present from overseas. Sat with Lance Fleming, the Dean and Chaplain of Trinity Hall.

> [Lance Fleming was the Director of the Scott Polar Research Institute, Cambridge until 1949, when he was consecrated Bishop of Portsmouth. Ten years later he was translated to Norwich.]

Thursday 10 June
Installation of General Smuts as Chancellor of the University. I was on duty in the Senate House as steward and took Audrey Space as my guest. Later attended the Honorary Degrees and took Julia Gorst; then on to the Garden Party at Christ's and took Pamela Maguire.

Tuesday 22 June
Uncle Harry arrived. Took him to dine in Hall and invited men into my rooms to meet him before and after.

> [The Rt Revd Henry Daniels, FB's mother's brother, was over from America representing his diocese of Montana, at the first post-war Lambeth Conference. In his autobiography FB said it was a great pleasure to entertain him at College. He also accompanied him to St John's College, where he confirmed some undergraduates for the Dean, Edward Raven. He went with him to Ely where they stayed with the Diocesan for the patronal festival and to Peterborough where they were entertained by the Archdeacon and Mrs Grimes. At Clopton Manor Tiny and Dame Mitchell received them in their usual generous style.]

Saturday 24 July
Showed the thirty-two members of the Ecclesiological Society round the College and had them to tea in Hall, then went in their coach with them as far as Mymms and stayed the night at the Vicarage. Uncle Harry arrived there and also stayed the night.

Sunday 25 July
Mymms. At 8 a.m. served Uncle Harry at Low Mass. He preached at 11 a.m. and I was MC. There was a photograph taken on the lawn afterwards.

Saturday 4 September
Cornwall. Staying with Miss Quiller-Couch at Fowey for the unveiling of the memorial to Q, at which I had to speak, then to Truro with the Bishop to stay with him.

~ 1948 ~

Wednesday 22 September
Barnet. Caught the coach to Hitchin. Walked thence to Gosmore, Preston, Whitwell, Kimpton (where the church clock struck 6 p.m.), Wheathampstead, Sandridge to St Albans – 18 miles in all, and no meal till I got home and nothing to drink since 11 a.m., not even water. Returned home by bus.

Wednesday 6 October
Cambridge. I entertained the Fellows' wives to dinner in the Prioress's Room then we retired to my rooms where the husbands joined us at 9 p.m.

> [This was the first of what became an annual event, known as the Freddy Feast. At that time the Fellows' wives were never entertained in College and indeed hardly ever appeared there except perhaps to pick up post. It was a grand dinner with the wives in evening dress and FB in white tie and tails. There were printed menus and flowers for the ladies to wear. The Freddy Feast continued until 1960 when the first official Ladies' Night was held in College.]

Thursday 21 October
Congregation for the Queen's Honorary Degree in the Senate House, where I was Steward.

[No further entries for 1948]

~ 1949 ~

Monday 3 January
Barnet. Walked to Galley Lane – a flock of about 150 bullfinches (or chaffinches) rose from a field as I went by and watched me from a tree.

Thursday 6 January
Old Christmas Day. Attended the liturgy at the Greek Cathedral, Bayswater – it was nearly full. The choir of men and women were in the north gallery. There were about twelve communicants, all of whom received standing; no one bowed or took any notice of the altar; no one, lay or cleric, knelt at any time.

Tuesday 11 January
Cambridge. A memorial tablet to Arthur Gray was unveiled in the Cloister followed by tea in the Prioress's Room.

Thursday 13 January
Went to King's College Chapel at 5.15. Ivor St C. Ramsay is the new Dean this term and he invited me to sit next to the Dean's stall, as before.

Wednesday 2 February
Geoff Ludford's twenty-first birthday party was held in my rooms.

> [Geoff Ludford was a brilliant mathematician who combined work with sport and was a member of the famous crew which won the Grand in 1947 and he was also a rowing Blue. He became Professor of Applied Mathematics at Cornell University, USA. His work on magneto-dynamic hydrodynamics (MHD) contributed to the discovery of layers parallel to the magnetic field extending from any obstacle in a cross flow, known as Ludford layers.]

Sunday 20 February
Jean Lindsay and Janet Matthews came to dine after which they spoke at the Rooster debate on the motion, "That women are always younger than men".

Wednesday 23 March
Barnet. Went to unaccompanied plainsong Evensong at St Albans Abbey with the Dean and three canons. Heard Gordon Slater's tune 'St Botolph' to 'Jesu, the very thought of three' for the first time. I jotted it down and it haunted me.

> [FB often recorded a tune in tonic-solfa.]

Tuesday 5 April
Wrote a short story titled *The Gypsy Queen*.

Wednesday 13 April
Walked to Kitts End and the Wash. The plum and blackthorn blossom was at its best. Elm suckers were in tiny leaf, hawthorn in full leaf and red poplar catkins at their best. At 8 p.m. attended Tenebrae at St Giles.

Monday 18 April
I was re-appointed Vicar's Warden at the Vestry meeting.

Wednesday 18 May
At the end of my French translation class I received what is called "a prolonged ovation". Later the Medieval Latinists presented me with a brass cockerel and a scroll with Latin verses on it.

> [The cockerel collection, started with the French one FB bought at Boulogne in the 1920s, had now grown to over five hundred and contained specimens from all over the world. By the time FB died the collection consisted of every size, design, material and colour and included such out-of-the way items as an earthenware cockerel about 2,500 years old from Cyprus, a brass cockerel some 500 years old from Ceylon, a witch-doctor's stick from East Africa, and a wooden cockerel from the Pitcairn Islands. Since then it has gone on growing as Muriel Brittain continues to receive gifts to the collection.]

Saturday 21 May
Had drinks in the Ghost Room with the crews who go into training tonight.

Wednesday 8 June
The May Races. Dined in the Prioress's Room with +Claude Petriburg and Mrs Blagden, +Edward Eliensis, Archdeacon and Mrs Grimes, P. G. Ward, Jean Lindsay and Janet Matthews. I proposed the Bishop of Peterborough's health and he replied.

> [Afterwards FB's guests stirred him up to tell a few stories about Q and he told them how annoyed he used to be if anyone called on him before lunch without an appointment. At first the caller would not hear a sound in answer to his knocking. After the third or fourth knock he would hear a mutter through the very thin door. After another knock or two he would invariably hear Q call twice on the Almighty and then exclaim dramatically, "Is there no peace in this blasted College?" Bishop Blagden was amused at the story. Afterwards he sent FB a letter that he kept because it was characteristic of its writer's delightful sense of humour. It was quite brief in expressing his thanks and ended, "We, at any rate, apparently unlike Q, found peace in your blasted College".]

Thursday 9 June
I was Steward at the Senate House for Honorary Degrees conferred on C. H. Dodd and Dame Myra Hess. [She was a professional pianist, best remembered for her concerts in the National Gallery during the Second World War.] At 8.30 p.m. I went to an outdoor performance of the primitive opera *Soul and Body* at Girton. Later, when I was undressing for bed, I was summoned by 'phone to a Highland Ball at the Dorothy with Jean Lindsay and Janet

~ 1949 ~

Matthews. With Jean I had the best dance I've ever had in my life; she was as light as a feather. Left at 3.30 a.m.

Friday 10 June
The Judo Club Annual General Meeting was held in my rooms.

> [FB was Senior Treasurer of the club. On 4 July he was in the chair at the Annual General Meeting and dinner of the Jesus College Cambridge Society at the Dorchester Hotel in London when C. B. Mortlock proposed the toast "The College and Freddy Brittain", since his name was inseparable from the College. He praised FB as a humourist and a scholar "with a genius for friendship".]

Saturday 16 July
Had all the College employees and their guests to tea in Hall.

Monday 22 August
Barnet. Took the bus to the Waggon and Horses, Ridge Hill, went through the farmyard and lay on the grass reading G. G. Coulton's *Medieval Panorama* till 8.30 p.m. except that I went back to the Waggon for tea. Went through Redwell Wood and down the long glen to the swallow hole at Redwell Edge.

> [A swallow hole is a cavity resulting from the solution of rock by the action of water and forming the entrance to a subterranean stream channel.]

Tuesday 30 August
After Evensong at St Albans Abbey and tea at the Black Cat, I called on Miss Archibald to introduce myself and she showed me over the Girls' High School.

> [The Dean of St Albans, the Very Rev Cuthbert Thicknesse (1887–1971), was chairman of the council of the school, an independent church public school with a high reputation in educational circles. The Dean had invited FB to join the council and he enjoyed the work very much. When setting out from Cambridge for council meetings he used to amuse (and at first startle) his colleagues by telling them that he was going to St Albans to see his thirty or forty mistresses and his five hundred and twenty-seven children.]

Monday 5 September
Dined at Bishop's College, Cheshunt and gave a talk on "Bogus Universities".

~ 1949 ~

[Bishop's was an Anglican Theological College in Hertfordshire.]

Wednesday 7 September
Took the train from Victoria to Newhaven and thence to Paris.

Friday 9 September
Travelled to Avignon, which made a very good centre for exploring Provence and Languedoc.

[On this trip FB renewed his acquaintance with Aix and its beautiful Cours, Mirabeau where the magnificent double avenue of plane trees rises to the housetops and dapples the wide promenade with myriad patches of light and shade. He went to Cavaillon, Carpentras, Vacqueras, Les Baux, Montpellier, Beziers, Carcassonne and Toulouse with their memories of the troubadours; to the grand Roman remains at Orange, Vaison, St Remy, Nime, Arles and the Pont du Gard; to Vaucluse, with its spring beloved of Petrach; to Tarascon with its memories of Aucassin and Nicolette and its modern memories of Daudet; to St-Gilles where he visited the saint's tomb; thence to the silent walled town of Aigues-Mortes, built on a Mediterranean lagoon by St Louis as a port from which to launch the Crusades. He travelled back through Les-Saintes-Maries, where the Mediterranean Sea washes the walls of the church in which Mistral's heroine died, and where the gypsies gather from all over Europe every year to venerate the tomb of the black saint, Sarah, the alleged servant of Lazarus, Martha and Mary.]

Wednesday 28 September
Lunched at St Albans with the headmistress of the High School and then spoke to the elder girls – about two hundred of them – on Q.

[Miss Edith Archibald, the Headmistress, was an ardent Scottish Episcopalian, a Highlander, and in politics a Jacobite. When her pupils produced a programme of *Tableaux Vivants* at the school one could be certain that Prince Charles Edward and Flora MacDonald would be included in it.]

Friday 7 October
Cambridge. Interviewing pupils. Took D. Lang to tea in the Small Combination Room, thus inaugurating it.

Saturday 5 November
Went by car to Peterborough for the Enthronement of the new Bishop, Spencer Leeson. [Bishop Blagden had retired.]

~ 1949 ~

Thursday 10 November
Dined at the Audit Feast at King's as the guest of Boris Ord.

> [Boris Ord was the organist of King's College Chapel and Organist to the University.]

Tuesday 6 December
Attended the year's mind requiem at St Clement's in memory of Bernard Manning.

[No further entries for December]

~ 1950 ~

Saturday 7 January
Barnet. In the evening we talked about "the good old days". Dad says the farm labourers at Stondon were paid only 10/- (ten shillings) a week till the 1914 war. Uncle Tom received a shilling more through being a shepherd. They got more, probably double, during harvest, but the extra was used at once in paying the year's rent and buying essential clothes. They certainly couldn't afford to keep a pig if they had any children at all. In bad weather most of them were "stood off" without pay. Neither he nor Mum tasted milk very often when they were children, except in tea and then it was always skimmed milk. When they married they could afford only skimmed milk and very little of that. Mother said her grandmother used sometimes to work in farm-houses and brought back the used tea-leaves in a tin to use again; also bacon rind as a special treat for one of her sons, who devoured it with great zest. The family who lived next to them at Clothall used to walk in to Baldock to buy a cod's head on which the whole family made their dinner. The father of the family, a farm worker, often went home to "a water-mess" for his dinner, i.e. bread soaked in water; and the farmer's wife used to mention the fact with a laugh in the hearing of my mother who was often at the house.

Friday 13 January
Cambridge. The Homerton section of the Battery came in.

> [Following Rooster terminology, FB's numerous girl friends were known as the Brittanic Battery of Beauty.]

~ 1950 ~

Friday 27 January
A. L. Rowse stayed the night but dined at Peterhouse. Men came in to see him later.

Sunday 29 January
The Rooster Exhibition of Really Modern Art was opened by A. W. Lawrence.

> [The exhibits included "The Bottomless Pitt" the side view of an 18th century gentleman with no behind, and "That Swine Heffer" an animal half cow, half pig.]

Thursday 9 February
At about 5.40 a.m. the Head Porter woke me up to tell me there was a dangerous fire on B Staircase. I dressed and went down but the Master soon told me to go in again lest I should get pneumonia as I was laid up with a chill. Watched the fire till nearly 7 a.m. from my rooms. It had been put out by then.

> [The fire was caused by an undergraduate trying to preserve the embers in his grate for use another day – such was the shortage of fuel at the time. G. A. F. Rainbow jumped from his window and earned himself the cock-nomen 'National Hero Rainbow'.]

Monday 13 February
Attended the funeral of Wilfred Knox at Pembroke.

Wednesday 15 February
Eric Kemp read a paper to the Neale Society and stayed the night.

> [Eric Kemp became Bishop of Chichester.]

Sunday 19 February
B. N. Bebbington dined with me in Hall. He then came to the Roost where, at a mock trial, I was tried for "trying to burn down the College".

Friday 3 March
At 5.30 p.m. I attended Stations of the Cross at St Benet's. Went to the Trinity Foot Beagles Ball at the Guildhall till 2 a.m. As I was entering the College, I bumped into A. C. Byron and G. R. Scott who came to my rooms until 3.15 a.m.

~ 1950 ~

Wednesday 20 March
Barnet. Visited Abbott and found him confined to bed. Made his bed and gave him a complete blanket bath.

Friday 31 March
At the Annual General Meeting of the Old Elizabethans I opposed the motion to adopt a bogus "coat of arms".

Thursday 4 May
Cambridge. Miss Bradley of Homerton came to lunch. Not realizing that my clock was at Rooster time she went on talking until 4.30 p.m. thinking it was only 3.30!

> [FB did not put his Cambridge clock forward for Summer Time. He usually referred to it as being at God's time but the diary shows its alternative title.]

Friday 12 May
Watched the College versus Lincoln Theological College at cricket on the Close. John Yates was playing for the visitors

> [John Yates became Suffragan Bishop of Whitby, then Bishop of Gloucester and finally Bishop at Lambeth.]

Sunday 14 May
Dined at Corpus. The Master told me that they had wanted me to be Proctor again and had wanted to nominate me but they felt each college should do its bit and therefore asked Geoffrey Styler to stand.

> [The Revd Geoffrey Marsh Styler was afterwards Dean of Corpus Christi College.]

Sunday 1 June
Held a Rooster sherry party in my rooms, followed by the comic procession and lunch in Small Hall. Women were admitted for the first time.

Saturday 5 August
Presented Wally Greenwood for his MA. In the afternoon I had the College servants and wives, husbands and friends to tea in Hall followed by a tour of the College and then ices in the Fellows' Garden.

> [Master Walter Greenwood worked at the Court of Criminal Appeal. On early retirement he went to Hong Kong as a Judge of the Supreme Court.]

Monday 7 August
Attended the Exceeding for the Name of Jesus.

Friday 18 August
Took the train from Victoria to Newhaven and then had a rough crossing to Dieppe. Arrived in Paris and stayed near the Arc de Triomphe.

> [After five days in Paris FB travelled on via Switzerland to Italy where he stayed at Cernobbio on Lake Como.]

Thursday 24 August
After dinner sat by the lake watching the moon and Jupiter disappear behind the hill next to Volta's memorial lighthouse.

Sunday 27 August
Attended "Sung" Mass at Cernobbio parish church but there was no choir and no one sang a note or said one syllable, except that the celebrant could occasionally be faintly heard but no word could be distinguished. The organ played all the time. After a siesta, took the motor ferry to Como and went by funicular to Brunate. Admired the grand view, had tea, and walked to Volta's lighthouse.

Tuesday 29 August
Went by ferry from Como to Moltrasio. Got caught in a storm on the way back across the lake, marvellous rainbow. Found a cable waiting from Frank to say that Mother is dangerously ill and advising my immediate return, but it is impossible to get back by fast train before tomorrow.

Wednesday 30 August
Cable from Frank to say that Mother died yesterday. Took the train from Como to Lucerne and there caught the 10.08 train direct to Calais.

Monday 4 September
At mother's funeral at St Giles I helped the Vicar and read the Lesson but could not finish it.

Wednesday 6 September
Burial of Mother's ashes at Mymms. After the service in church I carried the ashes, which were buried between the church tower and the gate, immediately north of the Austin monument. Went to Evensong at St Albans Abbey and called at Knightsland on the way home.

~ 1950 ~

[The Daily Telegraph
and
Morning Post
Fleet Street, London E.C.4.

Dear Dr Brittain,
I fear that we had all been expecting this news for some time, but it is none the less distressing. On every occasion when I had the honour of meeting your mother, she impressed me by her singular sweetness of character, coupled with a strength and a wisdom, which made her both a great and a charming lady. I can well realise how deeply you feel her loss.

I hope you will not think it impertinent if I add how proud both your parents were of you and what profound pleasure you brought into their lives. It is some comfort to know when one loses such a person, that one has not failed them.

As for your last paragraph, I have come to consider your father as a true and valued friend, so that any question of kindness does not really arise.
Yours sincerely
(signed) Colin R. Coote]

Saturday 9 September
Caught the coach to Rochester with about twenty Mymmsians, then on to Canterbury for lunch at the Fleur de Lys and Evensong at the Cathedral. The "Red" Dean read the second Lesson. Home by 8.30 p.m. and played crib.

[The Very Rev Hewlett Johnson was known as the Red Dean because of his Communist sympathies.
FB played cribbbage with his father every evening from now on whenever he was at home.]

Thursday 28 September
Attended the Enthronement of the new Bishop of St Albans, the Right Rev Michael Gresford-Jones, and had an excellent seat (by ticket from the Dean) in the front row at the north side of the presbytery at its west end. It was a very beautiful ceremony.

Monday 9 October
Cambridge. Helped to marshall the procession in the Senate House for the memorial service for Field-Marshal Smuts (Chancellor of the University), and then to Great St Mary's with E. E. Raven to usher people into their stalls. The church was full. Bishop Walsh [Assistant Bishop of Ely] gave the Blessing in black cope and mitre. The annual dinner for the dons' wives was held at 7.15 p.m. – fourteen attended this year.

~ 1950 ~

Thursday 19 October
Catalogued some of my cockerels. It was so warm and sunny in the afternoon that I sat nearly two hours in the Fellows' Garden. Denys Wilkinson came in later and proposed that Nehru should be nominated for Chancellor.

Wednesday 25 October
Margaret Deansley read a paper to the Neale Society in my rooms. The Primus of Scotland (John How) was present.

> [Dr Margaret Deansley, D.Litt. Lambeth, the author of books on Anglo-Saxon, the medieval church and of a biography of St Augustine, was professor of History at the University of London from 1942 to 1950.]

Sunday 29 October
Attended Chapel at 8 a.m. Took two Indians on a tour of the College. The Roost consisted of a parody of the BBC broadcast *Up Your Street*. Today I met Elizabeth Brittain (Homerton) for the first time.

> [FB liked to pass Elizabeth off as his cousin.]

Wednesday 1 November
All Saints Day. The Jesus "Tractarians" and fellow travellers met in my rooms with Leslie Brown present.

> [The Rev L. W. Brown was Chaplain of Jesus at this time. He then entered the mission field and went to South India, later becoming Archbishop of Uganda until he was succeeded by an African. Returning to the UK, he was Bishop of St Edmundsbury and Ipswich until his retirement to New Square, Cambridge. In spite of being almost blind he continued to be in great demand for counselling, Quiet Days, and preaching and was still an active member of the staff at Westcott House and at Great St Mary's church at the age of eighty.]

Wednesday 15 November
Went to Addenbrooke's Hospital for the distribution of certificates to Joan Scott, Sheila Shaw, Ursula Payne and other newly qualified nurses.

Saturday 2 December
Saw the boats start in the Fairbairn Cup Race, which we won in record time, then watched rugger on the Close. Arthur Wills [organist at Ely Cathedral] and his wife and several men came in for sherry.

[No further entries for December]

~ 1951 ~

Saturday 20 January
Cambridge. Jimmie Simpson (my GP) sent me into the Evelyn Nursing Home with influenza (and fear of pneumonia.)

Tuesday 23 January
Feeling better. Ivor Ramsay [Dean of King's College] came to see me.

Thursday 1 February
It was Guest Night in Hall, after which I sang about twelve songs in L. A Pars's rooms, with him at the piano, to an audience of about a dozen, which included my guest, R. W. Ladborough.

> [Dick Ladborough was a linguist and a Fellow of Magdalene College. He did brilliant impersonations, the best being of the Most Rev Michael Ramsay, also a Magdalene man, who was a close friend of his.]

Saturday 10 February
Barnet. Douglas Plank called to say that Gaffer Brown died at 4 a.m. Dad and I went to see Mrs Brown and interviewed the undertaker etc.

Thursday 15 February
Gaffer's funeral took place at Christ Church Barnet. I read the Lesson and the Sentences and gave a short address at the graveside. In fact, I officiated entirely, which is a very great privilege for a layman.

Thursday 15 March
It is a fine day (for a great change). Spring is very late this year, hardly a sign of it. There is the barest showing of green on the hawthorns but *nothing* else. Walked to the Wash, which was roaring like a great river after recent heavy rains. Played crib later.

Monday 19 March
Visited St Albans High School and met the new Headmistress, Miss Gent, for the first time.

Saturday 24 March
Easter Eve. Went to Frank's and watched the Boat Race on his television set. Oxford sank and Cambridge therefore did not finish. I sang the Exsultet throughout at the Easter Eve Ceremonies.

Friday 27 April
Cambridge. At 3 p.m. I went to King's in scarlet for the thanksgiving on completion of cleaning the Chapel and replacement of all the glass. [It had been removed for safety during the war.]

Saturday 5 May
Attended a Committee at the Old Schools [University Offices] to revise the form for Commemoration of Benefactors.

Monday 28 May
Went home and to the wood. The bluebells are very late this year because of the phenomenally cold, sunless spring. The roadside the whole way home is lined with masses of cow parsley in its prime.

Monday 4 June
Elizabeth Brittain and I held a sherry party in my rooms consisting of equal numbers of Jesus undergraduates and Homertonians, plus Frederic Raby and Alan Percival. We dressed Ron Ray as a woman, and had him announced as the Principal of Newnham, causing at first complete silence and then an outburst of laughter. A few minutes later the announcement, "The Principal of Homerton" caused the company to laugh at first, expecting another man dressed as a woman – but it was the real lady this time. Only Elizabeth, Frederick Raby and I knew she had been invited.

> [Miss Alice Skillicorn, CBE, affectionately known as Skilly, took the joke in excellent part.]

Wednesday 6 June
Took a car full of Homertonians to Ditton Paddock for the first day of the May Races. Afterwards Joan Scott came to dinner in my rooms.

Thursday 7 June
I was on duty as Steward at the installation of the new Chancellor, Air-Chief-Marshal Lord Tedder.

Saturday 9 June
It was a very full day indeed. Wrote nine letters etc., after which Barbara Northwood arrived, followed by Hilda and Anne Woods. Had a sherry party

followed by a lunch party for seven. Then went to the races, with tea at the Bigland Woods'.

> [Hilda and Gerald Woods and their two daughters lived in the Avenue at Barnet and became his close friends. They kept an eye on FB's home and family when he was at College.
> Gordon and Agatha Wood lived next to the Jesus Paddock in the house with the glorious view up the Reach to Chesterton. Every year they had open house during the May Races.]

Monday 11 June
We had a Rooster Cruise in the lovely sun with tea at Clayhithe.

Tuesday 12 June
I was on the go all day. Showed a party round the College, then went to the Natives' sherry party followed by the May Ball Committee dinner and to the Ball all night.

Wednesday 13 June
A Ball photo was taken at 6 a.m. Went to bed at 7.30 a.m. but slept little and was up again soon after midday for the Tripos examiners meeting at King's.

Wednesday 27 June
Barnet. Went to visit Abbott. He is worse mentally, i.e. he told me he always thought I was a Cambridge man.

Saturday 30 June
Attended Evensong at St Albans Abbey with the sun pouring into the presbytery and on to the great altar screen – it was most moving. Took the bus to the Waggon and Horses and walked home. The hedges in Packhorse Lane are full of dogwood in flower – yards and yards of it – also herb Robert, angelica, hogweed, comfrey, periwinkle, catchfly and elder.

Saturday 7 July
Henley Regatta. The College was beaten by Pembroke in the final of the Ladies' Plate. Gerald and Hilda Woods were my guests for the day and we went home together.

Tuesday 21 August
After seeing Abbot, went to Ridge Hill, on the brow of the hill and stayed there, resting meditating and reading; reclining against one of the shocks of barley till 7.30 p.m., except for tea at the Waggon, enjoying the same glorious view. Later the sun went in and the Abbey (with its flag flying), was backed

by black trees and hills. Then the sun came out behind the Abbey, but the Abbey itself was still black. It looked wonderful on a brilliant gold background of sun, like stage scenery.

Tuesday 11 September
A. R. B. Fuller and I made our first visit to East Grinstead where we looked in the church and at J. M. Neale's tomb. After lunch at the Dorset Arms we visited Sackville College, which is most charming.

> [J. M. Neale had been Warden of Sackville College, homes for elderly people.]

Monday 24 September
Went to St Albans. Sat on the Close opposite the west front, then sat in the Cathedral and read until Evensong. After tea at the Black Cat, went back to the Close and read again. I reflected on what a privilege it is to be able to read about the Middle Ages in this vast, grand medieval building. What would an American scholar give for it?

Tuesday 9 October
Cambridge. Interviewing students, after which I attended a Committee of College Stewards. J. Byrnell (conservative) and J. Charkham (labour), who are close friends, are sharing the set of rooms at the foot of my staircase this term.

> [Their sofa had Conservative literature at one end and Labour at the other but they rejected FB's suggestion that they should send out their manifestos in the same envelope!]

Tuesday 30 October
At the All Saints' Trustees lunch at Matthews Café I read the trust deed, as always since I was elected. As we came away G. A. Weekes said to me, "I was in the Cambridge University Press showroom the other day and looked at your *Medieval Latin and Romance Lyric*. I thought to myself if I could have written that I would die happy."

Wednesday 31 October
It has been lovely sunny weather of late. The leaves of the copper beech in the former North House garden are a wonderfully rich russet-brown; some of the honey-locust leaves are light green and the others golden yellow; the sycamore in Pump Court is a glorious mass of gold-yellow leaves.

Sunday 4 November
The copper beech has changed overnight into a practically bare tree.

Thursday 29 November
Went to King's for Evensong with the first ever *internal* floodlighting. The service was sung to Goss in E and Stanford's 'Beati quorum via' – there are only ten words in it but I love it more every time I hear it with its wonderful ending "qui ambulant . . .", the basses first, then the tenors coming in, then altos, then trebles, and lastly the higher trebles.

Friday 30 November
Dined at Ely Theological College, where I gave a talk after dinner on "The Episcopal and Academical Underworlds". Attended Compline and address by the Dean and stayed the night at the Bishop's house.

Thursday 13 December
Cambridge. Audit day and a stiff one, as usual. Up at 7.30 a.m. Read correspondence at breakfast then dictating letters and discussing business with the Manciple. The Audit Meeting took place from 10 – 11 and included the increases of pay for all employees. The Audit lunch for all Fellows was held in the Prioress's Room followed by continuation of the Audit Meeting. From 3.15–4 p.m. the seating for the Feast had to be re-arranged due to withdrawals caused by dense fog. Had guests to tea and at 6–6.45 p.m. I was changing and inspecting tables. Attended Commemoration of Benefactors in Chapel followed by sherry and looked out for guests and presented them to the Master. The Audit Feast took place at 8.15 p.m. in Hall followed by punch in the Combination Room, then I saw the Vice-Chancellor off at the outer gate. Went to Pars's rooms and did my usual turns until 2 a.m., when I made tea in my rooms. At 2.45 p.m. saw the outside guests off and got to bed at 3 a.m.

Sunday 16 December
Marking papers and at about 5 p.m. heard Great St Mary's bells in full peal, most melodious and haunting as usual. Looked though my window as they rang. Jupiter was high up over the black Gate Tower and the adjoining range with the plane [tree in the Fellows' Garden] towering over it, the black ilex massive to the right, and the wet flagstones in the Court reflecting the half-concealed lights from the Cloister and the lodge.

Saturday 29 December
After choral Evensong at St Albans Abbey had tea with the Sub-Dean (D. R. Feaver) and his wife at their house in Sumpter Yard.

[This was the first of many visits and the Feaver family became FB's close friends. Douglas Feaver left St Albans to become Vicar of St Mary's, Nottingham in 1960 and was consecrated Bishop of Peterborough in 1972. *Purple Feaver*, a book of his outrageous sayings, was published after his retirement.]

[No further entries for December]

~ 1952 ~

Saturday 2 February
Cambridge. Went to King's for Byrd's Five-part Mass for Candlemas. Called in at Heffers and R. G. Heffer told me he is going to publish my *Tales of South Mymms and Elsewhere*.

[After it was published the following review appeared in the Observer. "My prose treasure is *Tales of South Mymms and Elsewhere* by Frederick Brittain, and, its literary virtue apart, it has a particularly giftable value as a bedside book for the recipient's guest-chamber, being a featherweight to hold and beautifully printed. The contents are eight essays, so charming and spontaneous that, in two instances at least, I would not fear to say that the author, (one of our most learned and versatile dons) could hold a candle to Elia." Edmund Vale.]

Wednesday 6 February
King George VI died unexpectedly this morning.

Friday 8 February
Went to the Senate House in scarlet to hear the new Queen [Queen Elizabeth II] proclaimed by the Vice-Chancellor.

Friday 15 February
Again to the Senate House to marshal the University procession for the Commemoration Service for the King in Great St Mary's. There must have been four or five hundred senior members there.

Thursday 6 March
The Cambridge Writers' Circle met in my rooms and I read the winning entries in their competitions.

~ 1952 ~

Saturday 8 March
J. D. Simpson ordered me to the Evelyn Nursing Home as I have pneumonia. I went by ambulance at 5 p.m.

> [FB was in the Evelyn until 8 April. He lists his visitors each day – a great number, including the Dean of King's who celebrated the Eucharist with him. Edwin Abbott died on 28 March.]

Friday 23 May
At the J. M. Neale Society Bruce Dickins was elected President and A. M. Ramsay [later Archbishop of Canterbury] Vice-President.

Saturday 24 May
F. J. E. Raby and I went to see the Tripos papers given out. When we went to the women's section there were numerous grins and giggles from Joan Barbour and the other Girtonians.

> [During the Long Vacation FB received the following letter from Joan Barbour:

Dearest Freddie,
 ... I meanwhile have been learning again how to hull strawberries, weed flower beds, make beds, and wash dishes. It's strange how at Cambridge one gets into such a mental tailspin that the little bit of mending or half hour washing is a jealously saved treat, a small oasis in a desert of mental effort. Then as soon as one gets home again neither mending or washing appear nearly so delightful!
 Strange too how free Cambridge life is from real personal relationships. It abounds with acquaintances, people whose company one likes, whose conversation one enjoys. But it is on the whole completely superficial – how superficial one only realizes when back at home one is again submerged and battered by relationships that run so much deeper. Does one always feel that life is no longer one's own but a tennis ball for other people to play with, while inescapably you must always be doing the same to them?
 At Cambridge it is not so but perhaps that is a bad thing and artificial. I suppose life always offers abundant chances of hurting the people nearest one, just because it is the real person you are near, not the social person who is very hard to hurt.
 What a lot of woolly philosophizing! I had better leave off until I can talk sense.
      Much love
      (signed) Joan

~ 1952 ~

P.S. Why do you give parties to Girton Litt.D's? The Mistress of Girton can be charming if she stops being shy long enough. She described presenting the loyal petition to the Queen last term – and her description of the ornaments and furnishings of Buckingham Palace was delightful. Also the tale of mishaps to the Oxford delegation – when the Vice-Chancellor dropped the petition, the man behind him stepped on it, the third bent down to pick it up and the fourth tripped over him.]

Tuesday 10 June
Collected Janet Blood from Girton for the May Week Ball. Saw her back to Girton by 1.30 a .m. She is the youngest Ball partner I have ever had, being not yet 19.

Sunday 15 June
Old Members (1937 and 1938 vintage) were up for the weekend. Took them round after breakfast. They were most attentive and D. Glyn said he was "enthralled".

Wednesday 18 June
Went to the Senate House to see our men take degrees, followed by Degree Lunch in Hall. At 2 p.m. went with Frederic Raby to see Eleanor Duckett take her Litt.D (for which we examined her). Gave a tea party in my rooms in her honour.

> [Miss Eleanor Duckett was an American writer. She spent part of each summer in England staying at the Garden House Hotel in Cambridge with her friend the author Mary Ellen Chase.]

Saturday 21 June
Jennifer Woods and I went to St Michael's School in St Albans and took part in the procession across the Verulam meadows with servers, banners etc. with the Dean and Archdeacon in copes. The Abbey choir came out to meet us and sang the Litany in procession to the Abbey, there were perhaps three hundred of us. In the Abbey High Mass in full cloth of gold vestments was sung at the nave altar by the Dean with the Bishop pontificating. At the end there was a procession to the shrine of St Alban and prayers there. Returned home and rang up the Patriarch to congratulate him on his eighty-sixth birthday today.

Tuesday 24 June
Barnet. From 3 to 7 p.m. I sat in the field at the top of Ridge Hill under an oak, the hay laying round me in swathes. Read *The Pageant of Summer* again and some of Edward Thomas's poems.

~ 1952 ~

Monday 11 August
Took the train to Portsmouth and ferry to Ryde where F. J. T. Mew met me and drove me to his home, Kingston Manor, Isle of Wight. After tea went to see the local churches including Mottistone church and Manor where we had sherry with Lord Mottistone.

Tuesday 12 August
Visited Carisbrooke Castle. In the evening helped Francis Mew (Mayor of Newport) to crown the Carnival Queen.

Sunday 17 August
Went with all the Mew family to Cowes. They went yachting, I to Sung Mass at St Faith's then sat on the front and lunched at the Gloucester Hotel – first rate position, must stay there.

Tuesday 19 August
Left Kingston and went on to Ryde. Went into All Saints', a fine big church on top of a hill with a very prominent tower and spire. The architect is G. G. Scott the younger and better.

Friday 22 August
Barnet. Went to Wrotham Park where Julian Byng showed us the house, the portraits, the gardens and some of the Byng papers, and gave me tea.

> [The Byngs have lived at Wrotham for over 200 years, from the time of the ill-fated Admiral to the present day.]

Saturday 23 August
Sat in Ridge Hill top field reading and writing and dozing from 2 – 8 p.m. Not a soul about, only sheep.

SHEEPISH

Sheep have two languages – one audible, the other inaudible. I have studied and used the inaudible language for years, but it is only lately that I have become proficient at the audible one. Perhaps it was because of my known liking for both languages that the Ridge Hill sheep, when I re-appeared in their field after a fairly long absence, gave me such a cordial reception. I am sure it was cordial, even though (as in all ovine affairs) they stood at a distance and kept their features under strict control.

"Good afternoon, gentlemen," I said, "or perhaps I should say ladies and gentlemen."

"We won't bother about that," one of them answered, "but perhaps you wouldn't mind telling us why we've seen so little of you lately. You used to come here very often."

"You are right," I said, "I love this field, and it has one of the finest views in the county, but I've been kept away by the very bad weather."

To my surprise, when I said this the whole flock went into fits of controlled laughter.

"Pardon me," I said, "I feel rather hurt at this laughter. It seems quite uncalled for."

There was silence for a time, then one of them said, "We laughed because you said the weather had been bad."

"So it has," I said. "In fact, it has been shocking. Everybody knows that."

"Excuse me," said Sheep No. 1, "but your statement is untrue. The weather has been excellent this year."

"Yes," bleated all the others, "excellent."

"Excellent!" I protested. "How can you say that, when we've had nothing but rain and dull skies for months?"

"We have indeed," retorted No. 1, "and that is excellent weather. There are only two kinds of bad weather – frost and drought, both of which ruin the grass and deprive us of decent food. Rain is admirable. It makes the grass plentiful and tender."

"Yes," interposed Sheep No. 2, "and it soaks it in water too, so that we don't even have to stop feeding now and then and traipse off down to the pond for a drink."

"You forget," said No. 3 to the other two, nudging them and winking at them, "that he's mental – I mean, that he doesn't eat grass."

"Thank you for reminding me," No. 1 answered, in an undertone. Then, turning to me, he said politely, "I saw you coming out of the *Waggon and Horses* just now. I hope they gave you a good feed."

"They did indeed," I said. "The mutton was particularly good."

"The *what?*" asked No. 1. "I don't like the sound of that. It sounds very much like what your people call our people in France."

"You surely don't mean," said No. 2, glancing at No. 1 in astonishment, "you really can't mean that he –?"

I changed the subject quickly by saying, "I hope you like my new suit."

They examined it as closely as was possible from a distance of nine or ten yards. For some time they carried on a conversation in an undertone, then they all turned and stared at me and one of them said aloud:

"I must say that we thought better of you than this. To put it in plain Sheepish, we find that you are either a robber or a receiver of stolen property. You are wearing wool, which doesn't grow naturally on you people. You must have filched it from some of our people. That explains why some rude man, no better than a dog, threw us on the ground one day and fleeced us. What is worse is that you have tried to conceal the crime by changing the colour of our wool and mauling it into a different shape to fit your ridiculous body."

For a time I did not know how to answer this charge, and the whole flock stared at me in silence. At last, feeling that I must say something, I stammered,

"I really must apologize. You make me feel like a man who tried to pick my pocket the other day. When I caught him in the act he looked very sheepish."

"Oh! He looked handsome and intelligent, did he?" said No. 3. "It's hard to see how a thief caught in the act could look like that."

"I'm afraid I didn't mean exactly that," I said.

Upon this, there was a chorus of "What did you mean, then?" – "You said sheepish, didn't you? – "Yes, you certainly said sheepish." – "Yes, I heard you myself." – "So did I."

When I at length managed to make myself heard above all this bleating I said, "It would take me too long to explain what I meant. I've talked too much already. If I say any more you'll think that I'm like a sheep's head – all jaw."

At this point I realized, from their loud coughing that I had committed another social solecism, so I quickly changed the subject again and said,

"You will remember that the last time I was here you appointed No. 1 and myself a committee of two to compile a book, *How to Speak Sheepish in Six Months without a Master*. The publishers are clamouring for it, and we must get it done."

"Quite right," said No. 1. "We must get on with it. Those of you who are not on this committee can go and do a bit of feeding. You've been without food far too long – quite five minutes, I should say."

They took him at his word and left me alone with No. 1.

"I think," I said to him, "you once told me you were of Spanish descent."

"That is so," he answered.

"Then perhaps you will allow me to call you Don Carnero."

"Please do," he answered. "Now about this book. What we want is a series of questions and answers on matters that are essential to both ovine and human life. As I was never trained for secretarial work, you can do the writing and I'll supply the brains."

"Very well," I said. "I've selected a few important sentences from a Spanish grammar that I used to study. For instance, we might have this one: 'Give me the 249 sandalwood boxes inlaid with mother-of-pearl, which my great-grandmother's second cousin once removed gave to your step-father's snuff-maker's uncle on Shrove Tuesday, together with the pen of an aunt.' Don't you think that would be useful?"

~ 1952 ~

Don Carnero thought deeply for a while, flicked his ears, and said, "Not very. Let's have another."

"Well," I said, "here is a very important one: 'The postillion has been struck by lightning.' What do you say to that?"

"Cut it out," said Don Carnero, after considerable meditation.

"Here is an essential one," I said. "'Have you filled in your football pools?'"

"Don't be absurd," Carnero said. "Pools should never be filled in. Give me another."

"This is a good one," I said, looking down my notes. "'Please direct me to a good but inexpensive hotel.'"

"What's a hotel?" asked Carnero.

"It's something like a fold," I answered, "but bigger – a sort of covered field."

"How ridiculous!" said Carnero. "Drop that one."

"We must have this next one," I said. "'At what time is breakfast?'"

"What's breakfast?" Carnero asked.

"The first meal of the day," I answered.

"Don't be silly," said Carnero. "There's no first meal of the day. There's only one meal, and it goes on all day long."

"Sorry, Don Carnero," I said. "You must think I'm as mad as a sheep. I beg your pardon: that was a slip of the tongue. I meant as mad as a dog. Let me go on. According to all phrase-books for travellers, we must have this sentence: 'Waiter, bring me the wine list.'"

"What's a waiter? And what's a wine list?" Carnero asked, scratching his flank with one of his hind feet.

"A waiter is – he's a sort of shepherd, and a wine list is a list of coloured drinks," I answered.

"Then we certainly won't have that sentence," said Carnero. "I've been warned all my life against drinking coloured water. Now, time's getting on, and I'm feeling famished. I woke rather late this morning and hadn't been feeding for more than seven or eight hours when you arrived. I think it's time I suggested a few sentences for the book myself."

"Please do," I said. Under his expert direction we soon reached agreement about the really important sentences, and I give them here in English and Sheepish side by side:

	English	Sheepish
1.	Good morning. Good evening. Good night. Good-bye. Farewell. Cheerio.	Ba.
2.	How do you do?	Ba?
3.	Nicely, thanks. Not so bad. Middling. I can't complain.	Baa.

4. I have a pain in the abdomen.	
You give me a pain in the neck.	
My rheumatics are proper bad.	Baaa.
5. I like grass, turnips, and water. A little of	
what you fancy does you good.	Baaaa.
6 Confound that beastly dog!	B !

"It's time I went,! I said hastily. "Good-bye."
"Ba," said Don Carnero.

The Whole flock watched me in a cordial silence until I had regained the *Waggon and Horses* and shut the door behind me.

[FB had spotted a reference to *Babylon Bruis'd & Mount Moriah Mended* by the writer Angela Thirkell and had written to her about it. She replied.

Monday 1 September
1 Shawfield Street
London

Dear Dr Brittain,

How very kind of you to write and I am enchanted that my reference to the Great Work pleased you. I came across it first through a review in the *Manchester Guardian* (now defunct) and have never stopped giving it to people whenever it was reprinted. I should like to think that it had rescued them from the heresy of Children's Corners and Pathfinders – but the Devil is undoubtedly among us having great power. I grieve to learn of the death of your brilliant collaborator.

    Thank you again
        Yours sincerely
        (signed) Angela Thirkell

[Angela Thirkell (1891–1961) was the author of more than 30 novels set in 'Barsetshire' which dealt with the descendants of characters from Trollope's Barsetshire novels.]

Sunday 14 September
Cambridge. Back to College where the Coal Board Conference has just started.

[FB took three parties of conference people round the College on successive days. It was on one of these tours, which included his rooms, that a member of the party said that he knew a miner who carved in coal and he would ask him to carve a cockerel for the collection.]

~ 1952 ~

Sunday 21 September
South Mymms. At Evensong I held forth but had had no notice at all until the hymn before the sermon. Went home to play crib, as usual almost every night, with Dad.

Thursday 16 October
Cambridge. Monica Hutchings [Mrs Baber, who wrote books on the Dorset countryside] arrived to stay at 20 Maids Causeway. Took her to dine at high table at Girton as guests of Jean Lindsay.

> [Women did not dine at high table at Jesus in the 1950s, or indeed in FB's lifetime. Later in the week he took her to lunch at the Regent House where women were admitted.]

Wednesday 29 October
Dined at Magdalene with Dick Ladborough and in the Combination Room and afterwards Dick and John Betjeman came back to my rooms to talk.

> [Sir John Betjeman (1906-1982), English poet, broadcaster and writer who was an astute and sensitive social critic. He was viewed as a national institution and was passionate in his abhorrence of modern architecture. Betjeman succeeded Cecil Day Lewis as Poet Laureate in 1972.]

Thursday 30 October
Went to 99 Gower Street, London for a sherry party to celebrate the publication of *Spectator Harvest,* which includes my story Electra. Met Norman Birkett, Peter Fleming and others.

Thursday 13 November
Acted as steward in the Senate House at the honorary degree ceremony for the Duke of Edinburgh.

Sunday 7 December
South Mymms. I was cantor at Sung Mass, then home in lovely sun lighting up the silvery-feathery rime frost (and snow, lying for the past fortnight). At 3 p.m. went to a rehearsal of *Aladdin* in the Village Hall. Read both lessons at Evensong. Tried to walk home in the fog but completely lost my way as it was so thick and black and I could hardly see the ground at my feet and couldn't even see which side of the road I was on. Thought I might have to stay there all night but fortunately a bus crawled up, the only vehicle on the road, and I got a slow but most welcome lift home.

Tuesday 16 December
Cambridge. Audit meeting of the College accounts and Audit Feast. Afterwards went to L A Pars's rooms where I sang many songs.

Thursday 17 December
The annual lunch for the tenant farmers of the College was held today. Some of the farms have belonged to us for over 800 years.

[No further entries for December]

~ 1953 ~

Tuesday 6 January
Went with the Bishop of St Albans to Southwark Cathedral for the consecration of Leslie Brown [former Chaplain of Jesus College] as Bishop of Uganda by the Archbishop of Canterbury and about a dozen other bishops. Lunched at the Church Missionary Society House, Salisbury Square.

Wednesday 7 January
South Mymms. Dress rehearsal of the pantomime.

Thursday 8 January
Arranged chairs in the Village Hall for the first performance of *Aladdin*. I introduced into my part as Widow Twankey the songs 'You've got a long way to go' (topicalized) and 'Tiddley-om-pom' with 'A little bit of what you fancy' as an encore. It was a very successful show with a party on the stage afterwards.

> [There were performances on Friday and Saturday and on the last night about thirty people could not get in.]

Thursday 15 January
Cambridge. Dined with V. C. Clinton-Baddeley at the Arts Theatre restaurant and saw his pantomime *Cinderella* there.

Monday 19 January
Presided over a meeting to consider how to help to raise the £40,000 still needed for Ely Cathedral.

~ 1953 ~

Saturday 24 January
At the Congregation in the Senate House, + Leslie Uganda got his honorary MA.

Thursday 5 February
We had a Rooster expedition in two coaches to Great Shelford, where we gave our annual show.

Thursday 19 February
Talked to the crews at the Boathouse and afterwards took tea with the first boat in Chapel Court.

Monday 9 March
Went to the Oxford-Cambridge Judo match at the Guildhall in the evening.

Wednesday 11 March
Gillie Potter called. Joan Barbour came to lunch and Rachel Attwater to tea. Have a cold (*the first this winter*), so I was not out of my rooms all day.

Monday 16 March
The College Council elected R. T. Dart to a Fellowship.

[Robert Thurston Dart, whose early death in 1971 at the age of 49, robbed music of a leading scholar and performer, became Professor of Music at Cambridge in 1962. He was known world-wide as a harpsichordist and as conductor and musical director of the Philomusica Orchestra. He was an authority, editor and performer of the music of the sixteenth and seventeenth centuries, especially that for the keyboard. In 1964 he moved to the Chair of Music in London where he made some bold experiments in musical education and introduced a number of reforms.]

Easter Day 5 April
Staying at the Vicarage, I called Father Carleton at 6.30 a.m., opened the church, and rang the bells for the 7 a.m. service. At 8 a.m. went to church and was cantor at 11 a.m. Afterwards had the Bruce Robinson sherry in the Vicarage as usual.

[Bruce Robinson was a great benefactor to St Giles. The family, who lived in London, were very grateful when Allen Hay allowed their daughter, who died while she was still a child, to be buried at South Mymms. Their considerable monetary gift included provision for the Vicar and churchwardens to have a bottle of sherry on Easter Day in perpetuity.]

~ 1953 ~

Monday 6 April
I was cantor at Sung Mass at 10 a.m. followed by the Easter Vestry meeting at which I was re-appointed churchwarden. Had lunch at the Sub-deanery at St Albans and at 3 p.m. went to the Abbey. The nave was packed tight for the Youth Service and pilgrimage to the shrine, ending with the *Te Deum* before the high altar with choir and transepts packed with over 2,000 people.

Tuesday 21 April
Went by car to Ashwell, Radwell (the mill pool was lovely), Stotfold and Stondon where we visited grandfather's and grandmother's grave. Had tea at Shillington vicarage with Mr Farmiloe, who led the way to the Pasque flowers on Danes Blood Hill, Pegsdon, from which there is a delightful view all along the bare chalk hills and the wooded green-sand hills. On to Ickleford where we looked at the River Oughton and its charming footbridge and rippling stream, then to Arlesey where we got out of the car to look at the fast running river Hiz.

Saturday 25 April
Cambridge. Delivered the Wood Memorial Lecture on the Troubadours at Hughes Hall and sang songs. My audience included the Master of Magdalene, the Mistress of Girton, the Principal of Homerton, Professor Owst, several Girton dons, etc.

Sunday 26 April
Thirty-one of us went by coach to Little Gidding where we sang Evensong with Mark Ruston officiating.

> [The Rev Mark Ruston was Chaplain of Jesus College; he became Vicar of Holy Sepulchre, the popular Cambridge evangelical church, and was made a Canon of Ely Cathedral.]

Tuesday 5 May
London. Addressed the Annual General Meeting of the Additional Curates' Society.

Tuesday 12 May
Bob Pennyfather arrived for the Rustat Feast. I took him to lunch at the Regent House. Brian Wicks arrived later for the Feast.

> [R. Pennyfather was one of FB's shipmates aboard the *Egypt* during World War I.
> Brian Wicks, a Jesus man, became a veterinary surgeon and married Judy Bates, the daughter of the writer H. E. Bates.]

Tuesday 2 June
The Coronation of Queen Elizabeth II. Watched the Coronation at Westminster Abbey on television. After a cold dinner in the Combination Room about 150 undergraduates came to wine and dessert in Hall with the Fellows. The Garden and Cloister were impossible because it was so cold and wet.

Thursday 4 June
I was Steward in the Senate House for Honorary degrees for President Nehru, etc.

Saturday 20 June
Barnet. The Queen Elizabeth's Grammar School Founders' Day service was held in Barnet Parish Church, at which I read the second lesson. Afterwards went to the school for calling of the roll, recitation of the Chronicle, coffee, cricket and lunch.

Saturday 4 July
It was hot and sunny all day at Henley Regatta. The College won the Ladies Plate.

Tuesday 7 July
Barnet. Spent the morning amongst my books, especially Edward Thomas, W. H. Hudson, and Richard Jefferies. After tea I caught the bus to the Waggon and Horses and walked in the fields, along the ridge and among the corn. The wheat is now a bluish green with a golden tint.

Saturday 11 July
Cambridge. Visited Miss Edleston, who gave me the ring of her great-uncle by marriage, Dr H. A. Woodham of Jesus. Later conducted a tour of the College for about 60 County Borough Medical Officers of Health who are holding a conference in College.

Wednesday 12 August
Travelled by train to East Grinstead and had tea and attended Vespers at St Margaret's Convent. Dined and stayed at the Dorset Arms.

Friday 14 August
Went by the convent car (with Gates driving) to the Roadmender country – Mock Bridge, Shermanbury, Henfield and Ashurst, where I visited the grave of Michael Fairless in the churchyard.

> ["Michael Fairless" (1860–1901) is the pseudonym of Margaret Fairless Barber. She trained as a nurse for work in one of the worst London slums

~ 1953 ~

but when her health broke down she retired to a roadside country cottage in Sussex where she wrote *The Roadmender*, which she dedicated to "My Mother and the earth my mother, whom I love".]

Saturday 15 August
In the convent I saw Dr Neale's chalice and lunched with the assistant chaplain, Father Radford, then went by car with Sister Vera and her sister to Ashford and Godinton where we had tea with Alan Wyndham-Green.

Wednesday 7 October
Cambridge. Conducted many, many interviews today. After Hall we drank the health of B. D. Till, who was admitted to his Fellowship today.

[The Rev Barry Dorn Till had been elected Dean of the College. He left in 1960 to become Dean of Hong Kong Cathedral. Later he renounced his Orders and was appointed Principal of Morley College, London.]

Saturday 17 October
Barnet. Gave an address at Christ Church and unveiled a window in memory of John Brown ("Gaffer"), then to the Boys' School for the unveiling of a portrait of him.

Saturday 31 October
Cambridge. Took tea with Mgr Gilbey at Fisher House. Dined at Homerton as the guest of the Principal, followed by a concert there at which I read *Mesech* by the light of a candle.

Tuesday 10 November
Saw the *Lady at the Wheel* at the Arts Theatre, the first performance of the Cambridge University Musical Comedy Club of which I am treasurer. There was a party behind the scenes afterwards.

Monday 16 November
The Ely Cathedral Committee (enlarged to about 30) was held in my rooms. At a meeting of the Society later we elected Gwilym Lloyd George an Honorary Fellow.

[Gwilym Lloyd George, the second son of the celebrated Prime Minister, came up to Jesus in 1913 and prompted the following in the College Alphabet: "G is for Gwilym who pays for his brekker, with funds that accrue from the country's exchequer", his father being Chancellor at that time. He held Cabinet rank from 1942 onwards, first as Minister of Fuel, then as Minister of Food, and finally as Home Secretary and Minister for

Welsh Affairs. He resigned office in 1957, when he was created Viscount Tenby, and died ten years later.]

Saturday 5 December
Stanley Parker came to lunch, tea and Hall. He sketched me for the *Church Times*.

Sunday 6 December
Went to King's at 3.30 p.m., where roses and lilies were presented at the altar by the Provost during the singing of Rex Henricus.

[King's College was founded by Henry VI.]

Thursday 31 December
Dined with the Dame and Tiny Mitchell and Jean Savill at Prunier's, then went with them to the Chelsea Arts Ball at the Royal Albert Hall. Tiny was dressed as a chef, the Dame in early nineteenth century Venetian costume, and I in my Litt.D scarlet gown and bonnet. We had a box in the Grand Tier with eight other guests including Alan and Rosemary Burrough.

~ 1954 ~

Friday 29 January
Cambridge. The Alcuin Club Committee met in my rooms. They decided to publish a new edition of my *Latin in Church*. The Dean of Chichester was my guest in Hall.

Tuesday 2 February
Skating took place on the Backs.

Tuesday 23 February
Dined at Sidney Sussex College as the guest of Willcock, then read a paper to their Classical Society on "Some medieval and modern pronunciations of Latin".

Ash Wednesday 3 March
I was usher at the memorial service for W. R. Inge at King's. Fellows of Jesus sat on the north side and of King's on the south.

~ 1954 ~

Saturday 13 March
After the Commemoration of Benefactors Feast I did most of my usual turns plus some Gilbert and Sullivan and –

CAMBRIDGE AS SHE IS VISITED
"FAMILIAR DIALOGUES AND IDIOTISMS"
(*Cambridge Review, December 5, 1886*)

I. For to buy the Billet.

Commissioner, where buys one's self a billet?

By the slit, sir.

Here is "all trains North from Peterborough; East from Colney Hatch; to Hatfield conclusively."

Where is my Maps' Atlas? Demon! this map is on Mercator's projection. I can not to understand him. It must to endeavour one's self. Sir, I wish a billet at Cambridge; how much is he?

Four shellings seven pennies and half.

Here is a doubloon and three pistoles.

Next window.

The clerk has shuted the bureau's opening as a blusterer; you have not sended my dog's billet.

II. By the plateform.

Have you the every baggages? The trunk, the fishing-wands, and the hats box?

Yes, sir, I have its.

How long before the convoy depart?

A quarter hour's.

I will lunch myself once. A glass of sour, my dear. (This bar's maid is engaged one's self in familiar dialogues and idiotisms. It is haughty.) Have you any pullet, Miss? Give me immediately a stick's drum, some bosom and the lights inwards on a proper plate; also a lamprey, any garlic, some citrons and a bottle of the Oporto wine. Hark, the Guardsman who puffs his horn. "All the world to the vehicle." Here is a bill of exchange.

III. At the wagon.

Sir, you must not to fume.

Why not, sir?

It is not a fuming's box: she is at the train's end.

But, sir, she is many multiplied of women and children.

It must to do one's duty.

Here is a schelling.

It is all right, sir. Will you also a shawl, the day's leaf, and her Punches paper?

No, thank you sir, I will not to fall to sleep. Have you perhaps some heated water's tins?

By your leave, sir.

Demon! that is my toe's end. Here are the Billet-gatherer, the Puncher, the Lamp Slighter, the Overlooker, the Stevedore, the Head's Station, the Supercargo, and the Man-at arms in a three-cocked hat, holding the bare sword. What will you, gentlemen?

Sir, this is a wagon at first classes voyagers; you can not to voyage in her.

I will to pay a supplement by Cambridge. See the Hammerer and the Greaser who assay the wheels. The Engine-rider has mounted one's self. We prick.

IV. In route.

Sir, are you sportman?

Yes, sir, I play Picquet, Pope Joan, Ombre, Quince and Quadrille.

Know you also to play the little joke at Three Cards?

No, sir, I have not seen him among the Espagnishmen, the Turcos or the Swisses.

Mister is clever voyager; he will soon learn. See, I take the Trefoil's Dame, the Pike Three and the Heart Six. Here is an honest Farmer. He wagers to divine the Dame. He has achieved. Alas, that I am a foolish! I lose my money. Now, sir, will you to wager?

With zest, sir; here is a moidore.

That is not the Dame; she is the Three; but, sir, you shall try again. Fortune is seemed to some other womens what I know; she is changeable and too ficklish.

I perceive, sir, you are gallant man; you are no doubt so fortunate with the beautiful sex than by the cards'game.

Sir, you do to rouge me. I not boast what to be more lucky as some perfumed little-masters of the age; but it owes not to recount the histories outside the lyceum. Now, sir, it delays you to will back your loss, and, as tell us other Englishes, "do some hay, during the sun sparkle."

Here is my watch of Englishes make at the crow-bar, valuable from ten ducats.

She is not more worthier three lewis! She is in retard, she is foundered.

Alas, how I am not so fortunate than the countryman; I have lost again. Here is Cambridge. Do you descend?

No, sir, we continue to Newmarket.

Good morning, gentlemen.

V. For to see the sights.

Gentlemen is a stranger? is it permitted one's self to guide him?

Sir, I am delighted; I love too much some quaint old towns, so are they picturesque.

Yes, sir, here is the tramway, the Jerry Buildings, the Post Office, the Skating Cercle, the asphalto pavement, the Improvement Boarding.

Have you not also any Colleges?

Yes, sir, but we will not to show its. The plan of their architectures is antique, their buildings proportions harmonious, and the altogether gracious. Its were builded from men, which loved beauty so much than use – thing too reprehensible in the illuminated age.

And the students to which studies apply theirselves?

Such and such learnings:
> the latin
> the greek
> the jew
> the metallurgy
> the upper mathematics
> the doctors' commons
> the enthymem, etc.

Stay, sir, here is a fine edifice with some pretty columns and a imposing façade. Is he perhaps the Hotel of the Town, the Purse or the Exchange?

Alas, no, sir, it is the Fitz-William. It oughted to have builded one's self with yellow brick, with pointings of red and black over his windows for a relievo. It is shamful, it is a eye-smart.

It regrets me who I spoke. See again, what huge boots-manufactory!

No, sir, you have wrong again. He is the Technical Museum of Comparative Stratiology – very magnificent. Which bricks! which slates! Which elegance! Which voluptuousness!

Saturday 20 March
I presented one PhD, took one proxy MA and saw R. A. Almond get his Honorary MA.

[Almonds were the outfitters and robe-makers in Sidney Street, later taken over by Gieves.

In his Easter vacation, FB worked on lecture notes and on his autobiography, *It's A Don's Life*. He went often to the woods where there were daffodils in full bloom, the sallows all gold, a few anemones, hazels in tiny leaf, but the trees still very black and the ash buds jet black. He shouted at an accursed woman digging up daffodils with a trowel but, despite marauders, thought that the daffodils had spread a little in recent years perhaps because the fields between the farm and the wood had been ploughed.]

Saturday 1 May
Cambridge. Received a letter from Mymms to say the Patriarch is in hospital so decided to go home and see him.

Sunday 2 May
Saw the Vicar who was fully conscious and he said he was glad to see me and pressed my hand warmly on parting.

Monday 3 May
Cambridge. A meeting of the Jesus Tractarians was held in my rooms and Owen Chadwick presented a paper on Liddon and Bishop King.

Saturday 8 May
Victor Ross telephoned to say that the Patriarch died at 3.45 a.m. today. *Requiescat in pace.*

Tuesday 11 May
Went to Mymms and at 8 p.m. met the Vicar's coffin at the churchyard gate. I escorted it to the church and sang Vespers of the Dead. There was a watch in church all night and at 9 a.m. I conducted Compline and Mattins at noon.

Wednesday 12 May
Sung Requiem with the Bishop of Willesden (Gerald Ellison) as celebrant. I was Cantor and MC. At the end Father Whittingham performed Absolutions of the Dead. The Patriarch's burial was at 3 p.m. with the Bishop of London presiding, Father Whittingham conducting the office, with myself as MC.

Sunday 16 May
At the end of the morning service I delivered a memorial oration on the Patriarch.

> [FB ended his address as he had begun it, with the text: "We cannot be sad for long when we think of him for he gave us so much enjoyment in life, so much happiness, so much laughter. Even on the day of his funeral we laughed and laughed aloud when we were talking about him. How could we do otherwise when thinking of a man who gave us for so long and so unfailingly beauty for ashes, the oil of joy for mourning, and the garment of praise for the spirit of heaviness."]

Tuesday 25 May
Claude Havard (a medic) arrived and I took him to Hall. P. Gardner-Smith asked him, "What are you up for?" "An examination" Havard replied. "What

~ 1954 ~

in?" asked Gardner-Smith. "LLB" Havard said, to which Gardner-Smith replied, "I should have thought you could leave law to the lawyers".

Thursday 27 May
Ascension Day. Attended Chapel at 8 a.m., had breakfast in Hall, then went to King's for Byrd's 5-part Mass. A coffee party in my rooms became a sherry party. Went to the University Sermon at 2.30 p.m. and to Evensong at King's.

Tuesday 8 June
Went to a sherry party in the Gallery of Emmanuel in honour of A. J. Venn's completion of *Alumni Cantabridgiensis*.

> [This work in several volumes contains biographies of all members of the University, Part I up to 1752 and Part II up to 1900.]

Monday 14 June
At 10.30 p.m. took part (as every evening this week) in the ADC [Amateur Dramatic Club] late night music Hall show called *Snowballs at the Moon*. I did 'Captain Ginger'.

Thursday 17 June
The Bishop of Bangor (Jones) dined with me in Hall. P. Gardner-Smith said, "I once applied for a job at Bangor University College but I didn't get it. Inge told me I would have stood a better chance if my name had been Jones". The Bishop replied, "You would have stood an even better chance if your name had been Gardner-Smith-Jones with two hyphens!"

Wednesday 23 June
At the College Council meeting I stated that I didn't want to be re-elected Steward. I was elected Praelector and re-elected Keeper of the Records and of the Old Library and Muniments.

> [The Praelector took freshmen to the Senate House for matriculation before the practice was discontinued. He still presents graduates to the Vice-Chancellor or his deputy to have their degrees conferred upon them.]

Monday 5 July
South Mymms. Discussed the benefice with Mrs Hamilton at the Vicarage. Presided over a meeting of the PCC and got them to make a short list of four for the Patron and to agree to abide by her choice.

> [Mrs Hamilton was patron of the living and had lived with her husband at

~ 1954 ~

Cedar House in the village until his death, when she moved to Letty Green. George Sage, Succentor of St Paul's Cathedral, a bachelor, was appointed Vicar.]

Friday 9 July
Cambridge. I was X-rayed at the Cambridge Chest Clinic. Eric Heaton called about 10.30 p.m.

[Eric Heaton was Canon of Salisbury in 1954 and Dean of Christchurch, Oxford in 1979.]

Monday 13 September
Monday worked on the *Cambridge Review* 75th anniversary number.

Monday 20 September
The Senate House, the Old Schools and King's College Chapel were bathed in soft, golden, autumnal sun as was the vivid green grass – unusually vivid after a wet, sunless summer – and the sky was clear blue. There wasn't a soul about or a sound in the air. It looked just like an aquatint from Ackerman's Cambridge, a most moving occasion.

Tuesday 5 October
Took J. E. R. Young and his wife to King's for Evensong. As we came out I heard the Dean [Ivor Ramsay] describe me to the Youngs as "the life and soul of Jesus College and indeed of the whole University" – a gross exaggeration!

Friday 8 October
Attended Reverend Percy Ward's funeral at Harston.

[In his will Percy Ward left FB a lock of Coleridge's hair in a locket, which was kept in a small, decorated wooden box. FB bequeathed it to Jesus College where it is now on display with other Coleridgiana in the Old Library.]

Tuesday 19 October
Leon Bourdon, Professor of Portuguese at the Sorbonne, called to see a book in the Old Library. He stayed till 9.30 p.m., i.e. lunch, tea, Evensong at King's, sherry with J. B. Frend at Christ's, and to Hall and Combination Room at Jesus, then I took him back to the University Arms Hotel.

[This was typical of FB's boundless hospitality, but it did not equal the occasion when Gillie Potter, the radio comedian, came for lunch and stayed three days.]

~ 1954 ~

Five Mill Cottage
Highgate, N.6.

My dear F. Brittain, Sir,

So rarely is there encountered such kindness as that of the type which you have now for so long practised as to cause it to have become second nature to you, that I am quite unrehearsed in that unusual style of epistolary requital which the experience in question requires. Unequal to the task, then, one resorts to the stock of clichés, which abound about us today, withdrawing therefrom the naïve yet democratic, "'Ta', ever so!"; adding thereto the explanatory fact that he who writes this, and thus, is

Yours most gratefully
(signed) Gillie Potter

Monday 1 November
Returned to Mymms for the Institution of George Sage as Vicar. I presided at the reception afterwards in the Parish Hall and stayed the night at the Vicarage where I now rent a room, the first to the right along the corridor towards the church.

Wednesday 3 November
Cambridge. Took 111 freshmen to the Senate House to matriculate.

Saturday 11 December
Malcolm Muggeridge was my guest for the Audit Feast.

Thursday 16 December
Went to Bath and was met by June James who drove me round to see the chief sights. In the afternoon I gave away the prizes at Oldfield's Secondary Modern School, where June teaches.

Sunday 19 December
Attended the Girls' High School Nativity Pageant at St Albans Abbey. It was very beautifully done, with the two rows of 17-year old Pre-Raphaelite angels in white with haloes standing on the two walls in the lancets between the retro-choir and the Saint's Chapel.

Friday 24 December
The annual Bradshawe Sermon and Distribution of Bread and after Midnight Mass, with Flo Finch leading the way with an electric torch (as it was pitch dark), I carried the cross of evergreens and hyacinths and put it on the Patriarch's grave. I felt very sad all evening, my first Christmas Eve without him since boyhood.

[No further entries for December]

~ 1955 ~

[The Christmas vacation was spent at home as usual. FB read the page proofs of his new edition of *Latin in Church*, made a new index for it, and played crib with his father in the evenings. They played nine games on 4 January after heavy snow had fallen all day. At St Giles' George Sage made a few changes, e.g. they began to sing services "Full" instead of antiphonally with cantors.

Back at College FB met C. S. Lewis (1898-1963) for the first time over lunch at the Regent House. Lewis had been appointed Professor of Medieval and Renaissance English at Cambridge the previous year. FB also rehearsed assiduously for *Pantomania* or *Champagne Cinders* by Wendy Joyce, in which he played the Dame. This was the first production of the Cambridge University Pantomime Society and at the end bouquets were distributed to Wendy and the girls, but a cauliflower was handed up to FB, followed by a bunch of narcissi. On the second night when the Vice-Chancellor, the Mistress of Girton, the Principal of Homerton, etc. were present, he was given a leek.]

Thursday 3 March
My scarlet-lined black cloak arrived from Almonds. At the Alcuin Club Committee held in my rooms Bishop Dunlop [Dean of Lincoln] proposed me as Chairman in place of A. S. Duncan-Jones who died recently, but I declined. Took the Bishop and J. W. Poole [later Precentor of Coventry] to Hall and then to a Red Herring Shoal in my rooms.

Friday 11 March
Went to St Clement's for Stations of the Cross and then on to the old Anatomy School Theatre for the first English performance of Tennessee Williams's verse play *The Purification*.

Tuesday 29 March
Barnet. The trees are showing a little brown or gold today for the first time whereas hitherto they were black. Douglas Feaver and Kathie took me by car to Bedford. We had tea at a café in Ampthill on the way back and called on Professor Albert Richardson, PRA, who showed us round his house containing paintings by Reynolds, Gainsborough, Constable, etc., Louis

XV's ivory chessmen, Mrs Fitzherbert's furniture and Napoleon's signature.

Saturday 2 April
Bach's *St John Passion* was sung in the nave of St Albans Abbey, but I sat in the returned stalls in the nearly dark choir by myself.

Wednesday 27 April
Cambridge. The following dined with me in the Prioress's Room in preparation for tomorrow: Sir Godfrey Russell-Vick, QC; Mr Arthur Figgis; his junior, Dr E. V. Bevan (Treasurer of the CUBC); Dr McLellan (Pembroke); R. D. Burnell (ex Oxford University Boat Club and *Times* rowing correspondent); and Mr Cox of Francis and Co., the College solicitors.

Thursday 28 April
I was taken by car to Ipswich for a sitting of the Admiralty Court in which I, as Treasurer of the Jesus College Amalgamated Clubs, was representative defendant in an action by C. Wallman for damage to his motor boat at Grassy Corner during the May Races 1952.

Wallman v. Brittain

A CASE WHICH was heard in the Courts in May 1955 illustrated some of the lighter side of English Law.

In 1952 our fifth May boat, which had been bumped by a Fitzwilliam boat near "Grassy" Corner and was trying to get out of the way of the boats following, ran into a motor launch which was moored alongside the bank. This belonged to a Cambridge townsman, Mr Charles Wallman, who maintained that his boat had suffered damage to the value of £121.

He wished, apparently to sue the Jesus Boat Club; but, although the Club undoubtedly makes itself felt on the river, from the legal point of view it does not exist. It merely consists of those members of the Jesus Amalgamated Clubs who prefer to row rather than follow any other form of recreation. The rowing members of the Amalgamated Clubs are however, affiliated to the Cambridge University Boat Club, but this also does not exist from the point of view of the law. Mr Wallman might possibly have sued the Chancellor, Masters, and Scholars of the University of Cambridge but it was finally arranged that he should sue the Jesus College Amalgamated Clubs. The treasurer agreed to appear in Court to represent the Amalgamated Clubs, in order that the Court should not be crowded out by the appearance of the 332 members of the Clubs who were jointly liable.

As the accident had taken place on water, it was arranged that the case should be heard in the Admiralty Court. Apparently an Admiralty Court must sit within smell of salt water, and so the case was heard at Ipswich.

The Amalgamated Clubs were represented by the late Sir Godfrey Russell-Vick, Q.C. The particulars of the accident were read out in Court as though there had been a collision between two great liners in mid Atlantic. When an official proclaimed, "Direction and force of wind at the time, unknown. State of the tide at the time, unknown," a titter went round the Court. The hearing lasted from 10 a.m. till nearly 6 p.m, with a short interval for lunch.

... The Judge found for the plaintiff on the ground that the Jesus coxswain had been guilty of negligent steering.

Saturday 7 May
Cambridge. About 11 a.m. Arthur Sherborne, Sid Chilton and Lynton Whiteley [three choirmen from Mymms] arrived. I took them to lunch at Regent House, to King's at 5.30 p.m. and we dined in Frederic Raby's rooms. Later I took them on a short tour of the College including the Combination Room where Alan Percival was presiding over dessert. We sat at the other end of the table and talked awhile about Mymms etc. The unsophisticated Sid [a bus driver] got me to collect their signatures on his menu card so that he could convince his conductor next day that he really had done what he said.

Friday 13 May
Rosamund Essex (editor of the *Church Times*) came to dinner, after which she read a first-rate paper to the Neale Society on "Twenty-five years of Ecclesiastical Journalism".

> [In his vote of thanks FB referred to Rosamund Essex as the editor of the 'Tuppenny Pope', as the paper was known when it was priced at 2d. (two pence). She had never heard it called that but was delighted with the title.]

Monday 13 June
Gillie Potter was here a good part of the day with Stephen Williams of the BBC recording a talk between Gillie and myself. After dinner we went to *The Seasons* in the Cloister, then on to the First and Third Trinity Ball, dancing under the Wren Library and across the river on a small floor laid on the grass, with coloured lights in the trees.

Monday 4 July
Went with Tiny Mitchell and the Bishop of Ely to St Paul's Cathedral for the opening service of the new Convocation of Canterbury. We sat in the Minor Canons' Closet. Geoffrey Cantuar brought up the rear of the procession wearing his long scarlet train. The service was all in Latin, processional psalms, Litany, Veni Creator, Gloria in Excelsis, and Blessing by the Archbishop.

Tuesday 5 July
Mymms. By bus to the Waggon and Horses and sat in the top field where there are usually sheep but today a herd of bullocks was grazing. Several came near to examine me as I sat on the grass. One came close and closer and finally pressed his nose against mine. Another drew up, with the same intention, but the first glared at him and pushed him away with his shoulder and repeated the nose-rubbing.

Wednesday 20 July
Cambridge. I was Steward in the Senate House at the Opening meeting of the Conference of Principals of European Universities who came in procession in most beautiful and striking costumes.

Friday 19 August
Barnet. Dad painted the front of the house upstairs and down including the attic window this week.

> [Tolman, i.e. the old man as he was known in the family, was then eighty-nine years old.
>
> In early September FB attended the 1st International Congress of Language and Literature held in Avignon.]

Thursday 8 September
Mistral's Birthday. Attended Mass at Maillane where there was a choir of women and girls in Provencal dress singing paraphrases of the liturgy in Provencal (not twelve words of Latin could be heard), men and boys in costume formed a band of drums and pipes which played whenever there was no singing. At Mistral's tomb in the cemetery wreaths were laid, 'De Profundis' sung and speeches "Coupo santo". Then to his house, now a museum, more speeches by his nephew and others, and finally Vin d'Honneur with the blind mayor at St Remy and then back to Avignon.

Sunday 11 September
Mass at St Didier's – called "grand messe" but not one word was sung. A priest in the pulpit read a French translation of practically the whole of the Mass concurrently including the Collect, Epistle, Gospel, Sanctus, Agnus etc.

Tuesday 13 September
On the way home by train the country between Paris and Boulogne struck me as charming.

~ 1955 ~

Thursday 29 September
Took the chair at the Alcuin Club committee meeting at Church House, Westminster and agreed to ask W. K. Lowther Clarke to become Chairman of the club. Dined at Bedford House (YWCA), Baker Street with the Coffee Pot Club, a collection of young graduates living in London. I talked to them afterwards on Cambridge life.

Monday 17 October
Cambridge. Meeting of the College Council at which I am glad to record we elected Trevor Jones to a Fellowship.

Tuesday 18 October
[The magazine *Reveille* contained the following: "According to *Who's Who* the chief recreations of Sir Frederick Brittain of Jesus College, Cambridge are singing and acting. He also has a much stranger hobby. He collects models of the College emblem, a cockerel . . ."

FB's close friend, the Bishop of Ely said that he felt hurt not to have been told of the knighthood and sent him the cutting. FB replied:

Jesus College
Cambridge
22 October 1955

My Lord Bishop,
   I thank you for the cutting from *Reveille*, which your Lordship has kindly sent me. The alleged knighthood had been brought to my notice just before the royal visit to Cambridge and I had some hope that it might have been an intelligent anticipation.
   A couple of years ago, when I had been performing as Dame in pantomime at South Mymms, I saw a report in the *News of the World*, rather "splashed" as they say. That was during the Christmas vacation. I consoled myself on the way back to Cambridge that none of my friends there would ever read such a paper as the *News of the World*. I discovered my mistake within 100 yards of the railway station, when greeted by the Professor of Anglo-Saxon. During the next few days I found that apparently the majority of the dons of the University of Cambridge study the *News of the World* with great care. I now find to my profound astonishment that the episcopate study that revolting weekly *Reveille*. My learned friend, Sir Godfrey Russell-Vick, QC, who is with me at the moment, deplores with me that the Bishops have nothing better to do than to study *Reveille*.
   My learned colleague and friend, Dr Frederic James Edward Raby, who is a Companion of the Most Honourable Order of the Bath and I may add,

a Failed BA, wishes me to convey to your Lordship his pained astonishment.

I have the honour to be, My Lord Bishop,
> Your Lordship's most obedient servant,
> Frederick Brittain.]

Saturday 22 October
On duty for the honorary degree on Albert Schweitzer (who has done so much for the people of Africa.) The Senate House was packed from end to end and hundreds were unable to get in.

Monday 24 October
My 62nd birthday. Recorded a talk, *Report from Cambridgeshire*, for BBC overseas transmission on 1 November.

REPORT FROM CAMBRIDGESHIRE

The "shire for men who understand", as Rupert Brooke calls Cambridgeshire, is always beautiful. It is never more so than at this time of year, when the leaves are changing colour. I am speaking from my rooms at Jesus College, Cambridge. Just under my windows there is a honey-locust tree. It is a lovely sight at the moment. Half its leaves are a delicate light green, the other half are a bright gold. At any time now a sharp frost may strip the trees throughout the county in a single night, but at present they are flashing with scarlet, maroon, and gold.

Every parish church and chapel in the county has held its harvest festival by now. That applies to the big magnificent churches in the fens to the north of Cambridge and to the more modest village churches to the south, where (as Miss Rose Macaulay writes)
> "the pale downs tumble, blind, chalk-faced,
> "And the brooding churches squat."

It is only in the college chapels at Cambridge that there has been no harvest thanksgiving. There is nothing new in that. College chapels are much more conservative than parish churches; and harvest festivals, which began little more than a hundred years ago, haven't reached college chapels yet.

Everyone has heard of our great cathedral at Ely, about 16 miles from Cambridge. I couldn't get there this year for the cathedral festival on St Etheldreda's Day, which falls on October 17th. I always go if I can. I enjoy the journey over the apparently endless level of the fens, with their straight willow-fringed roads and their great fields of stoneless black earth, each field surrounded by a deep banked ditch. I love to watch the mighty cathedral drawing nearer and nearer out of the distance, growing bigger and bigger, raising superbly under the vast unbroken arch of the fenland sky, and riding the fields like a great ship at anchor.

What have we been talking about in Cambridge lately? Well, there have been two outstanding events. The first was a visit from the Queen, who came to open the new buildings of the University Veterinary School. They are over in the fields towards Madingley Hill. The other outstanding event was a visit from the famous Albert Schweitzer, who has done so much for the people of Africa. He came to receive an honorary degree from the University. The Senate House was packed from end to end and hundreds were unable to get in. I was on duty there. My job was to check members of the University as they came in – to see that they were wearing the proper academical dress, for instance. Most of them were; but (as usual) there were a few who were not. Some were wearing their hoods inside out, others had them turned back to front, or were guilty of some other minor irregularity in academical dress. I don't mind saying that I even caught a Professor or two . . .

Tuesday 1 November
Lectured as usual but in scarlet today [All Saints' Day]. Hall dinner was an Exceeding with dessert in the Prioress's Room afterwards.

[While he was Steward, FB revived the Exceedings (Minor Feasts) to celebrate St Radegund's Day on 11 February, the Name of Jesus on 7 August and All Saints' Day on 1 November.]

Friday 9 December
Innumerable callers stopped me from marking scholarship exam scripts.

[The entries for every day in College list the names of hordes of visitors. It is not often that, as for today, they appear to have been too many to mention.]

Thursday 15 December
The scholarship examiners held their final meeting in my rooms. Vivian Cox, Leslie Bricusse and Frederick Raphael came to discuss a proposed film of Cambridge life. [The film was *Bachelor of Hearts*.]

[No further entries for December]

~ 1956 ~

Friday 13 January
Went to the Royal Academy to see the Exhibition of Portuguese Art and into St James's Piccadilly, which has been wonderfully restored by Sir Albert Richardson. Then to a meeting at New Burlington Place with the editor of *Victoria Encyclopaedia* for which I am writing articles on Medieval Latin Literature.

Monday 23 January
Cambridge. Went to King's at 5.30 p.m. I felt very moved with all the books and papers cleared away from Ivor Ramsay's vacant stall next to mine and the sweet, impersonal voices of the boys sounded gentle and melancholy.

> [FB's close friend Ivor Ramsay, the Dean of King's had taken his own life by throwing himself down from the tower of King's Chapel.]

Tuesday 3 February
Went with Nigel Phillips, his guitar, and Frederic Raby to Girton for a Medieval Banquet. I dressed as a Troubadour, Phillips as my Joglar, and Raby as the Bishop of Ely. After dinner I sang Troubadour songs, "Orientis partibus" and "Multi sunt presbyteri".

Saturday 4 February
Barnet. Home for the day, as it was Dad's 90th birthday. Frank and Elsie, the Tyrwhitts and Cis Wall [a cousin] came for tea.

Friday 17 February
Cambridge. W. L. H. Duckworth's funeral was held in Chapel, after which we "circumnavigated the whole College" as D. J. V. Fisher said.

> [i.e. the usual custom of following the coffin of a former Master round the courts was carried out.]

Saturday 3 March
Tea at Bene't House, where there was an interesting discussion on plainsong and I put forward my conviction about the influence of the French language being too strong for Solesmian theories. I was very glad to find agreement.

~ 1956 ~

Sunday 11 March
Had tea at Neale House, Huntingdon Road [the Cambridge house of the Community of St John Baptist sisters] where I gave a talk on "The Academical and Episcopal Underworlds".

Tuesday 1 May
Gave a dinner party in the Prioress's Room for Frederic Raby, the Dean of Ely and Mrs Hankey, Owen and Mrs Chadwick, Mrs Prior, Professor C. S. Lewis, John Dickinson and Valerie Pitt of Newnham.

[Frances Hankey wrote afterwards:

"Patrick and I had a very happy evening and I'm sure everyone else did too, and your farewell comment that you would like life to contain a long trestle table down which one could move a convivial spirit was a charming remark to come from an exhausted host.

It was a great pleasure to hear you begin the Feast by saying Grace. Never abrogate that right when you are at the head of your own table. No guest can give the same effect of seemliness. Will Spens refused to ask the Archbishop of Canterbury to say Grace at his table because he knows that the host should always do it, and can only delegate it (if necessary) to his parish priest. I never realized until your dinner how right he was".]

Saturday 5 May
Presided over the Anglo-Catalan Society's dinner in College, made a speech of welcome, then took them in the twilight round the Fellows' Garden, Combination Rooms and Hall.

Monday 21 May
Dealing with A. J. Austin's testimonial correspondence [as every day in the coming weeks].

[Captain Austin was retiring after many years as Head Porter. One of his duties was to write a report for the Senior Tutor on the happenings of the previous night. For example his statement for week ending 6 March 1932 recorded that on the Friday night there was "A large party (about 40–50) in Mr Reed, T. W.'s rooms, mostly rowing gents but some others brought in put more life into it. Very noisy and singing and shouting could be heard all over the Court. Two windows broken and branches broken off trees but the party kept within the rules and there was no general smash-up".]

Tuesday 24 July
Went to a performance of *A Midsummer Night's Dream* in the Fellows' Garden at Trinity Hall, a wonderful setting with the river wall and trees for background.

Saturday 4 August
Professor Leslie Martin was admitted to his Fellowship in Chapel.

> [Sir Leslie Martin became an Honorary Doctor of Letters at Cambridge in 1991. The following is a translation of the citation he received:
>
> AFTER the Great Fire the citizens of London turned to Sir Christopher Wren. Three centuries later, after the devastations of war, they turned to our honorary, Deputy and then Chief Architect to the London County Council. The schools and houses whose building he planned are now the silent fabric of the city. The Royal Festival Hall speaks forth in more eloquent witness. We welcomed him to Cambridge as our first Professor of Architecture, and he founded the research centre now named in his honour as the Martin Centre for Architectural and Urban Studies, and he placed Cambridge in the forefront of architectural teaching and research, and at the same time changed the whole direction of architectural education in this country. Some, if they seek his monument, may find it in Lisbon, where he has designed the Gallery of Contemporary Art; others in Glasgow, where he built a new home for the Royal Scottish Academy of Music and Drama; others in the libraries, auditoria, and halls of residence with which he has enriched many a University. But you and I will find it beside the Cam, in Harvey Court of Caius, or in the Gallery of Kettle's Yard, or in the Music School, whose concert hall has earned the applause of listener and performer alike; or by the banks of the millpond at Great Shelford, where he has converted the old mill and barn into his studio and home.
>   I present to you
>   Sir JOHN LESLIE MARTIN, M.A.
> Emeritus Fellow and Honorary Fellow of Jesus College, Emeritus Professor of Architecture, Royal Academician, gold medallist of the Royal Institute of British Architects.]

Sunday 5 August
E. M. Forster and two Italian ladies ("fans" of his) came to my sherry party.

Wednesday 12 September
Barnet. A fine day, most unusual this year. Walked through Cutthroat Lane to the Wash where the stream was a roaring torrent. Saw succory in bloom for

the first time there. Some corn is being cut today but very few fields yet touched and the corn is spoiling.

Friday 2 November
Cambridge. Presented Pat Jenkin for his MA and Michael Zander for his BA.

> [Patrick Jenkin, a barrister, was elected Conservative MP for Wanstead and Woodford in 1964 and appointed a Privy Councillor in 1973. He held several Opposition and Government posts before being elevated to the peerage in 1987.
> Michael Zander became Legal Correspondent of the *Guardian* in 1963 and Professor of Law at the London School of Economics in 1977.]

Thursday 8 November
I took eight of "Freddy's Foreign Legion"; 5 Italians, 1 Swede, 1 Dutch and 1 Swiss to the Rooster Hen Party.

> [Professor Muriel Bradbook, Fellow of Girton College (of which she was Mistress 1968-1976), was a guest at one of FB's dinner parties on 20 November 1956. A few days later he received the following:
>
> Dear Freddy
>   I'm ready
>   To admit
>
>   Your Dinners
>   Are winners
>   And fit
>
>   For Queens
>   And Kings
>   Of highest station
>   You dine us
>   And wine us
>   (With a pink carnation)
>
>   And with charm
>   Enough to warm
>   The most depressed and raise to heights
>   Memorial.
>   Excuse the platitude,

~ 1956 ~

>Accept the gratitude
>For your delightful party, of
>>Your obliged,
>>>Respectful,
>>>>Muriel

Girton College,
21 November 1956.]

[No further entries for 1956]

~ 1957 ~

Saturday 2 February
Cambridge. Lunched at the Lamb at Ely with Mrs Camille Prior and Dick Ladborough, then in scarlet to the enthronement of Noel Hudson as Bishop of Ely. [The Bishop had been translated from Newcastle and was at Ely until 1963.] Dined as the guest of R. Y. Jennings at the Candlemas feast at Trinity.

>[FB's friend, Frederic Raby, was now ill in the Evelyn Nursing Home – for the next week or so he went twice, and sometimes three times, a day to visit him.]

Thursday 21 February
It is turning colder after wonderfully mild weather ever since New Year.

Monday 25 February
Moses I Finley was elected to a Fellowship.

>[Moses I Finley became Professor of Ancient History at Cambridge in 1970 and was Master of Darwin College from 1976 to 1982.]

Saturday 2 March
It was a lovely day today. We finished Head of the Lents. Went to the Bump Supper and then to the bonfire on the Close.

Saturday 9 March
Attended Evensong at King's and then visited Alec Vidler in his rooms until the King's Guest Night commenced.

[A. R. Vidler had been elected Dean of King's in place of Ivor Ramsay. He had been on the staff of the Oratory House, Cambridge (1931-38) then Warden of St Deiniol's Library, Harwarden, until he became a Canon of St George's Chapel, Windsor in 1948.]

Sunday 17 March
Delivered a lecture to the girls of the Priory School, Lichfield, on the Troubadours. Had tea with the headmistress, Miss Gent, then sang songs to them accompanied by a girl pianist and guitarist. Dined at the boarding house of the school, then told stories to the boarders, e.g. 'Pigs Trotters'.

Wednesday 20 March
My medico, Henry Batten, found that I have emphysema but no sign of disease in the heart or lungs and I am "much younger than my age". The plum blossom is in its prime throughout Cambridge.

Thursday 18 April
Attended the Royal Maundy Service in St Albans Abbey, distributed by the Queen. Had a fine seat in the presbytery. The Abbey and Chapel Royal choirs sang S. S. Wesley's 'Wash Me Throughly' and other anthems.

Sunday 21 April
Easter Day. Took Muriel Cunnington to St Albans and to tea at the Sub-deanery.

Saturday 1 June
Went to Jesus College, Oxford, where I will stay until Tuesday. Watched the last two divisions of the Eights from the Jesus barge. Before the Bump Supper several Fellows warned me to be prepared for noise etc. I told them afterwards that compared with some Bump Suppers I had attended at Jesus, Cambridge before the war this was almost like a dinner in a Trappist Monastery!

Sunday 2 June
Attended College Chapel at 8 a.m., the University Sermon at St Mary the Virgin at 10.30 a.m. and College Chapel at 6 p.m. followed by Hall at 7.30 p.m. Dessert was in the Old Bursary followed by coffee in the Upper Common Room. Sat there till nearly midnight with Idris [Foster] egging me on to tell stories about Jesus Cambridge characters. I made them double up with laughter.

~ 1957 ~

Monday 3 June
Had breakfast in my rooms before going to Cuddesdon where John Pulford showed me round the theological college and the beautiful parish church. Lunched at the College sitting next to the Principal, E. G. Knapp-Fisher.

Wednesday 3 June
Cambridge. Cambridge Footlights May Week Revue called *Zounds* is the worst I have ever seen. About 80 sherry glasses and 10 beer tumblers were used in my rooms today.

Saturday 13 June
Took the motor coach to Little Gidding. There were about 200 on the pilgrimage led by Bishop Walsh and Owen Chadwick delivered the sermon.

Saturday 3 August
Presented D. R. Shackleton Bailey for his Litt.D.

> ["Shack", as he was known, University Lecturer in Tibetan, was a Fellow and Director of Studies in Classics at Jesus from 1955 until 1964 when he emigrated to the Department of Classics at Harvard University.]

Monday 4 November
Dined at Trinity with John Burnaby after which he and I and Holloway of Queens' judged the nine entries for the Seatonian Prize.

Saturday 30 November
The Senate House re-opened today after cleaning and re-lighting. A tea party was held in the Council Chamber to celebrate.

[No entries for December]

~ 1958 ~

Tuesday 21 January
We had snow this morning, the first this month, not one flake before.

Saturday 1 February
With Richard Bainbridge to King's for a Candlemas Pageant in the ante-Chapel.

~ 1958 ~

[Richard Bainbridge was a popular member of the Jesus High Table. He took part in most college activities, was a keen supporter of the Chapel and the Roosters, and Red Herrings remember him for his sparkling contributions to their deliberations. As a marine zoologist he invented the Bainbridge Fish Wheel, a device which adds to the knowledge of fish movement and migration. At his time there was no vacancy among the Fellows of Jesus for a biological scientist so he was elected to a Fellowship at Corpus Christi College in 1963 and later became its Senior Tutor. He died suddenly in 1987, and his obituary states "...Richard was a devoted Christian with a superb talent for friendship. ...For several years he was a Proctor and one feels confident that any malefactor he "progged" would emerge from his proctorial interview a wiser and richer man even if he was 6s. 8d. the poorer . . ."]

Monday 3 March
Dined at the Arts Theatre and then saw the English première of Orff's *Catulli Carmina*, which was excellent.

Sunday 9 March
It snowed today and I am in bed with a chill. Roosted from my bed.

[During FB's frequent attacks of chest infections the Roosters met as usual in his rooms with the door to his bedroom open so that he could take part.]

Monday 10 March
Held a sherry party for the Roosters to meet the Bishop of Ely.

[As Visitor to the College the Bishop would have been invited to accept the office of Exalted Justiciar to the Roost.]

Saturday 22 March
Attended John Maxwell Edmonds' funeral service in Chapel.

[FB was the co-executor of his (J. M. Edmonds' estate) and many times had to answer queries about his famous couplet, which is so often quoted (and more often misquoted) on war memorials (see 1920 for the correct version.)]

[While on a visit to Jesus College, Oxford in May FB visited the Cowley Fathers, walked along the towpath with Idris Foster and had tea under the apple trees in an Iffley garden. He dined at Christ Church as the guest of Denys Wilkinson, Professor of Nuclear Physics at Oxford and later

~ 1958 ~

Vice-Chancellor of Sussex University, and at Keble College as the guest of the Warden, Eric Abbot, who became Dean of Westminster in 1959.]

Friday 20 June
J. M. Cohen of Penguin Books came to discuss my doing a *Penguin Book of Latin Verse*.

Saturday 5 July
Last day of Henley Regatta. I was in Humphrey Playford's launch behind our first crew in the final of the Ladies' Plate in which they beat Christ Church, Oxford. My guest for the day, Joan Barbour, drove me back to the Vicarage.

Sunday 6 July
Mymms. We moved back today to the restored and repainted chancel, which looked magnificent. The Bishop of Willesden (George Ingle) preached and dedicated the new carved altar rails in memory of the Patriarch. Mr Gowar and I wore our new blue Readers' scarves for the first time.

Thursday 10 July
Worked at Gray and Brittain [the history of Jesus College, which he had been asked to revise and continue] all day in the field above the Waggon and Horses. The hay has now been machine-gathered into cubes.

Monday 29 September
Attended Stephen Smalley's ordination at St Paul's Cathedral. Lunched at Lloyd's with M. J. (Bunje) Langton and then had a meeting with Alan Hill at Heinemann's to discuss Gray and Brittain.

[S. S. Smalley became Precentor of Coventry Cathedral in 1977 and Vice-Provost in 1986. The following year he became Dean of Chester.]

Saturday 8 November
Muriel Cunnington arrived on her way to Peterborough and lunched with me in my rooms.

[The end of this year was to be momentous in FB's life. George Sage had resigned the living at South Mymms to take up an appointment at Addington Palace, and the Rev E. P. Clare, a married priest from Hampstead, was appointed. FB, not wanting to force himself on to the new incumbent at the Vicarage, had consulted his old friend Mrs Blake about finding another room for him in the village. This gave Florence Blake an idea. "I would have him here", she said to Muriel Cunnington, "but he must stay somewhere with the telephone". Muriel knew at once that she was expected to offer him accommodation at Ingham Lodge. She was fully occupied as Chief Pharmacist at Westminster Children's Hospital, as well as supervising a business inherited from her father, so she rather grudgingly replied that he could have the dining room and a bedroom but he needn't think that he was going to be looked after in any way. Florence then produced one of her splendid 'bon mots' in words of warning "You don't have to go giving him the glad eye, you know, because he's silly with girls". She was also good at mixed metaphors. On one occasion Muriel, driving her in London and impatient in a traffic jam, was told "Now, my dear, you've got to remember you're not the only fly in the ointment". Another day when Muriel visited her Florence recounted that Mrs—— had been to see her but she, Florence, was out. "I wasn't sorry", she said. "I'm not sort of inundated with her." As things turned out FB did not become Muriel's lodger. As usual the diary is extremely reticent about matters of the heart, but some of FB's letters reveal how fast feelings developed between them.]

Tuesday 30 December

5 The Avenue
Barnet

Dear Muriel,

Simultaneously with your lavish consignment this morning there came a letter from the United States. It began: "My dear Freddy" and ended "Yours ever, Muriel". As I wasn't at the moment associating Muriel with America I was puzzled for a while. Then I realized that the letter came from a somewhat elderly Fellow of Girton, who is temporarily in the USA, named Muriel Clara Bradbrook. I have a fellow-feeling with her, as we are both numbered among the few Cambridge Doctors of Letters. Obviously, I reflected, as she started by calling me *her* dear Freddy, I should look stand-offish if I began my reply without a "My". Further reflection convinced me that, as I like you more than I do her – and I by no means dislike her – it would be illogical for me to begin my letter to you without a "My". After all, I reflected, if you object, I am sure you, with your customary politeness, will find a way of saying so without beginning "Hi, you! What the – do you mean by this familiarity?" So I start afresh –

My dear Muriel,

It was very kind of you to send me these lovely apples (which have gratified Tolman as well) and these most acceptable gloves . . .

~ 1959 ~

Monday 12 January

Jesus College
Cambridge

My dear Muriel,

Since I got back this morning I have had about a thousand things to do and have become immediately immersed in my other life, the Cambridge life. Which of the two is my dominant life? Robert Gittings, who used to be a Fellow here, once boldly asserted that South Mymms is dominant in me. That was a bold statement seeing that here I am almost regarded as the embodiment of Jesus College.

On the other hand, it is when I am at Mymms, particularly in my sheep field at the top of Ridge Hill, that I realise the truth of Kipling's lines most keenly:

> Deeper than our speech or thought
> Beyond all reason's sway,
> Clay of the pit whence we were wrought
> Yearns to its fellow clay

Few people realise – I think you are one of the few, as you have I imagine the same feeling yourself – how deeply, how unreasonably (I would even say how desperately) the clay of the South Mymms area yearns to me. That awful Mrs ———-, awful for this one remark only – once astonished me by saying (after reading *Mostly Mymms*), that she was surprised to find that country so very near London could have such a hold over anyone. Astonishing woman! Can't she understand that London is like a great invading army and that it is the people who live on the frontier of an invaded country that are perhaps the most furious about the invasion? She could never understand W. J. Cory's lines:

> All beauteous things for which we live
> By laws of time and space decay
> But O, the very reason why
> I clasp them is because they die

I enjoyed the weekend very much. You, dear Muriel, were very kind to me and I am most grateful.

Love,
    Freddy.

Wednesday 14 January
>My dear Muriel,
>
>... I am going to Hall in a few minutes closely wrapped in my scarlet-lined, thick black cloak. So far I haven't been out of my rooms today, it is the worst possible weather for my bronchitis and emphysema. When my friend Old King Cole [E. Cole, a friend of his brother] drove me up the other day he remarked that his medico had warned him that he must be careful or he would have a chill one day, pneumonia the next, and a coffin the day after that. Then Old King Cole added that my case is very similar to his.
>
>Love,
>>Freddy.

Monday 26 January
>... I am glad you saw *Bachelor of Hearts*. I liked it *very* much more than I feared I would and said so to the producer, Vivian Cox, at the sherry and sweetmeats party afterwards. I think I told you that it all began at a lunch-party in my rooms at which I entertained VC, Leslie Bricusse and Frederick Raphael ... I thought the Cambridge photography admirable and the whole film very entertaining.
>
>I am still in bed. My chief Sawbones has just been in to see me and Sister Brady [the College nurse called Sister Broody in the Roost] calls twice daily, so you see I am still "in bed with the doctor and the nurse", as Shakespeare says in one of his lost plays. ...

Friday 6 February
>... I have an idea, dear. On 18 March I have to give a lecture on the Troubadours and to sing some of their songs at Dean Close School, Cheltenham where a recent pupil of mine (and an Old Elizabethan) is now an assistant master. Do you feel like running me there? ... I have been offered accommodation at the Headmaster's house and surely he could accommodate you too ...
>
>11.30 p.m. Since I can find no St Muriel in Baring-Gould's *Lives of the Saints* in 17 volumes I've just discovered the obvious saint's day for you – July 12th St Epiphana, a Sicilian woman martyr probably about 250 AD.

[Muriel's birthday fell on the Feast of Epiphany.]

Thursday 12 February
>... I am very glad that you would like to come to Cheltenham. From there we could easily work in a run to Gloucester and even to Ross-on-Wye where I have never been and would very much like to go ...
>
>I never like to miss Evensong on Ash Wednesday at King's as they

finish up with Allegri's *Miserere*, which makes my hair stand on end with its sheer beauty and fills me with immortal longings. When I got there yesterday I found that the service had been at 4 because of a broadcast. However I hope to hear John Blow's immortal anthem *Salvator Mundi* at King's on Sunday. It is wonderful, sublime and does literally make me tingle all over. He has been overshadowed by his great pupil, Henry Purcell, the greatest musical genius this country has ever produced, but I don't think Purcell wrote anything to surpass *Salvator Mundi*.

You know how people shockingly misuse the world "literally" by using it when the real meaning is "in all senses *except* the literal". For instance, I read recently that "When Marie Corelli went to live at Stratford-on-Avon she literally took Shakespeare to her bosom". (There must have been a great row in the town when they saw her digging up Shakespeare's bones and clasping them. Why didn't they send for the police and a mental specialist?) However, the story I am coming to appeared a year or two ago in the *Church Times*. It was copied from a parish magazine, which said, "We are all so sorry that our Vicar is leaving us. The young people will be particularly sorry because he was literally the father of every child in the parish". (I wonder what the population of the parish was?)

Love,
Freddy.

Wednesday 18 February
Caught the train to London in bright sun but much fog there. Had tea with Muriel in the pharmacy of Westminster Children's Hospital and then we went to Dame Mitchell's sherry party at the Dorchester. The fog was so thick when we left that we each decided to go home without dinner. Muriel took me to the Strand and I got a taxi to Liverpool Street and caught the 8.50 p.m. train to Cambridge.

Friday 20 February
My dear Murielita,

I am reading for the nth time Coleridge's poem *Kubla Khan* and am much struck by the line "As if this earth in fast thick pants were breathing": but surely the earth would need a very large pair? "Fast" presumably means unshrinkable which (considering what laundries are like) is incredible.

Thank you, dear, for your letter received this morning with its account of your adventurous journey home from the Dorchester, a good piece of descriptive narrative. I wonder why on nights like that there aren't a larger number of robberies and murders than usual. Perhaps there are. I ought to have gone with you.

I am so glad you enjoyed that Dorchester party. I think you met Bud

Mitchell's wife, but not, I think, Alan Burrough's wife. They are sisters. Their father, now dead, was Captain Bruce who was the navigator on Captain Scott's celebrated Antarctic expedition. They are nieces of the late Lord Trent who was elected Honorary Fellow of Jesus because we felt that his old College ought to do something to show Cambridge's appreciation of his being the founder and first Chancellor of a new University (Nottingham). His name was John Boot, son of Jesse Boot, the first Baron Trent, who started Boots Cash Chemists.

By the way, it would be a great help if you would please number the pages of your letters, not merely the leaves as in incunabula, which is confusing. On Friday evening I stole away to the service of Stations of the Cross at St Clement's – a simple service, eminently suited to my very simple mind. My thoughts went back to boyhood with Allen Hay conducting the Stations of the Cross at South Mymms. I can see him now, nodding to me to start the unaccompanied singing of the *Stabat Mater*. Strange that after all those years, I have to lecture on that poem (among others) in my Medieval Latin course . . .

Well, Murielita, lita, lita, the gramophone needle has got stuck. I think I must call you Lita sometimes in Spanish style.

Love,
    Freddy

Tuesday 3 March
Cambridge. Peter Anson dined with me in the Guest Room (plus the Dean of Ely and Mrs Hankey) before he read a paper to the Neale Society.

[Peter Anson, the author of *Bishops at Large* (Faber and Faber), exchanged letters with FB concerning the ecclesiastical underworld as together they sought to expose bogus bishops and bogus universities. One such character was His Sacred Beatitude Mar Georgius, I, DD, DCL, Lord Patriarch of Glastonbury, Prince Catholicos of the West, Apostolic Pontiff of Celtica and the Indies, Prince de Mardin, Exarch of the Order of Antioch for Britain, Ruling Prelate of the Order of Corporate Reunion, Prelate Commander of the Order of the Crown of Thorns. (These are merely a selection of his titles.) He was also head of the Western Orthodox University, which claimed to confer any and every degree, also knighthoods and other titles of honour. An entertaining letter from Anson to FB tells of a man who, when the validity of his Holy Orders conferred by a bogus bishop was questioned, replied that he had evidence of his Orders but they were written in Syriac. An expert was consulted and the document was pronounced to be, as claimed, in Syriac; however, it was not a statement of Holy Orders but a recipe for curry! Peter Anson, who lived at Montrose in Scotland, would sometimes sign his letters to FB, Mar Petros, Patriarch of the Picts and Catholicos of Calcedonia.]

Friday 6 March
My dear Murielita,
   Thank you for your account of the Conservative Dinner. I shouldn't be surprised if some of them start asking you when I am going to join the Conservative Association. You will then have to tell them the ghastly truth. (I imagine you will enjoy studying their faces)....
   Pardon me if I point out an error in your use of English. You say "It is very kind of you to invite Barbara and I. It isn't. I couldn't invite "I", I can invite "me". It doesn't matter if 5 million people come between the verb and the object the latter must be "me", eg "between you and me and the gatepost, or "between Bill Brewer, Jan Stewer, Peter Gurney, Peter Davy, Dan'l Whidden, Harry Hawk, old Uncle Tom Cobleigh and ME".
   Please understand that I mention it only because I know you would wish to be right. The error in question was until recently a mark of illiteracy but it is increasing like creeping paralysis. I shudder to say that I have even heard dons using it. . . . I am sure you will always get it right now, you are so quick on the uptake . . .

Saturday 14 March
Barnet. Frank and Elsie came and we discussed the future of Dad and Mog. Afterwards Dad suggested that Mog and he should enter homes.

Tuesday 17 March
Muriel called with the car and we went via Amersham to Oxford where we lunched at the Mitre with Idris Foster. We went on to Cheltenham, passing the signpost to Adelstrop we turned off and went in the church there.

[Edward Thomas's poem "I remember Adelstrop" was a favourite of FB's]

Wednesday 22 April
Jesus College
Cambridge

My dear Murie,
   "They had swallowed us up quick", the psalmist says and that is how I have felt since I got back here – the wave of things to do overwhelmed me . . .
   What a vacation the Easter one was! There has never been one like it. I am most grateful to you, dear, for all the help and loving comfort you gave me. You helped me tremendously in what was a trying enough crisis for me

~ 1959 ~

as it was, but without you it would have been much more painful to carry out that breaking up of the family and the old home. Tolman had been a trial in more ways than one, yet it was sad . . .
  Much love dear Murielita,
    Freddy

[During the Easter vacation FB and Muriel had decided to get married in July. Practically no one was told, as they wanted a quiet wedding.]

Monday 25 May
Cambridge. Duncan McKie was elected a Research Fellow. In Hall the Master [Dr Tillyard who had returned after sick leave with a heart condition] said that he had just been given a new drug for his heart. P. Gardner-Smith said, "They put Manning on a new drug for his heart. He died next day."

Wednesday 27 May
Jesus College
Oxford

  . . . I have been having a very good time here. The Summer Eights are on. I was on my way to the river yesterday when I heard the Cathedral bell ringing for Evensong so I decided to take it in on the way. Among the canons present was Henry Chadwick, a good friend of mine at Cambridge (his original University) till last autumn. He waited for me and took me to his house in Tom Quad where we talked for an hour so I didn't get to the river at all. [Henry Chadwick returned to Cambridge in 1979 as Regius Professor of Divinity.]
  I have just lunched "on" Idris at the Randolph. He enquired after you and I gave him your warm regards. You asked me if I would tell him about us. I didn't think I should have the courage to do so yet but when he asked me questions about the Vicarage I told him and he said he was delighted. He said he'd thought about it last March when he saw us together and thought how delightful it would be . . .
  You know my Rooster spelling is ffreddy? Idris says I should now spell it ffffreddy – ff for Freddy, f for "felix" and f for "fortunatus".
  Much love, darling,
    Freddy.

Tuesday 14 July
10 years' mind of Muriel's mother. Betty Birks came to lunch. She tells me that she and Humphrey Playford are getting married.

~ 1959 ~

Friday 24 July
South Mymms.

> [The Clares had insisted that FB should not vacate his room at the Vicarage and they also invited Frederic Raby to stay the night at the Vicarage as he was to be best man at his marriage to Muriel the next morning.]

Saturday 25 July
A glorious day. At 7 a.m. served E. P. Clare at Mass. At 8 a.m. got married. 8.45 a.m. Nuptial celebration of the Eucharist at North Mymms. After the wedding breakfast the six guests dispersed. We lunched at the Lantern Café and then went to Drury Lane to see *My Fair Lady*, the tickets being a present from Murie's friend and bridesmaid, Margaret Dawson.

> [As the newly married couple drove from South to North Mymms they were spotted by Flo Finch, the Vicarage's daily help, on her way to work. She was known as the village gossip and some said that if Flo didn't know about something it wasn't happening. "People are about early this morning, Vicar", she greeted him, "I've just seen Dr Brittain and Miss Cunnington in a car". "No, Flo, you haven't," EP replied. "Of course I have, I know them, known them all their lives". "No, Flo, you have seen Dr and Mrs Brittain, I've just married them", at which she let out a piercing shriek and dashed off to the village shop to spread the news]

Tuesday 18 August
David Peters [a Jesus man and History master at Nottingham High School] came to lunch. He had heard nothing of our marriage so I introduced Murie as my old landlady and said "She's just got married". David said, "Oh yes, well I hope she'll be very happy". To which I replied, "Yes, I hope so too. You see, she's married me". David went quite pale with shock and sat down abruptly. I said, "Have some sherry", but Murie said, "He looks as if he needs brandy". Later he said to me, "I hadn't seen her before but I know you couldn't have done better". Walter Wright [FB's solicitor and friend] came to tea in the garden. On leaving he said, "She's a peach".

Saturday 22 August
We gave a sherry party for about 40 people at Ingham Lodge.

Monday 24 August
Visited Eleanor Farjeon at No. 10 Perrins Walk, Hampstead and spent nearly an hour with her.

~ 1959 ~

[Eleanor Farjeon was born in 1881 and was the author of many books and also plays with her brother Herbert. The visit was in response to the following letter, which FB received after Eleanor had read Sheepish.]

20 Perrins Walk, N.W.3.
Dec. 4th 1958

Dear Dr Brittain,

Ba? Baa.

In other words, I'm doing nicely and can't complain, though I shan't be clear of wheezing until [these] fogs stop coming and going. I needn't tell you how one settles down hopefully at night during convalescence, and wakes knowing, before one sees, that there's mist in the air again. But all the same, BAA.

Don Carnero tickled me risibly: I needed the vocabulary, for I've never known a sheep really well. Goats (which I unBiblically prefer), and cats in profusion. A Tortoise, which never spoke but knew whenever I was lunching on lettuce in the garden. Sundry dogs belonging to others, because my cats wouldn't let me. A lion-cub who conversed with me by telephone. But never a sheep.

Perhaps if I'd walked Ridge Hill instead of Amberley Mount I should have met the talking breed.

If ever the keenest of Edward Thomas fans is in London, I'd love to ask him to come to Hampstead for an hour. I scarcely go out now, and my days of going away are over I think, but my corner of Hampstead is worth seeing for its own sake, a hayloft adjacent to an ancient Right of Way which I happen to own; and I can plant apricots and gooseberries along the edges as long as I leave three-feet of path down the middle for Sir Frank Soskice to walk on. And if you happen not to talk in cat-tongue, I will send Mr. Benignus Malone out to the Cherry tree Robert Frost plucked a green cherry from when he was here last year in June, and carried back with him to Vermont. Did you meet him that month, I wonder, when his Honours were falling thick upon him. I asked him how many American Universities had bestowed degrees on him. "Oh – about thirty." "I hope they gave you something nice to remember them by." "Oh, I got something very pretty to remember them by! You see, over here they just give you a Hat. But there you get a little silk hood, all of different colours. Now I've had those thirty hoods cut up and made into a very pretty crazywork quilt."

That story will come into Book Four, if I live till I'm ninety.

Well, might you come next June and pick a green cherry?

Yours always,
(signed) Eleanor Farjeon

~ 1959 ~

Tuesday 1 September
Murie and I went by car to Godinton.

[Part of the Brittains' honeymoon was spent at Godinton Park, the stately Kentish home near Ashford of FB's former pupil Alan Wyndham Green. As soon as they got inside the park gates they stopped the car and FB dressed Muriel up as a nun. They then drove up to the front of the house. Leaving her in the car FB got out, fetched Alan to the door and told him that Muriel had not been able to come after all. "However", he said, "I haven't come alone. You remember the two nuns who came with me last year?" "I should think I do", he answered, laughing. "Well", I said, "one of them has come again this year – Sister Monica". He looked up and there Sister Monica apparently was, looking very demure at the steering wheel of the car. He grasped the situation after a few seconds, but afterwards he generally addressed Muriel as Sister Monica whenever they went to Godinton.]

Friday 25 September
Attended a meeting of the Girls' High School Council at St Albans. We decided to abolish the boarding houses.

Monday 5 October
Cambridge. The Fellows' wives came to dinner with Murie and myself in the Prioress's Room. At the gathering in my rooms afterwards inscribed silver candlesticks were presented to Murie and me.

Thursday 8 October
There was a meeting in Chapel to elect a Master. D. L. Page was elected at the second vote.

[Denys Lionel Page, an Oxford man, became Regius Professor of Greek at Cambridge in 1950 and retained the Chair on becoming an active and sympathetic Master of Jesus. With his wife, Katie, he made the Lodge a centre of social life as well as taking a great interest in sport. A Fellow of the British Academy, he was President from 1971 to 1974 and was the first master of the College to receive a knighthood. He died in 1978. In the weeks following his election Professor Page was wont to complain jocularly that no one was interested that Jesus had a new Master; all they could talk about was that Freddy Brittain had got married.]

Sunday 11 October
Murie's three months' leave from the hospital ended today. She left for home, weepy.

~ 1959 ~

Friday 16 October
Attended Dad's funeral at Garston crematorium at which I assisted E. P. Clare.

Saturday 24 October
My birthday and Murie came up for the weekend. We had a sherry party; the Master and Mrs Page stayed to dinner.

Thursday 3 December
Went to Liverpool Street where Murie met me. We dined at 81 Ashley Gardens with Sir William and Lady Haley plus Mr and Mrs Iolo Williams, Sir James and Lady Mann, Sir Douglas and Lady Logan and Sir Oliver and Lady Franks.

> [Sir William Haley was Editor of the *Times*. He was later elected an Honorary Fellow of Jesus. Sir Douglas Logan was Principal of the University of London 1948–75. Sir Oliver Franks, later Baron Franks, OM, was British ambassador at Washington at the time. He was Provost of Worcester College, Oxford 1962–76 and Chancellor of East Anglia University 1965–84.]

Monday 14 December
Henry Batten [FB's GP] called and ordered me into the Evelyn Hospital where I stayed until 2 January with bronchitis, asthma and pneumonia.

> [He was so ill that Muriel was allowed to stay in the Evelyn with him; thus their first Christmas was spent in hospital. Their usual hundreds of Christmas cards arrived and were duly hung up on strips so that no inch of wall in FB's room was visible.]

[No further entries for December]

~ 1960 ~

> [Henry Batten had decreed that, in view of the seriousness of FB's illness, he should spend the worst of the winter in a warm climate. The Brittains decided to take a cruise to Madeira and Teneriffe, spending about ten days in each place. Muriel resigned her job at the Westminster Children's Hospital and they sailed on the Greek Line ship QSS Arkadia on

~ 1960 ~

5 February. Madeira was luscious and green – bouganvillea cascaded everywhere – which was not surprising in view of the heavy rainfall. In spite of the weather, they explored Funchal, the capital, on foot and in a bullock sledge. They visited the Museum of Sacred Art, the Cathedral and had tea near the statue of Henry the Navigator. Taking a taxi to Monte and the Balcony, they returned by toboggan over the cobblestones.]

Monday 15 February
We went to Camera de Lobos where a small girl took us round the church, which was decorated with hundred of arums and other flowers for the feast of N. S. de Fatima. In the afternoon we went to Machico and on leaving the church saw the pathetic funeral procession of an infant coming up the path, the grief-stricken young father carrying the small white coffin himself.

Monday 22 February
Arrived at Teneriffe to stay at the Hotel Mencey at Santa Cruz – we have a top floor room with a grand view of the town and the hills behind.

Friday 26 February
Went by bus to Puerto de la Cruz and lunched at Hotel Taora. We were back by 6 p.m., tearing along scores of hairpin bends with no wall between us and a 500-ft drop.

Sunday 28 February
Attended the Anglican Church service conducted by a Lay Reader, then to Mass at the church of La Concepcion. Two vernacular hymns were sung by a choir of women and girls, the first to Dykes *Horbury* – d r ms s fm, m.rm f m, mll s f m, and the second to L. Bourgeois's melody for Psalm 42 in the Genevan Psalter 1551 – lld-r m-r dt ts, d-r-m f m r d. ll m m s fm rm.

[While in Santa Cruz they overheard the following story. A very rough Rugby player arrived at the pearly gates and, trembling, replied to St Peter's question about his occupation on earth: "I played Rugby for Hull Kingston Rovers". "Come right in, lad", said St Peter, "We can do with thee, we're playing 'ell tomorrer".]

Tuesday 1 March
Visited Oratava, Icod with its Dragon tree hundreds of years old.

Thursday 3 March
With six others we went by car to Esperanza. Amazing views all along the main ridge of the island with wonderful views towards both seas thousands of feet below. Los Azulejas, Llano de Ucanca with its volcanic rocks, Villaflor,

Medano (on the south coast where we lunched), Grandadilla again, Guimar, Condelaria and home about 6.15 p.m.

Saturday 5 March
It is very hot and we stayed round the town all day. News reached us that Dorothy Philpot died yesterday. RIP.

> [News of national interest also reached them on this trip. The waiter at their hotel in Madeira had expressed surprise when FB asked for a local paper. "But it is in Portuguese, Sir". "Yes", said FB "that's why I want it". One day, while reading it, he suddenly shouted "Good Heavens! I don't believe it. It *can't* be". Muriel of course, unable to read Portuguese, begged: "What? Tell me". "Well I never. Tony Armstrong-Jones is engaged to Princess Margaret". Lord Snowdon, as he became, had come up to Jesus College in 1948 to read Architecture but he lost interest in his course and, determined to become a photographer, he was asked to leave. As he had done for so many others before (and since), FB pleaded for him to be allowed to stay up but could not persuade the College authorities. Before going Tony had called to say goodbye and FB had said to him, "My advice to you is, don't be in a hurry to get married". When recounting this interview later FB would end, "So you see he took my advice. He waited many years and then married a princess". Perhaps it was just as well that FB did not live long enough to see the break-up of the Royal marriage.]

Monday 7 March
We left Tenerife on board the Arkadia at 2 a.m. and on waking found we were at Las Palmas in Grand Canary. Took a taxi to Tafira, Sta Brigida (glorious road lined with geraniums, interspersed with bouganvillea) and Caldera de Bandana where we looked down into the crater. Back at the city we attended part of Vespers in the Cathedral and left at 6 p.m.

Tuesday 8 March
Out of sight of land all day.

Wednesday 9 March
Tied up at Casablanca and spent the day shopping and sightseeing in the Law Courts at Place de la Mosquee.

> [They left in the evening and on the way home passed Cape St Vincent, Cape Finistere and Ushant – reminiscent of FB's voyages during the First World War. On their last night on board FB's breathing became very bad and the ship's surgeon administered adrenalin, as did his own GP when they arrived home. Gradually he recovered and spent the rest of the

~ 1960 ~

vacation working on his *Penguin Book of Latin Verse*, entertaining numerous visitors at Ingham Lodge and driving with Muriel round the villages of Hertfordshire. At Tewin they visited Alexander Nairne's grave, which reminded FB of the stories Nairne used to tell of his experiences as a parish priest at Tewin. On one occasion a member of his congregation came to him in a great state because her neighbour had "called her all the b's". Nairne was puzzled by this phrase but on reflection decided that the woman was telling him that her neighbour had sworn at her. "So I said to her, next time this happens, just go back into your house and shut the door" and she replied, "Thank you, Rector, I will." Continuing the story Nairne said, "After she had gone I thought about this curious expression for some time and decided that she must have been referring to swear words all beginning with the letter B. But, do you know, that try as I might, I could only think of *three*". The thought of the saintly Nairne racking his brains to think of swear words beginning with B kept the Combination Room amused for a long time.]

Monday 18 April
Easter Monday. Back to Cambridge and started moving from C staircase to 13 Chapel Court.

[Derek Taunt, Fellow of the College and University Lecturer in Mathematics, had kindly offered to exchange rooms with FB in order that he might be on the first floor instead of the second and on an easier staircase. There were, of course, no women resident in the College so Muriel slept at 7 Malcolm Street.]

Wednesday 27 April
Attended Chapel at 8 a.m. and in the afternoon took Murie to the Boathouse. Went to a dinner in the Prioress's Room in the evening with Alan Hill of Heinemann's as host to celebrate the publication of the revised *History of Jesus College* (by Gray and Brittain). Five undergraduates came in to sing afterwards and I had to sing 'You've got a long way to go'. The singers came to my rooms and stayed till midnight.

Sunday 1 May
Chapel at 8 a.m. followed by Mattins at 10.30 a.m. and Litany. A short Roost and sherry party was held in my rooms at which Murie was confirmed in her office as Deaness etc.

Wednesday 4 May
Attended the Examiners' meeting for Tripos Part I. Murie and strolled at Trinity among the double cherry blossom in its prime.

~ 1960 ~

Tuesday 7 June
Watched the boats from the Pike and Eel, Chesterton, then went to Muriel Bradbrook's sherry party at Girton. Dined in the Jesus Fellows' Guest Room as guest of the Eclectics; John Smith, John Morrison, Fraser Alexander, Colin Tully, John Turner, Ian Streat and Clive Oxley.

Thursday 9 June
On duty as Steward in the Senate House at the Honorary Degree ceremony for Boris Ord, etc.

Wednesday 10 August
Worked on the *Penguin Book of Latin Verse* [as all this vacation]. Dined at Bishop's College, Cheshunt and talked to them on "A Layman looks at the Church".

Saturday 13 August
Murie finished her locum at Clare Hall [the chest hospital in South Mimms] at lunchtime and started one at Beynon's pharmacy at Potters Bar in the afternoon.

Monday 29 August
Margaret Dawson took the typescript of the Penguin Book to the publishers.

Tuesday 6 September
Went to Broadcasting House in London for a rehearsal at 11.15 a.m. and then recording of my talk on "My Grandfather" for broadcast.

Thursday 8 September
Today was one of the few fine days we have had this summer. Murie and I went to St Albans and through Luton to Clophill where we looked at the delightful little River Flitt from its bridge and went into the church, which seems to hum with activity. We went through Maulden to Ampthill where we lunched at the White Hart and then called on Sir Albert Richardson who was leaving for Greece at 3 p.m. but very kindly insisted on taking us round his house.

Friday 16 September
We dined with Zelie Timins at the Rotary House Hotel, Marylebone and then went to *Das Rheingold* at Covent Garden Opera House.

Friday 23 September
Saw *The Trials of Oscar Wilde* at the Regal Cinema, New Barnet.

~ 1960 ~

Sunday 25 September
Staying with Alan Wyndham Green at Godinton. We went to the Sung Eucharist at Canterbury Cathedral and talked to the organist, S. Campbell, after the service. *Generations* and *Nations* were sung with "shons" instead of "ci-ons" by order of the Chapter, he told me.

["Ci-ons" were FB's 'betes noires' so this pleased him greatly.]

Wednesday 28 September
Went to the Old Elizabethans Annual Dinner (at which I was guest of honour) at the Salisbury Hotel, Barnet. Michael Fairey [an Elizabethan and a Jesuan] proposed my health. I suppose I took 15-20 minutes in my reply.

Thursday 29 September
Murie and I went to Cambridge for the first Ladies' Night. Had sherry at the Lodge, dinner in Hall, then sitting out in the Prioress's Room and dancing in the Master's dining room.

[The College Council had decided that the presence of Fellows' wives should be recognised by an official function, which replaced the Freddy Feast.]

Friday 30 September
Murie ran me to Simpson's-in-the-Strand for the JCCS Annual Meeting and Dinner with the new Master in the Chair. I spoke later in response to cries of "Freddy" and included the story "We're playing 'ell tomorrow". Eric Abbott waited afterwards to meet Murie when she came to pick me up and after a few minutes talk we drove him home.

Monday 3 October
The Rev Peter Baelz, the new Dean of Jesus, [afterwards Professor of Moral and Pastoral Theology at Oxford and later Dean of Durham] was admitted to his Fellowship with toasts afterwards in the Combination Room..

[The Rev Barry Till had vacated the deanship for that of Hong Kong.]

[No further entries for 1960]

~ 1961 ~

Monday 2 January
In bed this week with bronchitis. Preparing lectures later

> [FB had repeated attacks of bronchitis this term but between them he continued lecturing, supervising, dining and entertaining as much as ever.]

Saturday 21 January
Cambridge. We gave a sherry party, which included Leslie Fielding and an Iraqui.

> [Leslie was an Old Elizabethan who rose to a high position in the Diplomatic Service. In 1987 he was made Vice-Chancellor of Sussex University.]

Wednesday 1 February
Miss Constance Babington-Smith came to lunch to talk about her edition of the letters of Rose Macaulay.

Saturday 18 February
South Mymms. Visited Highgate School. After coffee with C. H. Benson we went with him to inspect S. T. Coleridge's tomb and to see the Headmaster. Gerard Lang called in the late evening and found me much better than a week ago.

> [Dr Lang was FB's GP when he was at home. They shared the same interests and became close friends.]

Good Friday 31 March
We listened to my recorded broadcast talk "Steve Fairbairn" and at 2 p.m. to a service broadcast from Great St Mary's, Cambridge.

Saturday 1 April
On television I watched Cambridge (despite all the prophets) defeat Oxford easily in the boat race.

~ 1961 ~

Easter Monday 3 April
Nature is *very* forward – several weeks before time. Our cherry tree below the lawn is in perfect bloom.

> [This tree, planted early in the century, survived until one of the great gales in 1989.]

Tuesday 5 April
Working at my broadcast script on "May Week in Cambridge".

Thursday 20 April
Cambridge. Raymond Williams came to breakfast.

> [Raymond Williams had just been elected a Fellow of Jesus College and became Professor of Drama at Cambridge University in 1974. When FB died his will stated that the next Fellow of the College to proceed Litt.D should have his best scarlet gown. He had two, one for ceremonial occasions in the Senate House and one for feasts, in case soup got spilt on it. Raymond Williams was the next Fellow to become Litt.D and he was pleased to accept the gown. On his death in 1988 his widow, Joy, kindly agreed to a similar arrangement enabling the gown to be inherited by Geoffrey Harcourt, Fellow of the College since 1982, and a Socialist like FB and Raymond Williams. The "apostolic succession" thus continued.]

Friday 28 April
Writing obituaries for the Jesus College Annual Report. At 4.30 p.m. Murie and I went to King's Cliffe for the celebration of the bi-centenary of William Law's death. It was very well done with an excellent sermon delivered by Owen Chadwick.

> [William Law (1686–1761) ordained in 1711, was the publisher and author of the *Serious Call to a Devout and Holy Life*. He declined to take the oaths of allegiance to George I. He published the first of his practical treatises on Christian perfection in 1726, founded a school for fourteen girls at King's Cliffe the following year and retired to King's Cliffe in 1740. The Law family was still living in the house opposite the church in the 20th century. Muriel's father's family had lived at Cliffe for generations and their, and FB's, old friend Charles Blake had come from there to work at Ingham Lodge in 1901. He had previously worked for the man he described as "old Tommy Law". In early May, while staying at Clopton Manor with Tiny and Dame Mitchell, the Brittains went to church at King's Cliffe where the Rector showed them the Cunnington tombs in the churchyard and entries in the parish registers.]

Ascension Day, Thursday 11 May
Attended the Sung Eucharist (Byrd's five-part Mass) at King's. We picked up Frederic Raby and Dorothy Whitelock on the way. [The three doctors were in their scarlet gowns]. There was a coffee party in my rooms afterwards, which included various undergraduates and five ladies from Brookmans Park. This became a sherry party, followed by lunch in the Prioress's Room plus John and Blanche Grimes [the Archdeacon of Northampton and his wife], Professors Walter Ullman and Muriel Bradbrook, and Dorothy Whitelock. Then we all went to the University Sermon at which the preacher was David Isitt.

Wednesday 17 May
Cambridge. Gave my last lecture as University Lecturer. [FB had just passed the retirement age of sixty-seven.]

Friday 19 May
Recorded my talk on May Week at the BBC, which will be broadcast on 28 May. Lunched at the BBC Club with Mrs Capel, the producer of all three talks.

Saturday 20 May
Murie and I dined with the Vice-Chancellor and Mrs Herbert Butterfield at Peterhouse Lodge. Also present were Philip and Mrs Sinker, Professor and Mrs Mansergh, Miss Megaw, W. Sartorin and wife, P. R. Baelz and A. K Cragg (tomorrow's University Preacher).

Tuesday 23 May
Murie and I went by car to Oxford to attend Hugh Lloyd Jones's inaugural lecture as Regius Professor of Greek.

[Hugh Lloyd Jones had been a Fellow of Jesus College, Cambridge from 1948–1954.]

Wednesday 24 May
Oxford. Walked round the town to Blackwells [bookshop] etc. in the morning then watched the Eights from the Jesus barge. Attended Evensong at the Cathedral and dined with Denys Wilkinson at Christ Church.

[Christ Church, known to all at Oxford University as "The House" was jocularly called "The Hovel" by FB. A member was once quite offended by this. "Some *hovel*", he said.]

Wednesday 31 May
Murie and I went to Saffron Walden and lunched at the Training College. We then went on to Newport, Quendon, Stocking Pelham, Brent Pelham, Great Hormead, Hare Street, Braughing, Puckeridge, Wadesmill, Bengeo, Essendon and home to South Mymms. It was a most lovely ride.

Thursday 1 June
South Mymms. The South Mymms Women's Institute paid their annual visit to Ingham Lodge. I talked to them about a Cambridge don's life.

Monday 5 June
Cambridge. Attended Chapel at 8 a.m. and Court of Twerpery at noon. [A Roosters committee meeting.] At 4.20 p.m. I attended a meeting of the College Council and at 8.30 p.m. the Annual Dinner of the CU Heraldic Society. [FB was its Treasurer.]

Tuesday 6 June
Went to the CU OTC wine and cheese party in St John's Wilderness and on to the madrigals on Trinity Backs for a little while.

Wednesday 21 June
At the College Council I was re-elected Praelector and Keeper of the Records.

[On 2 July FB suffered a coronary thrombosis and was in Potters Bar Hospital until 13 August. At first he said he couldn't go to hospital as he and Muriel were leaving for Henley Regatta in a few days! Then, when he began to feel better, he asked if he could write as he had intended to spend the vacation bringing the *Jesus College Boat Club History* up to date. In 1961 six weeks' bed rest was the treatment for his condition and the request was refused. Not to be beaten, he asked if he could dictate and this was allowed. All the relevant Minute Books were obtained and Muriel spent every day in FB's hospital room writing down names and weights of crews and results. The staff, on looking in, would be amazed to hear FB saying, "Lady Margaret bumped Sidney", or "Jesus IV was bumped by Christ's III", and would beat a hasty retreat. The whole exercise proved to be wonderful occupational therapy and the history was completed more quickly than it would have been if FB had not been ill.]

Thursday 17 August
We drove through the Lower Village and along the old coach road lingering by the field of golden-brown wheat ready to cut, magnificent with silvery oats

behind and clover behind that. The late summer wild flowers are lovely everywhere.

Wednesday 30 August
We went to St Albans, Sandridge, Coleman's Green and the ford over the Lea below Wheathampstead – a most beautiful and glorious sight in the bright sun; then on to visit the church at Ayot St Peter, and to the ford over the Mimram.

Thursday 31 August
G. Lang brought Dr Hayward, a cardiologist, to see me. He gave a good report and advice about the future.

Saturday 30 September
Lunched at West Hill, Highgate with Paul, Ruth and Martin Sinker.

> [Paul Sinker, a Fellow of Jesus College from 1927 to 1949, joined the Treasury after the war and became Head of the Civil Service Commission and Director-General of the British Council. He was made CB, KCMG, and an Honorary Fellow of the College. He died in 1977.]

Tuesday 17 October
Went to Ely for the St Etheldreda's Day procession and Sung Eucharist in the Cathedral with the Bishop celebrating. It was splendid, with the Cathedral robin joining in at the top of his voice and perched on the top point of the cross over the choir screen.

Saturday 4 November
Cambridge. Gillie Potter and four friends called. Professor and Mrs Gombrich came to lunch before I presented Professor Gombrich for his ex-officio MA.

> [Ernst Hans Joseph Grombrich, the Austrian-born British art historian, was Slade Professor of Fine Art at Cambridge from 1961–63 and was elected an Honorary Fellow of Jesus in 1963. He was Director of the Warburg Institute and Professor of the History of the Classical Tradition in the University of London from 1959 until he retired in 1976. FBA and FSA, he was knighted in 1972. His books include *The Story of Art* (1950), *Art and Illusion* (1960) – an influential study of the psychology of pictorial representation, and *The Sense of Order* (1979).]

Sunday 19 November
A Rooster "Hen Party" was held in East House, which was excellently decorated for the occasion.

[There were no female Roosters until the College admitted women in 1979 but they were invited to the annual Breakfast-at-Lunchtime in May week and to a hen party, usually held during the Michaelmas Term.]

Thursday 23 November
In the Combination Room after Hall, P. Gardner-Smith, whose wife had been dead for about a year said, "Would you be very shocked if I told you that I was going to marry again." I replied, "Not at all. I congratulate you. Do I know the lady?" "Know her?" said Gardner-Smith, "Of course you know her. She's out of the same stable – my wife's niece".

Friday 24 November
Murie and I attended Evensong at King's where we saw the Rubens painting for the first time.

[The large Nativity, later so familiar over the high altar in the Chapel, was at first placed in the nave against the choir screen.]

Thursday 30 November
Murie and I went to P. Gardner-Smith's wedding at St Mark's Church, Cambridge.

[It was an unusual wedding. The bride arrived first accompanied by her uncle, who, after the ceremony, invited the entire congregation to go into the vestry. When the registers had been signed the happy pair walked down the aisle, not arm-in-arm but with the bridegroom slightly in front, or "leading the bride by a canvas", as some rowing onlooker expressed it! Elizabeth née Leeke, gave Perks, as she called him, more than twenty years of happily married life and nursed him devotedly when he became frail in body, though he was razor-sharp in mind until his death in 1985 at the age of ninety-seven.]

Saturday 2 December
The Fairbairn Dinner-Dance was held at the University Arms Hotel. It was a most enjoyable evening.

[No further entries for December]

~ 1962 ~

Monday 1 January
South Mymms. There is 12 inches of snow everywhere.

Sunday 7 January
Went to Mattins at North Mymms. The Colne is in full deep stream at Water End, both above and below the swallow holes and sweeping wide under the bridges by North Mymms church.

Monday 8 January
The snow had gone this morning and everything is green.

Tuesday 16 January
A meeting was held in our library at Ingham Lodge to consider publication of a joint history of Potters Bar Urban District.

Friday 26 January
Cambridge. James Owen, the new Chaplain dined with me. His first remark was, "I have heard a lot about you from Katharine and Victor Ross".

> [Canon James Owen, a Trinity Hall man, had served a curacy at the London church attended by Allen Hay's eldest daughter Katharine and her husband. He went on from Jesus to become Chaplain of Nottingham University and then returned to Cambridge as Vicar of St Mary-the-Less.]

Thursday 8 February
Peter Anson arrived to stay with us at Holbrook Road. [The Brittains were using Miss Skillicorn's and Dr Sargent's house while the ladies were abroad.] At 8.30 there was a meeting in the Prioress's Room to discuss Communion of Non-Conformists in Chapel.

Monday 12 February
South Mymms. At last there are snowdrops in masses in the garden but only one aconite.

> [The following, cut out of *The Lady* magazine and date unknown, was found in FB's desk after he died.]

See the choir boy aconite, singing in the snow
A carol to the newborn light, with golden head aglow
Merry, innocent and tough, and round his head a ruff
(Stephanie Gifford)

Wednesday 7 March
Cambridge. We slept at 2 Maids Causeway for the first time.

[The Brittains were now renting the College house on the corner of the Four Lamps roundabout at the end of Jesus Lane.]

Thursday 15 March
Received a letter from Tom Langton to say that enough money has been received to start printing the *Jesus College Boat Club History*. Chris Schneider, Miles Roberts, Mark Moreton and John Nash all came to lunch as they are helping Murie to paint the rooms at 2 Maids Causeway. After lunch we went to Long Reach and saw A. V. Cooke win the final of the Fairbairn Junior Sculls.

[Arnold Cooke became an oarsman of world-wide repute.]

Friday 16 March
The Commemoration of Benefactors service in Chapel followed by the Feast in Hall. Afterwards went to Pars's rooms where I sang, in costume, 'We nuns of St Radegund', 'The Sound of the old Chapel Bell', 'The Tri-tripos' and 'Save a little one for me'.

Wednesday 18 April
I was overhauled by Dr Hayward in Harley Street. He gave a very encouraging report. We went on to St Vedast's Rectory, Foster Lane, EC, where we lunched with C. B. Mortlock in his delightful house and then looked into the church, superbly restored in the most admirable taste by Dykes Bower.

[It had been bombed during World War II and was going to be reconsecrated the following week.]

Thursday 19 April
My *Penguin Book of Latin Verse* was published today and the Times had its third leader on it.

This Ageless Language
"Neither should it be forgotten" wrote POPE JOHN XXIII in his recent constitution *Veterum Sapientia*, "that Latin has a noble and

characteristic conformation, a concise, varied and harmonious style, full of majesty and dignity, which contributes singularly to clarity and solemnity." His encomium prefaces a reassertion of the place of Latin in the life and work of the Roman Catholic Church, and it does not allude, naturally enough, to those features of the language which serve no ecclesiastical purpose. Some of what the Pope omits to mention the Penguin manages to suggest, for the anthology of Latin verse issued today under that imprint shows how this ageless language clothes more than the Roman virtues ancient or modern; how its modulations encompass the ardours or languors of profane love, the misanthropy of satire, the harsh accents of scurrility: how it entertains the vernal venery of the *Cras amet* . . ., the compact intricacies of medieval hymnody, and the glorious anger of the twelfth-century "Archpoet", who wrote what is perhaps the greatest of all songs of genius's defiance to the culture that nourished it; how a theme or even an image (like AUSONIUS'S of the falling rose as the paradigm of love's urgency) soars like a rocket to scatter over the literature of Europe its dissolving stars.

An anthology which begins with NAEVIUS (*fl.* Third century B.C.) and ends with ALLEN RAMSAY (*ob.* 1955) emphasizes the longevity as much as the variety of the language. Its longevity is perhaps exaggerated. The Renaissance for all its scholarship and excited reinstatement of the classical originals paradoxically marked the end of Latin's literary development and the end is nowhere more conspicuous than in verse. The poets migrated to the vernacular leaving Latin to the mercy of the verificators. Even with the *Gradusae Parnassum* the ascent became laborious and the labour was in vain for the heights were found to be untenated. No muse likes living at the top of a flight of steps. Latin verse became the preserve of learned dexterity, of scholarly *jeud' esprit*. Sometimes the exercises have a charming freshness, as in Henry Vaughan's little parable of the Salmon which is given in this collection. But neither invention nor inspiration has survived.

If the living tree, spreading its roots, exfoliating in unexpected places at unexpected season, has become mere timber, it does not on that account deserve to be cast aside. Timber has uses too. As POPE JOHN asserts, the rigidity of its forms and the loss of its capacity for spontaneous development make Latin in some respects a singularly appropriate language for doctrinal formulations and liturgical expression; while its neutrality is one point in its favour as a medium in which to conduct the central business of a universal church. Nor does its claim to secular consideration rest wholly on the genius of the writers who have informed it. It is still the best instrument for the study of European culture in depth. Its cadences echo backwards and forwards in time, penetrating layer upon layer of European consciousness, exhibiting the turmoil and the continuity of the tradition, like the stones of the Eternal City from which its influence sprang.

Easter Day, Sunday 22 April
South Mymms. Went to church at 11 a.m. and a silver wafer box was dedicated in memory of Frederick Roland White. I gave a preliminary short address from the chancel step.

Monday 30 April
Cambridge. Went to Bertram Mills Circus on Midsummer Common and talked to Bernard Mills in his caravan. As usual he couldn't (or wouldn't) come to dine at High Table.

> [Bernard Mills was an old member of the College but on none of his annual visits to Cambridge had FB been able to persuade him to dine in Hall.]

Monday 14 May
South Mymms. The apple blossom at Ingham Lodge is in its prime, also milkmaids and narcissi in the paddock where our newly planted weeping willows are showing leaf. The limes along the Barnet-St Albans Road are a most beautiful, vivid light green. The bluebells in Rectory Lane [Shenley] are a "sun-lit water", and there are great masses of stitchwort everywhere.

Thursday 17 May
Gerard Lang drove me back to Cambridge as he was coming to the Rustat Feast as my guest. Plumb of Christ's College sat on my right and C. H. Dodd was facing me. We used the Upper Hall for the first time after a feast.

Tuesday 22 May
The New Building Appeal Committee was held in the Master's Lodge. [The new building became North Court.] At 3.30 p.m. Peter Pilkington [later successively Headmaster of the King's School, Canterbury and St Paul's School] arrived with thirty-seven of his Mothers' Union from Bakewell for a tour of the College and tea. [FB said to Muriel on seeing them approach 13 Chapel Court, "Here's Peter and his Bakewell tarts".] Took Murie to dine at the Union after which we listened to the debate.

Thursday 24 May
Eustace Tillyard [former Master] died this morning. I was kept busy at the telephone, etc. arranging details of the funeral at the Master's request. At 8.45 p.m. Murie and I went to a "Swarry" for junior graduates at the Lodge.

Monday 28 May
Bruce Sparks was admitted to his Fellowship in Chapel.

~ 1962 ~

[Bruce Sparks was the College's first Director of Studies in Geography and became successively Steward, Senior Tutor and Financial and Tutor for Admissions. His success can be measured by the examination results during his time, which were the best for many years. On the financial side he seemed to enjoy dealing with tutorial accounts and found pleasure in finding resources for undergraduates on a tight budget. He was an amateur cabinet maker of outstanding ability and he had a delight in, and an encyclopaedic knowledge of, all types of wood. He died in 1988.]

Tuesday 29 May
I was on duty in Chapel as usher at Eustace Tillyard's funeral, after which we went round the Courts. The coffin was wheeled through each of the College courts in turn with Stephen Tillyard and the Fellows walking behind.

[The retiring age for Masters having been introduced, the custom of wheeling the Master's coffin round the College was extended to the funeral of a former Master in this case, but was not continued when Sir Denys Page died in Northumberland in 1978. It was revised for Professor David Crighton's funeral in 2000.]

Ascension Day, Thursday 31 May
[The usual "Scarlet Brigade", Dr Frederic Raby, Professor Muriel Bradbrook, etc. plus some undergraduates went to the Sung Eucharist at King's. At lunch they were joined by a Mr & Mrs B., an Australian couple. Mr B. announced that they had been to Stratford and seen "A Midnight Summer's Dream", adding weightily "I don't know about you people here but for me Shakespeare is one of the immortals". Muriel Bradbrook, Professor of English and an authority on Shakespeare, said quietly, "Yes, Mr B. I'm inclined to agree with you".]

Wednesday 6 June
South Mymms. The oaks are all gold with catkins. Dined with Alan and Enid Hill at the Garrick Club. Jimmy Doggart came up and spoke to us in the lounge before dinner. He was in a party of members of the Club who had just returned from Epsom, it being Derby Day.

Wednesday 13 June
Cambridge. Went with George Cockram [a friend from the FB's World War I days aboard the hospital ship *Egypt*], his wife and two Canadians to the Jesus Paddock and saw the 1st and 2nd division races on the river. Our first boat started second, at Ditton it was about its distance behind Lady Margaret, and Trinity was only about ½ - ¾ length behind us but we went Head at Morley's

~ 1962 ~

Holt. Drove round the Backs and had the Cockrams to dinner, they then left for Ely and Scotland.

Friday 15 June
Went to the Paddock and saw our first boat row over Head. Met Mrs Sully (née Evans) whom I had coached when she was in the Newnham boat.

Saturday 16 June
Had a sherry party in my rooms for graduates, took them to lunch in Hall and at 2 p.m. presented them for degrees. They included S. S. Prawer who was proceeding Litt.D.

> [S. S. Prawer became Taylor Professor of German Language and Literature at Oxford and a Fellow of The Queen's College in 1969.]

Monday 18 June
Watched the "Crocket" match between the Roosters and the Boat Club on the Close. At 2.45 p.m., with about 40 persons on board, the Viscountess Bury launch left for Clayhithe and we had tea at Fen Ditton Barn on the way back. John Nash provided entertainment most of the time with his "tough" achievements, e.g. catching hold of the bridges as we passed under and swinging from them before dropping back into the stern of the boat. It was a very enjoyable outing.

Tuesday 19 June
Conducted a tour of the College this morning. Presided at the May Ball Committee sherry party and dinner and went to the Ball at 10 p.m. There was a midnight Roost in my rooms with every inch of floor space and standing room occupied. Peter Mitchell-Heggs and Ian Fergusson were made Companions of the Red Herring and Simon Banks was installed as President.

Friday 22 June
Attended Evensong for Readers at St Lawrence Jewry in the City at which seven new Readers were admitted. Bishop Lunt of Stepney delivered the sermon. It is a most beautiful church very recently restored. Afterwards we had coffee in Grocers' Hall.

Monday 25 June
Staying at the South Strand Hotel, Angmering-on-Sea. Called to see Chippy MacDonald later [a shipmate from World War I days].

~ 1962 ~

Tuesday 26 June
Emma Gordon drove us in her Jaguar to Chichester Cathedral where we admired the recently replaced medieval stone choir screen. After tea we went to Kingston Manor and selected some furniture which Emma has given us for 2 Maids Causeway.

Tuesday 3 July
Arrived at the Red Lion Hotel, Henley for the Regatta. It was very cold and I was glad to wear my thick winter black and scarlet cloak for the first two days, then it got warmer.

Tuesday 17 July
South Mymms. The lime blossom this year is perhaps the most abundant I have ever seen anywhere; the scent most delicious and the blossom so numerous that the trees look very lovely.

Thursday 26 July
The New South Mimms bypass opened today for the first time.

> [It was later up-graded and became the M25 motorway. Next day the Stevenage bypass opened and it became the A1.M.]

Monday 30 July
Murie started a fortnight's pharmacy locum duty at Clare Hall Hospital.

> [FB liked to tell friends that he sent Muriel out to work and he stayed at home and lived on her moral earnings.]

Bank Holiday, Monday 6 August
Opened the Annual Fete at Ridge, this year it was held in the field on the north side with a wonderful view of the church. Rain got heavier as the day progressed and the weather was very cold. Had to light a fire in the library to keep warm in the evening.

Monday 13 August
Went to Madam Tussaud's [Wax Works Museum]. Lunched at Hampstead, after which we went to Keats's House – delightful, it is kept in perfect condition, in a pretty garden. It was a perfect day for our first visit.

Wednesday 15 August
Went to Abinger Manor near Dorking to stay with Bob and Joy Clarke and Mary Clarke and her mother.

Thursday 16 August
Visited the "prehistoric dwelling" in the field below the Manor, after which we went to Thorpe's fine, big second-hand bookshop and the Cathedral in Guildford. Later went to Abinger church and to Wootton church to see the tomb of John Evelyn, the diarist.

[The Brittains spent their summer holiday in the West Country. At Nether Stowey they visited S. T. Coleridge's house and then went on to Minehead to stay with Percy Waters (another shipmate from FB's World War I days aboard the hospital ship *Egypt*), and his wife Mary. They visited the Dean and Mrs Thicknesse, who had retired from St Albans Abbey to Porlock, and had tea with Sir Harold and Lady Scott. Sir Harold was a Jesus man and the civil servant who had been involved in formulating the air raid precautions for Greater London during World War II. For the first part of the war he was Permanent Secretary to the Ministry of Aircraft Production. In 1945 he was made Commissioner of Police for the Metropolis and the smooth working of the Coronation of Queen Elizabeth II was mainly due to his skilful organization.]

Monday 24 September
South Mymms. Went by car to Sarratt Green and down the very long, steep hill to Sarratt Bottom. We soon came to a lane ending in a dead end. Then we climbed over a stile and came to a wooden bridge, two planks wide with one handrail, over the delightful, clear-flowing Chess. We sat at the mid-point of the bridge with our legs nearly touching the water for nearly an hour, eating our lunch and revelling in the river in its low meadows with wooded hills rising rapidly on each side.

Wednesday 26 September
Dined with John Whalley and family in New Barnet and then I spoke to the Church of England Men's Society on the origin and history of church customs, services and costume.

Monday 1 October
Cambridge. Nancy Eastham arrived today from France.

[Nancy Eastham was an American law student who became the Brittains' "lodger" at 2 Maids Causeway. While with them she met Frank Iacabucci, a Canadian of Italian parentage. They later married and had a charming family in Canada where Frank rose to great heights in legal circles, becoming a Justice of the Supreme Court of Canada. Nancy and Frank often returned to the UK for conferences etc. He never forgot the bread and cheese lunches they often shared with FB and Muriel when FB would say,

"We've got two kinds of bread, yesterday's and today's, which will you have?"]

Monday 15 October
Went to Clopton Church, Northants for a service followed by the burial of Tiny Mitchell's ashes in the churchyard. Had tea and dinner at the Manor House.

Thursday 18 October
Took the chair at the small Guildhall for the opening of St Clement's Bazaar by Murie, who was deputizing for Dame Mitchell.

> [FB pointed out that he really could not introduce Muriel, indeed he really should not speak to her himself, as they had never been properly introduced. He had first seen her at South Mymms when she was in her pram and her mother had said, "What do you think of my baby?" and he had been embarrassed and hurried on.]

Sunday 28 October
At 10.30 a.m. attended Mattins in Chapel. The choir was in cassocks for the first time (or rather the second as they started last night when I wasn't there.)

Sunday 4 November
Went to Evensong at Linton Parish church where the nave was completely full and both aisles largely so. There were thirty-eight men and boys in the choir and there was a procession at the end with two stations. It was all most moving and delightful.

> [This was the first of many visits to Linton church. The Brittains struck up a friendship with the Vicar, Father Harry Crichton who had started life as a carpenter and then became an officer in the Church Army. Turned down by five theological colleges on account of his lack of formal education, he persisted and was eventually ordained. He was a born parish priest and his services were a joy. After Linton Father Crichton went to Sevenoaks and finally to the glorious wool church at Lavenham, Suffolk. He died in retirement at Bury St Edmunds.]

Sunday 18 November
We attended the dedication of the new organ by the Bishop at St Albans Abbey. Afterwards we had tea at Peter Hurford's [organist at the Abbey.]

~ 1962 ~

Tuesday 27 November
Cambridge. Went to the Upper Hall to view Sir William Coldstream's portrait of the Master [Professor Sir Denys Page]. At the buffet luncheon, which followed, Gardner-Smith said, "Now we had better get a decent photograph taken of the Master so that future generations will know what he looked like".

Saturday 1 December
Innumerable callers all the morning made it impossible for me to get on with any work as I had hoped to do.

Saturday 8 December
Murie and I left Cambridge for home where the hall had been repainted white and the stairs carpeted in deep red. Went to the so-called "Santa Claus Fayre" in the Village Hall. It was very pleasant being greeted by many old friends.

Saturday 22 December
The Vicar and six choirboys came round playing carols on the handbells returned to the church after about fifty years absence. All came in for drinks and baked apples.

Monday 31 December
There is deep snow everywhere. Saw the New Year in in bed, and began it by giving Murie:
> A pinch and a punch for the first of the month
> A smack on your little Mary for the first of January
> A drop of water for the first of the quarter
> A box on the ear for the first of the year.

~ 1963 ~

Monday 4 February
Cambridge. There is thick snow and it is freezing hard. Went by car round the Backs where people were skating and walking on the river. Murie tried to go home to Mymms but were turned back by snowdrifts after Foxton.

Saturday 9 February
Held a sherry party for graduates etc. then presented Ian Stewart and others for their MA's.

[B. H. I. H. Stewart became a Conservative MP in 1974 and Economic Secretary to the Treasury in 1983. He was created Baron Stewartby of Portmoak in 1992.]

Sunday 17 February
Wrote a hundred New Building Appeal Letters.

[The College appeal for North Court was now in progress. FB wrote 1,600 individual letters by hand. He called it doing his knitting and whenever there was the prospect of a free half-hour with Muriel and her friends he would say, "Do you mind if I bring my knitting?" The letters brought in the requisite amount of money and also replies from old members delighted to hear from him and demanding news of their contemporaries, so that he had to write hundreds more in reply.]

Ash Wednesday 27 February
It thawed during the day and Midsummer Common became a big lake. There was a hard frost again at night. Finished reading [Thomas Hardy's] *Tess of the D'Urbervilles*, a very fine gripping novel revealing deep knowledge of human nature, much superior to *The Mayor of Casterbridge*.

Friday 15 March
The Commemoration of Benefactors Feast. The choir sang Grace from the balcony for the first time.

Thursday 21 March
Went to Putney for the unveiling of a memorial to Steve Fairbairn at the Mile Post by Viscount Bruce of Melbourne, followed by tea at the London Rowing Club.

Saturday 23 March
We joined a Hickie Borman and Co. tour at Victoria and went on the boat train arriving at Venice on Sunday morning.

Sunday 24 March
Had Breakfast at the Hotel Principe then to Low Mass with sermon at St Lucia nearby. Boarded the Yugoslav MC Jadran and put to sea at 2 p.m.

Monday 25 March
Arrived at Dubrovnic (Ragusa) a lovely medieval walled stone built town. There was not a fragment of litter to be seen anywhere. Everyone was obviously very well fed and clothed.

~ 1963 ~

Tuesday 26 March
Arrived at Corfu and went by horse cab round the town. Looked round and went into St Spiridious church

Wednesday 27 March
We had a very rough night at sea. Our porthole came open, the sea rushed in and the oranges we have been given (the size of footballs) flew about like cannon balls. The captain decided not to go on to Crete as intended but dropped anchor in harbour at Milos.

Friday 29 March
Arrived Crete (Heraklion) and visited Knossos in the morning. Went to the evening office at the church of St Nicholas, which was packed. A woman standing beside us crossed herself at least 400 times in 15 minutes, purely mechanically.

Saturday 30 March
We arrived at Rhodes and went ashore by ourselves. We took a bus along the seashore (the water was Cambridge and Oxford blue) with masses of flowers all the way (big yellow oxalis, red anemones, mimosa, pear blossom, almond blossom and judas trees in full bloom) to the little village of Paradeisi where the bus reached its terminus. At a little café, where we took coffee outside, we were given a great welcome by an unofficial Reception Committee. The people spoke only Greek except that the landlord spoke Italian. He and I talked in that language and he translated to the others. He borrowed the next door neighbour's superior WC for us to use and we were presented with carnations, freesias and two gigantic lemons. The village idiot was brought out and introduced to us. When we left the landlord charged an absurdly small sum for the coffee etc. which we had consumed and I had difficulty in getting him to accept more. He stopped the bus for us outside his house so that we did not have to walk the 80-100 yards to the proper stopping place.

Passion Sunday 31 March
Arrived at Mykonos and tied up. We walked round the beautiful clean, stone-built, completely white-painted town except for outside staircases in blue, green and red. Lunched on board ship and continued on to Tinos where we visited the Church of the three Hierophants and went to part of the Stations of the Cross at the Roman church.

Monday 1 April
We went ashore at Thasos and out into the attractive country with its loaded donkeys, sheep bells, hills and flowers. When we put to sea we passed close to

Mount Athos where we could see a number of its monasteries at fairly close quarters.

Thursday 4 April
It was a lovely day today. We arrived at Katakoto and went by coach to Olympia, its ruins were enveloped in masses of daisies, ox-eyes, asphodel, herb Robert and orange blossom.

Sunday 7 April
We experienced considerable roll in the Adriatic. Arrived at Venice and went to St Mark's for the latter part of Vespers with the Cardinal Patriarch presiding.

Holy Saturday 13 April
South Mymms. Went to see the Bishop in the Ramryge Chapel in St Albans Abbey then to Evensong and the blessing of the Easter Garden.

> [Bishop Michael Gresford-Jones was FB's Confessor to whom he went each year in preparation for his Easter Communion.]

Monday 22 April
Cambridge. We had sherry at Pop Prior's and dined at the Arts Theatre before seeing Peter Ustinov's *Photofinish*, a most original and brilliant play with first-class acting.

Saturday 18 May
Dined at the Commemoration Feast at Downing as the guest of Ilya Gershevitch and sat between him and Portway.

> [Colonel Donald Portway, CBE became Professor of Chemical Engineering at Khartoum University when he retired as Master of St Catharine's College at the age of seventy. He was a Swimming Blue, the only man to win his weight four years running in Oxford versus Cambridge boxing and probably the only one to command combatant troops in the field. His autobiography *Militant Don* was published in 1964.]

Ascension Day, Thursday 23 May
After a lunch party we all went to the University Sermon. It was packed full of out-of-the-way theological technical terms, e.g. schizo-hermeneutics and at least one heresy. Found out later that the preacher was becoming a Unitarian.

~ 1963 ~

Friday 24 May
Returned home so that Murie and her cousin Marjorie Townend could go to the 75th anniversary gathering of Old Girls at Queen Elizabeth's Girls' School, Barnet.

Saturday 1 June
Cambridge. After the CU Coxswains' Society garden party in the Memorial Court at Clare College and the Rhadegunds' sherry party on the Close, we dined at the Union.

> [The Rhadegunds were founded in 1874 as a club for the top sportsmen at Jesus College.]

Hangover Sunday, 9 June
At the Rooster lunch in Upper Hall I presented Denys Wilkinson, FRS for the installation as High Steward of the Roost after Claude Havard had jocularly opposed it.

> [Denys Wilkinson held the office until it was proposed that Sir Alan Cottrell, Master of the College 1974-86, should take it as he was on the spot and extremely gallinaceous. Denys agreed, saying that he was willing to give way to an older man.]

Monday 10 June
By car to Grantchester and had tea at the Orchard with four or five Roosters who had come up by punt.

Tuesday 11 June
It is very hot. Took a tour round the College. Gerard and Winifred Lang arrived for the May Week Ball. There was dancing in the Cloister, in Pump Court, in the ground between First Court and the hockey field and (on grass to a steel band) in the Fellows' Garden. At the Midnight Roost in my rooms I was installed as Lord Protector [of the Roost for the vacation period.]

Wednesday 12 June
A buffet supper was held in Hall followed by a cabaret by Lance Percival at 2 a.m. Got to bed from 3 – 5.30 a.m. then up for the 6 a.m. photograph in First Court.

Saturday 15 June
Attended the Queen Elizabeth Grammar School Founders' Day celebrations, made a short speech and unveiled a tablet to Harry Mayes (Curley) and

stayed to lunch with the Masters and some of the Governors. [Harry Mayes had been the school porter.]

Sunday 23 June
South Mymms. Murie and I lunched at the Waggon and Horses after church and then walked up the side of the field of green corn behind the pub to the top of the hill. The sky was as clear as could be so we had a grand view across Hertfordshire into Bedfordshire.

Tuesday 2 July
Left for Henley to stay at the Red Lion until Saturday.

Thursday 4 July
Sandhurst beat our crew in the Ladies' Plate by 3-ft.

Friday 5 July
After the races we held a Roost in the almost empty Enclosure and I, as Lord Protector received 'gallage', then Chris McDouall rowed us across the river to the Red Lion and the others came round by the bridge and had drinks with us.

Saturday 6 July
Heavy rain fell without ceasing all day long – the worst weather I have ever known for Henley Regatta, inches of water in the Enclosure so we didn't go to the races at all.

Monday 8 July
South Mymms. Field's man came and cut the grass in the paddock. We picked raspberries and gooseberries.

Tuesday 23 July
It was a lovely drive to Cambridge, particularly in the open, hedgeless country between Slip End and Walkern where the roadside was one glorious herbaceous border of scabious, knapweed, vetch, meadow sweet, thyme, poppies, lady's bedstraw, and white campion.

Thursday 25 July
Our 4th wedding anniversary. Went to St Mark's, New Barnet for 9.30 Eucharist. Muriel's parents were married there in 1917. We gave a small Madeira and sherry party in the evening.

Friday 26 July
Attended the AGM of the Hertfordshire Society. The Society's tie was on sale for the first time. Major-General Sir George Burns, the President,

thanked the Chairman, Lord Brocket, for his magnificent gift of a gross of the ties. "Now I didn't know what a gross was", said Sir George, "But I'm told that it is 144 dozen". Lord Brocket plucked at his sleeve and whispered to him. "What?" said the President, "Not 144 dozen? Well, whatever it is, it's a very generous gift."

Tuesday 30 July
Cambridge. Had my hair cut but had to wait about 20 minutes during which the wireless was playing the most platitudinous music possible, so when I took my seat I said "What do you charge for a haircut? If I pay you sixpence more will you turn off the noise?" The barber agreed.

Sunday 4 August
In the Combination Room Alan Sharpe asked after Muriel adding, "Perhaps I should have said Mrs Brittain?" When asked why he replied that P. Gardner-Smith had said recently "I don't like to hear Fellows referring to other Fellows' wives by their *Christian* names. They'll be going off to Paris with them next."

Friday 9 August
Left for home with Murie's new gold dress and the cockerel curtains for the library, just made from the material that I had kept since 1957.

Sunday 11 August
The Vicar still being in hospital, the celebrant at 8 a.m. was the Archdeacon [Graham Leonard, later Bishop of London.]

> [St Giles, South Mymms was at this time still in the diocese of London. It transferred to St Albans when Middlesex was no longer a county and the village became part of Hertfordshire.]

Thursday 15 August
We gave a sherry party at Ingham Lodge to say farewell to the Dean of St Albans, the Very Rev A. K. Matthews, who leaves in September. He came in his gaiters with representatives from several local parishes. The party went with a swing from the very beginning to the very end.

Monday 26 August
We had a very heavy shower in the evening accompanied by one of the best rainbows I have ever seen. It was exciting to see Dancers Hill behind the "end of the rainbow".

~ 1963 ~

Friday 4 October
By car through the Lower Village to the first lodge whence I walked right through the woods to North Mymms church where Murie picked me up. It was a most enjoyable walk, which I hadn't taken for a very long time. Vincent Robinson would have said "The autumnal tints of foliage" were most beautiful. At 8.15 we went to the village hall at North Mymms for a harvest supper.

Saturday 5 October
Went with Murie to a Quiet Afternoon for Readers at St Lawrence Jewry conducted by the Rev A. Bridge, followed by Evensong with intercessions led by the Bishop of Stepney.

Sunday 6 October
We went to Colchester to lunch and tea with Albert and Christine Pirnie and afterwards to Denham and its magnificent church, which was luxuriously decorated for the harvest thanksgiving with a huge, solid, corn cross suspended from the roof. At 5.50 p.m. about forty people had already taken their seats for 6.30 Evensong. We continued on to Flatford Mill and Dovercourt where we stayed the night at the Trust House on the sea front.

Monday 7 October
As the ferry from Harwich doesn't take cars, we had to go right round the Orwell estuary to get to Felixstowe, where we visited Mr and Mrs W. H. Richardson.

> [Mr Richardson, a retired London City Missioner, had run the Mission Hall at South Mymms. He was also scoutmaster and a great influence for good on the young people of the village.]

Tuesday 8 October
Returned to Cambridge via Sudbury, Long Melford, Cavendish, Clare and Haverhill. Dined in Hall, Hugh Trevor-Roper was a guest, being here to elect a Professor of Modern History.

> [Hugh Trevor-Roper, won international fame for his book *The Last Days of Hitler* (1947), a vivid reconstruction based on research on behalf of British forces in occupied Germany. He was Regius Professor of Modern History and a Fellow of Oriel College, Oxford until his appointment as Master of Peterhouse, Cambridge in 1980. In 1979 he was created a Life Peer and took the title Baron Dacre of Glanton.
> Charles Wilson, FB's friend of long standing amongst the Fellows of Jesus College, was elected to the Professorship.]

~ 1963 ~

Saturday 2 November
After a short Congregation at which I presented three MA's and two BA's (including Arnold Cooke's) we managed to drive to the Pike and Eel (taking EVC) in time to see Jesus row a dead heat with Pembroke in the final of the Cox'less Fours. Went to the Fours dinner and made a speech.

Saturday 9 November
Saw *Queen B* at the Golders Green Hippodrome, a comedy by Judith Guthrie with Dame Sybil Thorndike in the title role and her husband, Sir Lewis Casson, as her faithful butler. We went behind the scenes afterwards by invitation and met Dame Sybil and Sir Lewis.

Wednesday 13 November
Cambridge. In the Combination Room Creswick entertained us with stories of thefts from the University Library.

Thursday 5 December
Paul Adamidi, our only Albanian member of the College so far I think, called and stayed for lunch. I hadn't seen him since he came up in 1922.

> [Paul Adamidi became a close friend of King Zog and after Zog's death, King Leka appointed him Honorary Chamberlain to the King of the Albanians with the title Paul Adamidi Bey Frasheri, the latter being his family name.]

Saturday 7 December
South Mymms. We moved back into the lounge at Ingham Lodge which Fred Hall [the Brittains' caretaker] had decorated "rose coral" from the picture rail to the chair rail and mushroom from there to the floor.

> [They had seen this colour scheme on a visit to Salisbury Hall at London Colney and had decided to try it as a change from the dark brown paper and paint which had been there previously.]

[No further entries for December]

~ 1964 ~

Friday 3 January
South Mymms. Gerard Lang came to supper after which we argued about the Papal claims till 11.45 p.m. Measurement of time: 2½ hours = 1 Gerard.

> [Gerard Lang was FB's general practitioner at Mymms and he and his family were practising Roman Catholics. Gerard was a regular visitor, not only for medical purposes. The two friends would talk far into the night so that on one occasion Muriel interrupted them with the stern warning, "Freddy's doctor said that he should go to bed early!"]

Thursday 9 January
Getting ready for this evening's party. Murie had acquired a sleeveless jacket to wear over her gold dress in which she looked very smart. Thirty-three "locals" came – Gerard and the Nevels stayed till nearly 11 though the invitation was for 8 – 9.29 p.m.

Sunday 12 January
Snow, so did not go to church but watched the Sung Eucharist from Liverpool Parish church on television. The celebrant faced the people across the altar. This is fairly common now.

Friday 17 January
Cambridge. At a Meeting of the Society [the Fellows] decided to have a ladies dinner in Hall at the beginning or end of Lent and Easter Full Term in the same conditions as an ordinary High Table dinner but at a different time or place from the undergraduates.

Sunday 1 March
Rang up Margo Dawson pretending to be a fictitious Captain Llewellyn with a Welsh accent. She was taken in for quite a time, in fact I had to tell her who I was.

Wednesday 11 March
The crocuses in the Fellows' Garden under the Oriental Plane tree are wide open to the sun in thousands – a wonderful sight. There is nothing to equal them in Trinity Avenue or at King's.

~ 1964 ~

[The huge Oriental Plane tree grew from a seed brought back from Thermopylae in 1802 by Edward Daniel Clarke, Fellow of the College.]

Thursday 19 March
South Mymms. John and Diana Welch came to dinner. He goes shortly to be Manager of Heffers, Petty Cury, Cambridge.

Easter Day, Sunday 29 March
The temperature in London was 7° lower today than on Christmas day.

Tuesday 14 April
We went to Godinton to stay with Alan Wyndham Green. After tea, as my sciatica was unpleasant, Alan pushed me in a wheel chair round the grounds among the thousands and thousands of daffodils in full bloom. H. E. and Mrs Bates came to sherry. We hadn't met them before.

[H. E. Bates (1905–1974) is best known for *Fair Stood the Wind for France* (1944), *The Jacaranda Tree* (1949) and *The Darling Buds of May* (1958) which became a popular TV series. FB had long admired H. E. Bates's works and had a collection of them, especially those dealing with the countryside.]

Wednesday 22 April
Went to Oxford for a Gaudy at Christchurch as guest of Denys Wilkinson who came back from Egypt this afternoon but he can't go to the feast as he has mumps. Canon Greenslade took me to the Senior Common Room. I sat between the Headmaster of Marlborough Grammar School and Sir Harry Melville, head of the Department of Scientific and Industrial Research, who deals in millions. Found him most genial. On rising from table talked a little to the Headmaster of Stowe (Drayson) who revealed himself as a former pupil of mine, also with Sir Goronwy Edwards. In the Senior Common Room I talked with Witton-Davies, Archdeacon of Oxford who was very pleasant and with Fr Gilling, formerly the curate of Little St Mary's, Cambridge.

Thursday 7 May
We left home for College via the bluebell woods near Ayot, taking Mrs Long of Brookside with us for a day in Cambridge. She much admired the "hysteria" in full bloom in First Court.

Wednesday 13 May
Staggered to hear that G. F. Roberts died suddenly early this morning. The following came to dinner: the Dean of Ely and Frances Hankey and the Revd

~ 1964 ~

C. Copsey, Vicar of East Grinstead, who afterwards gave an excellent talk to the J. M. Neale Society about JMN as a man and a scholar. Two of the Sisters of St Margaret were there. I was delighted to find that they disliked as intensely as I do the substitutions by Bede Frost for Neale translations in the Office Books of St Margaret's.

[Fulton Roberts, a Fellow and Director of Studies in Medicine at Jesus, also played a full and vital part in the life of the College. During his years as Steward the kitchens were rebuilt and the Upper Hall created out of two sets of dons' rooms at the top of Hall staircase. At the time of his death (from meningitis) he was Bursar overseeing the construction of North Court, the first new building in the College since 1930.]

Friday 15 May
We went by car to Grassy Corner and lunched there. It was a perfect May Day, not a wrinkle on the water and only one swan.

Saturday 30 May
South Mymms. Men came and fitted up our summer-house in the paddock near the pond. Frank and Elsie came to tea, after which we all sat in the summer-house and discussed what to call it. As we couldn't think of anything suitable, Murie suggested that we should call it Gawda, i.e. Gawd-a-God-knows.

[FB alleged that when his father did not know the answer to a question he would reply "Gawd-a-God-knows". Brian Wicks later wrote this poem:

> There's a Gawda in our garden and when the evening's cool
> We sit and watch the wildlife as it thrives upon the pool.
>
> We've an Elsan in our Gawda but it's not quite what you think
> For our outlook's rather broader and we keep it stocked with drink.
>
> As in quiet contemplation we sip our Rooster tea
> The Stately Home of Brittain towers up in majesty.
>
> We are happy in our Gawda but longer grows the grass
> What can we do to keep it down? I know, we'll graze our 'arse.

This pronunciation of horse was a reference to a farmer friend of Brian's who always pronounced horse 'arse, as in "The 'Arse of the Year Show" and "Now the weather's better I'm leaving my 'arse out in the field."]

Monday 8 June
Cambridge. At the termly meeting of the Society, A. H. M. Jones's [Professor of Ancient History] proposal to allow women guests to Hall dinner during

Full Term was turned down. Dart [Professor Thurston Dart] gave notice that at the next meeting he will propose that the Council consider what steps to take to turn Jesus into a mixed College.

Sunday 14 June
Paul Sankey [Jesus man and RC priest] drove me to St Edmund's House where he said Mass for my intention. At the Rooster Breakfast-at-Lunchtime I introduced the new Bishop of Ely (Edward Roberts) who was then emperched, orderized and installed as Exalted Justiciar and did 'gallage'. I tucked my silk square of material, woven with Red Herrings, across his purple stock for the ceremony. When he sat down his wife said, "That's a very nice present they've given you" and he, not knowing that I only meant to lend it to him for the day, put it in his pocket and took it home.

Monday 22 June
Attended Sung Eucharist at the High Altar of St Albans Abbey to celebrate the golden jubilee of Dean Thicknesse's ordination to the priesthood. There was a large congregation for this moving service, which was followed by lunch at the Pré Hotel.

Monday 13 July
We went to Sarratt Bottom and lunched on the bank of the River Chess where watercress, forget-me-nots and willow herb were in abundance. Went back home for tea in the Gawda.

Monday 20 July
Went with Gerard Lang to All Saints' Convent London Colney, where we inspected the magnificent Chapel of which the western extension was consecrated only about two weeks ago.

[All Saints' was then the home of an Anglican community but later became a Roman Catholic Pastoral Centre.]

Friday 24 July
Gerard Lang presented me with a Red Herring square to replace the one that the Bishop of Ely had walked off with on Hangover Sunday.

[While the Brittains were on another delightful visit to Godinton, Frank and Tumpty Coulton came in for drinks and FB recounted the saga of the WC:

A young couple about to be married were looking for a house in the country. After satisfying themselves that it was suitable they made their way home. During the journey the young lady was very quiet and thoughtful and when asked the reason, replied that she hadn't seen the WC. Edward hadn't noticed one either so he wrote to the owner of the house asking where it was located. The ignorant old landlord did not know the meaning of WC but came to the conclusion that it meant the Wesleyan Church, so he answered as follows:

Dear Sir,
   I have great pleasure in informing you that the WC is situated about two miles from the house and is capable of holding 250 persons. This is an unfortunate situation for you if you are in the habit of going regularly but no doubt you will be glad to know that a great many people take their lunch and make a day of it. Others who can't spare the time go by car and arrive just in time. It will also interest you to know that my daughter was married in the WC. In fact it was there that she first met her husband. I remember the wedding well on account of the rush for seats. There were ten persons in the seats that two usually occupy and it was wonderful to watch the expressions on their faces. My brother was there too. He has gone regularly since he was christened. A wealthy resident in the district erected a bell over the WC to be rung every time a member entered. A bazaar has to be held every year and the proceeds help to provide plush seats as its members feel this a long felt want. My wife and I are getting old now and do not go as regularly as we used to. It is six years since we went last and I assure you it pains us very much not to be able to go more regular.
   Yours faithfully,
        ————]

Friday 31 July
Cambridge. Went to Evensong at King's. The Rubens picture is now behind the high altar (which looks about knee high by comparison) and the panelling has been stripped from the east wall and from the side walls as far as the stalls.

Saturday 1st August
Presented John Turner [former Organ Scholar] for his MA degree – my only candidate today and my last presentation as Praelector.

Sunday 2 August
The very moment after the Blessing at the end of Evensong in Chapel there was a terrific outburst on the organ and awful discords. P. Gardner-Smith said, "Just as you're saying your prayers all HELL'S let loose", followed by "that man ought to be sent down".

~ 1964 ~

Tuesday 18 August
Dear Dr Brittain,
Thank you so much for your card – so glad to know that you enjoyed the broadcast.
Yes, indeed – vive them all!
bless you, – bless you!
Sincerely yours
(signed) Sybil Thorndike

[FB wrote on this letter: I had written to her after Murie and I had listened to her broadcast about her career and her opinions. She had mentioned her Anglicanism, her socialism. I had ended my card with "Vivent le theatre, l'anglicanism, le socialism, et le vingt-quatre Octobre." (our common birthday.]

[On 31 August the Brittains went on a most delightful holiday via Burford to Gloucester and then on through Monmouth and Llandovery to St David's. They were so staggered by the beauty of the Cathedral with the admirable taste of all its fittings (7 altars) that when their time was up at the full guest-house where they were staying they asked the Dean if he could suggest somewhere else for them to stay. He suggested the Priory, a convent and guest-house run by the nuns of the Order of St John the Evangelist from Dublin. Breakfast was silent as it was taken with the nuns and this proved a severe test for the Archdeacon of Oxford (formerly Dean of St David's) who was also staying there. He launched at once into animated conversation as soon as the door closed behind the last nun to leave.

Leaving St David's with great regret, they went via Fishguard, Nevern and Lampeter to Aberystwyth. At the pier they had a cup of what seemed to be a mixture of tea and blackcurrant jam in a cardboard cup and sat on hard metal chairs with the backs at too obtuse an angle to be comfortable. The floor and table was littered with tea, dead matches, cigarette packets and dirt. They drove out to look at the National University of Wales and the new buildings still in progress.

Returning home by a glorious drive through the mountains to Rhayada, New Radnor, Kingston and Leominster, they stayed at the Diglis Hotel, Worcester, in a fine bedroom overlooking the garden and the river. They visited the Perrins Museum of Porcelain and went to the reject shop there and bought a gold Worcester tea service and other items to replace the silver they had lost in the first devastating burglary at Ingham Lodge. Gerard Lang was to comment, "The Brittains have lost their silver but they have bought gold."]

Saturday 17 October
Cambridge. Went to the Senate House and introduced Ilya Gershevitch to the various officials and sat by him to prompt him during his first Congregation as Praelector. Afterwards went on to the Pike and Eel to watch the boats.

Poppy Day, Saturday 7 November
We went with Graham Harris [Muriel's first cousin once removed downwards, staying for his half term from Cheltenham College] round the town to see the Poppy Day fun. This included an undergraduate selling "filthy postcards" (plain cards rubbed in mud), and the Chaplain of Jesus, dressed as a stage parson selling for 6d a copy, 'Save the tower of St Mangold and All Wurzels", which I had written at twenty-four hours notice.

Monday 16 November
Went to the Audit Room at King's for the first performance of *A Victorian Evening*. Pop (Camille) Prior produced it, in costume. The book was by the Rev M. J. Plumley, Professor of Egyptology, who played the part of the father of a Victorian family with Pop as grandmother. I, as great uncle Adolphus, wore a fiery red moustache and contributed 'Captain Ginger'.

Tuesday 17 November
The second performance of *A Victorian Evening* – to a very enthusiastic audience. I had a terrific reception and had to give 'Seaweed' as an encore. Lady Lee, the wife of the Master of Corpus, came and thanked me afterwards.

Thursday 26 November
Mild weather with a temperature of 59°F and brilliant sunshine for much of the day. Watched the Fairbairn Cup Race (forty boats and only one division this year). Jesus I finished second. At 7.30 p.m. there was a Roosters Annual Dinner in Upper Hall. It was noisy, particularly the rowing men, but not rowdy, and never out of control.

> [The Boat Club were not allowed a dinner during the Michaelmas Term as they had the Lent and May Bump Suppers. They got over this by being invited to the Roosters Annual Dinner on the President's Official Birthday (Fairbairn Cup Day) as paying guests.]

Saturday 28 November
Dined with the Rowing Club as a guest as also was Maurice Zinkin. P. Marsh, a South African, in proposing "The Guests" said that when he came up the only Jesuans whose names were known to him were Steve Fairbairn's and mine and that we were the two best known Jesus men anywhere. Maurice Zinkin in responding said that when he was up thirty years ago I was "the life

and soul of the College" and I still am. I proposed "The Club" and referred to the reference to Maurice in *Chanticlere* [the College magazine] of his time.

> There is nothing either good or bad
> But Zinkin makes it so.

Sunday 29 November
Attended Sung Eucharist at St John's College Chapel, sung most beautifully to Palestrina's *Aeterna Christi* with K. Sutton as celebrant and S. Sykes, the youthful new Dean, as Gospeller. At 6.30 p.m. we went to the centenary of the consecration of All Saints' church [opposite Jesus College and therefore known at one time as St Opps]. The Bishop of Ely delivered the sermon and afterwards we went to the vicarage for coffee where Murie and Mrs Newton Flew made the first cut in the centenary cake with 100 candles on it.

[Keith Sutton (Jesus 1954) became Bishop of Lichfield and Stephen Sykes became Bishop of Ely.]

[No further entries for 1964]

~ 1965 ~

Friday 15 January
Cambridge. At the meeting of the Society the chief subject was the neglect by some Fellows of the duty to come into the Combination Room after Hall. I listened to Evensong broadcast from Guildford Cathedral, which was admirable. The psalms were sung more slowly than we had ever heard before and gained very greatly by this.

Sunday 24 January
Sir Winston Churchill died at 8 a.m. There was a sherry party in my rooms followed by the Roost's, a "Grains Trust". Bruce Ponder wrote afterwards to say that he had "left no prune unstoned" to discover something.

Tuesday 26 January
South Mymms. A. R. B. Fuller, [librarian of St Paul's Cathedral] came to supper. He bellowed, bawled and blared – mostly about having a state funeral for anybody. At St Paul's, he said, all are agitated primarily about the adequate provision of dykes [lavatories] at Winston Churchill's funeral.

~ 1965 ~

Saturday 30 January
From 9.30 a.m. to 1.40 p.m. we watched Winston Churchill's funeral on television – magnificently done.

Friday 19 February
"Bats" Fuller came to supper. He consumed one whole smoked haddock, scalloped eggs in cauliflower 'au gratin' (two helpings), one pineapple fritter, stewed rhubarb and ground rice, one orange and about half a pound of grapes.

Sunday 21 February
We watched Mass from the RC church at Epsom on television. The choir sang a psalm in English at the Introit, a layman in lay dress stepped up to read the Epistle, a priest in surplice and stole said the Gospel in English (as was the Epistle), the Nicene Creed was said in English, the Sanctus and Agnus sung in Latin. The canon was silent.

Sunday 28 February
Cambridge. Hangover Sunday sherry party and Rooster Lunch though it was a Day for Fasting and Humiliation because we had finished only fourth on the river, having been Head of the Lents for the six previous years.

Thursday 11 March
It was a superb day so went to the aconite wood near Abington. The flowers were wide open in the sun, making a golden carpet. A. D. Traill and his wife called later.

[Sir Alan Traill became the second Jesuan Lord Mayor of London in 1984.]

Tuesday 16 March
South Mymms. It is the season of "March many weathers" with wind, showers, thunder and lightning and patches of sun, during one of which the magnificent cock pheasant, which has been round here for some time, stalked grandly across the paddock and disappeared next door.

[FB sent John Betjeman a copy of the 'William Dowsing Report', along the lines of *Babylon Bruis'd & Mount Moriah Mended*, which the Dean of St Albans had asked him to do on the Abbey. He received the following reply:

~ 1965 ~

Friday 26 March

43 Cloth Fair
London, E.C.I.

Dear and golden Doctor,
   Oh, how I have enjoyed on recovering from flu your gorgeous report on St. Alban's by William Dowsing. I wish you would do such noble work to the City churches here in London, and your beloved native Middlesex. *You are one of the great men of the age*, and it was a joy to hear from you.
   Yours,
      (signed) John Betjeman

Friday 9 April
South Mymms. The Rev John Bryan, Rector of King's Cliffe, Northants, brought some of his parish registers recording the baptism of Murie's great-great-great-grandfather Humphry Cunnington and of his son John Cunnington.

Tuesday 13 April
Zelie Timins came to tea. We took her to Evensong at St Albans Abbey. When the Sub-Dean started reading the first lesson at apparently the wrong place the Dean interrupted him with a loud "Where are you?"

   [Mrs Timins was a formidable lady and widow of Douglas Timins, a Jesus man. Both were considerable benefactors to the College.]

Sunday 2 May
Cambridge. In Chapel James Owen celebrated from behind the altar as was done last Sunday for the first time.

Tuesday 11 May
Two masters of Queen Elizabeth's School, Barnet who had come up with the school cricket team to play against the College, came to lunch. Murie and I watched the match and took tea with the teams in the Pavilion. When play ended both teams and their supporters came to my rooms for wine. There must have been nearly forty of them. [This was an annual event for many years.]

Friday 21 May
In the Combination Room I sat next to the Master who was entranced with my stories about Edleston, the Intercollegiate University and *Episcopi Vagantes*; an utterly and amazing new world to him, he said.

~ 1965 ~

Monday 14 June
Looked on at the 'Crocket' Match between the Roosters and the Boat Club on the Close. V. G. Clinton-Baddeley and a number of the performers in his *Pride of the Regiment* came to sherry. Took him to Hall and then to the play.

Thursday 17 June
It is the twenty-second anniversary of my having given up smoking at 8 p.m. on Thursday 17 June 1943. Today I weighed only 11st 6 lbs, my lowest for years.

Saturday 26 June
We went to Ely to attend the Festival Evensong of the Friends of the Cathedral. The choir was huge and came from all over the diocese. The gigantic Wills conducted with a long baton from a high throne outside the choir gates, the choirs being under the Octagon. It was awful.

Friday 2 July
Henley Regatta. Saw our Ladies' Plate crew beat 1st and 3rd Trinity in the semi-final of the Ladies. We went to Choral Evensong in Cookham parish church and heard Bryd's Great Service and Wm Smith's Preces that they sang unaccompanied without a choirmaster beating time. It was astonishing and delightful to find this in a village church. If these things can be done in village churches why not in cathedrals?

Saturday 17 July
Today was the official opening of the new North Court. We had a buffet lunch in Hall and Upper Hall with the biggest crowd in the Cloister where there was a marquee. At 2.30 p.m. the new Court was opened with a speech by the Master and another by the Bishop of Ely who ended with prayers. The Old Members (1066–1930 vintage) who were up for their Reunion weekend, had tea in the Fellows' Garden, then Choral Evensong in Chapel and dinner in Hall.

Tuesday 20 July
Murie went to the Arts Theatre for world premiere of *Howard's End* from E. M. Forster's novel of the same name.

Tuesday 27 July
Frank Collieson of Heffers came to consult me about a new edition of their *Guide to Cambridge*.

Saturday 7 August
I presided in Upper Hall for the Name of Jesus Exceeding. The numerous candles lit halfway through, the Death Silver and the other silver made a lovely display.

[Alderman Death, Mayor of Cambridge in the 1890s, left his silver to the College in gratitude to the Senior Tutor, H. A. Morgan. It seems that there had been rowdy behaviour by undergraduates at a concert in the town and the Mayor had had them evicted. Next day they went round to his house in Maids Causeway with the intention of wrecking it but the Senior Tutor heard of the plan and stopped it.]

Friday 13 August
South Mymms. Mr William Narraway, the artist, lunched with us and stayed till 3 p.m., having taken many snapshots of me.

[FB was Narraway's first Cambridge sitter – afterwards he painted many University worthies as well as the Queen (five times) and Princess Anne. Narraway's official portrait of FB was commissioned by the Old Members of Jesus College.]

Sunday 15 August
The Vicar (E. P. Clare) preached a very good sermon on the Assumption stating how, some years ago, a Pope had nearly killed the proper observance of feasts of the Blessed Virgin Mary by making belief in her bodily assumption an article of faith.

Monday 16 August
I sat for W. Narraway till 1.45 p.m. when we all lunched in the Gawda, and I sat for him again until 4.30 p.m. Afterwards, I took a Siesta in the long deck chair and finished reading T. Yoseloff's *Laurence Sterne*, an excellently written, well-argued defence of Sterne.

Tuesday 24 August
At Godinton. Rain kept us in after lunch, not that it matters here, there is so much to see.

Thursday 26 August
We left Godinton, regretfully as always, and went via Headcorn and Sutton Valence and much wandering by unsignposted roads through woods to call at Brasted Park Theological College. Peter Staples of Linton showed us round the fine, classical building with recent chapel etc. added; but we, like Peter, disliked the slack discipline there, e.g. only one silence a week and that from after 10 p.m. Compline only, and even then not strictly observed.

Friday 27 August
South Mymms. Murie went to Enfield and brought Dominic and Mario (two of her paper boys) back to tea. Then Dominic cut the lawn and Mario did some weeding. Douglas Elson joined us for supper. The boys enjoyed both meals to the full (very full).

Sunday 12 September
Staying at the Southgate Hotel, Winchester. We went to the Sung Eucharist at the Cathedral, then to Wolvesey and had sherry with the Bishop and Mrs Allison, her daughter and son, Sherard. That night I dreamt I walked into a room where a black cat, licking its left foreleg, was the only occupant. I said, "Good morning cat". The cat, without looking up, replied "Good morning". "How do you like it here?" I asked. Putting his leg down the cat said, "Not much. I've been to worse places but to many better. The people here seem to think that all a cat wants is one square meal a day." "May I ask what else a cat expects?" I said. "Nothing big but bits and pieces. I admit there was no written agreement when I came here, but it was clearly understood that there were to be bits and pieces, not exorbitant when you consider the work a house cat is supposed to do" he said. "You mean", I replied, "mice and all that?" "Yes" said the cat, "and many more things". "What are you going to do?" I said. "I'm leaving", said the cat, "they can get some other cat to do the job".

Monday 13 September
Left Winchester and went on to Sidmouth via Bridport and Lyme Regis. We went on to Ottery St Mary and into the glorious church there.

Wednesday 15 September
Came home via Salisbury. The newly painted Mompesson tomb in the Cathedral is a magnificent sight with its brilliant colouring. We looked at the side chapel ticketed "Chapel of the Mothers' Union and of St Thomas of Canterbury".

Saturday 18 September
Gerard took Murie and me to Coventry to see the new Cathedral. We had lunch with Joseph Poole and his wife at the Precentor's house, and then he showed us thoroughly over the Cathedral with which we are much impressed though there are a few things in it we dislike.

Wednesday 20 September
We went to Goff's Oak, Little Berkhamsted and Epping Green where we started a picnic lunch in a field but the wasps forced us to finish it in the car.

> Lovely picnic weather with a north-easterly breeze
> You want skins like leather to keep off the wasps and the bees
> There are flies in the butter and paraffin in the cheese
> And we'll all freeze together with a Primus between our knees.
>
> (Sung to the tune of the 'Eton Boating Song')

Friday 1 October
Back to Cambridge. Went to a party in Downing to celebrate the publication of R. J. White's *Dr Bentley*. Stood talking a little with S. C. Roberts and Angela Wilson. After a minute or two she said "I'm going into the other room, it's so dull in here". "Thank you! Thank you!" said SCR. At Jesus the new Fellows J. M. Dunn, J. E. Roseblade and J. Cameron Wilson were admitted.

[John Dunn, who had come from King's College, returned to it the following year as Fellow and College Lecturer in History. J. E. Roseblade, a Trinity mathematician, later took on all FB's College posts, i.e. he was Praelector, Keeper of the Records and Honorary Secretary of the Jesus College Cambridge Society. Cameron Wilson, a modern linguist and a pupil of FB's became Admission Tutor for Sciences as well as doing an immense amount of pastoral work in the College.]

[From 5th – 9th October FB sat for his Narraway portrait. Encouraged by the artist, several people called to see it including undergraduates and staff from the College Office. The Head Porter was enraptured with it and told how Buxton, a gate porter, coming to deliver letters had said, "Good morning, Doctor" to the portrait and then, surprised at getting no answer, looked up and saw his mistake.]

Friday 15 October
I lectured to the Huntingdonshire Historical Association on "English History of the late Victorian and Edwardian times as portrayed in popular song" with vocal illustrations.

Wednesday 27 October
Professor Plumley gave an admirable lantern talk to the Neale Society on "The Church in Egypt today".

Saturday 6 November
We attended the marriage of Elizabeth Lang [Gerard's daughter] and Nicholas Candy at the "Papisticle Conventicle", Potters Bar, which was very well conducted by "Pastor" Moriarty. At the reception I proposed "The

Bride and Groom" introducing the imaginary history of the bride's great-great-grandfather, Old Lang Syne.

Sunday 14 November
James Owen brought the Sacrament to me in bed. We had undergraduates to dinner and two other freshmen called to ask if the Roost Sabbatical was being held.

Thursday 25 November
Gordon Simpson [his Cambridge doctor] brought Hugh Fleming, a cardiologist, to see me. He took an electrocardiogram of me.

Saturday 18 December
Gerard drove us to Evensong at St Albans Abbey. John Betjeman was in the congregation and I had a little talk with him afterwards. He said, "Do you go in for a kitchen table and the celebrant standing behind it at South Mimms church?" When I said "No" he replied, "Excellent" and went on to tell me that he had given away about 15 to 20 copies of my *Mostly Mymms*.

[No further entries for December]

~ 1966 ~

Thursday 20 January
South Mymms. There was frost and fog all day. I read *It's a Don's Life* to Murie for criticism [and for the next week or so.]

Monday 14 February
Cambridge. Trevor Jones rang up to say that the College Council had today decreed that Murie may live in College with me. We accordingly had a little celebration at supper.

> [This was the first time in either Oxford or Cambridge that a wife had been allowed to share her husband's rooms in an all-male college. It was a great and generous concession made in view of FB's poor health and the wish of the Council that he should be able to remain resident in College for as long as possible.]

Thursday 17 February
Humphrey Payford called to take the rowing collection away.

[FB had disposed of his library of books on rowing to Henley Regatta where they are now housed at the Regatta headquarters.]

Saturday 19 February
The Rooster Bizarre Bazaar was held in the Junior Parlour at which I conducted the Clawktion (auction). There were various ingenious side-shows, e.g. indulgences and relics for sale.

Tuesday 8 March
Murie and I left Ingham Lodge in bright sun for Cambridge via the Beane Valley. Stopped at Waterford to look at the Beane, the weeping willows in emerald leaf, and the ducks basking in the sun. At Watton-at-Stone we bought sandwiches and a bottle of Spanish rosé wine and on through Walkern, Cromer, Rushden to Wallington where we enjoyed a picnic lunch at the top of the hill.

Tuesday 15 March
Murie helped me to receive Mrs Agar, Miss Leversidge, and Miss Benevilli and then I took them to the Supervisors' Dinner in Hall, the first official dinner with gowns to which women had ever been invited. The annual Ladies Night is without gowns, there are no College guests and it is in effect, a wives dinner.

Monday 21 March
Murie and I left for the Skinners' Hall in the City where at 6 p.m. a wine party began for the presentation of my portrait, painted last autumn by William Narraway. It was a delightful party and one of the great days of my life. About 150 men and a dozen women were present. Tom Langton made an excellent speech and then called on "The Venerable Bolly" (J. du B. Lance, Archdeacon of Wells) to make the presentation which he did admirably.

Monday 28 March
Finished reading *The Kaiser* by Virginia Cowles. It is well written except for some displeasing Americanisms, e.g. "the Kaiser was rather silent at the beginning of dinner due to indigestion".

Friday 1 April
South Mymms. On drawing the curtains I looked out of the window and said, "Well, I've never seen *that* before?" "Seen what?" said Murie. "A rabbit sitting in a tree". Murie scrambled out of bed and rushed to the window before remembering that it was April Fools Day.

Good Friday 8 April
Heard a beautiful rendering of the Litany and Ante-Communion from the Temple Church on the wireless, then on TV saw a new rendering of Stations of the Cross from the RC church at Islington. The officiant wore a wide-sleeved surplice down to the ankles and a purple stole. There were readings from the Bible and apparently extempore narratives of the fourteen Stations interspersed and not one Ave, Pater or Aminae fidelium. There was a striking description of Simon of Cyrene wondering why he, "a respectable working man should be dragged from his dinner hour to help in the public execution of a criminal". I found it very helpful.

Monday 18 April
The House of Lords Seal
As from Ripon

My Dear Freddy

I was *delighted* to get your letter, for which many thanks. Thank you for what you say about my interventions (as one should say at the Vatican Council). I am glad that you approve of them. I fear there is a conspiracy going on to ruin (a) the Bible (see NEB – which I think *appalling*), (b) the Prayer Book, and possibly (c) The Church of England. A few of us try to oppose this; but I feel the forces against us are strong, especially among the younger clergy, who seem very restless and discontented – at least some of the time.

I am delighted to hear that you and Madame are now living in Jesus. I shall be in Cambridge on April 30th, is there any chance of my calling upon you? I shall be spending two nights at Emmanuel and returning to Ripon on the Sunday. There is much that I should like to talk to you about.

I was interested in your P.S. about the Anglican-Methodist proposals and have sent it on to the Dean of Carlisle who is on the Committee. I know he will be glad to read what you and Prof. Jennings have to say.

You will see that I am writing to you on grand notepaper. I have just arrived in London to read Prayers (not apparently to pray) on 4 successive days. I am quite glad to know that I shall be here for the Opening of Parliament on Thursday – a function at which I have not previously assisted.

I am writing a "popular" book on this Vatican Council and am [writing] a less popular one later on, so life is full but interesting.

With love
  Yours
   (signed) John
   (+ John Ripon, né Moorman)

Thursday 21 April
Cambridge. We had the first sight of the sun since Easter Day. Dom Fabian Glencross from Worth Abbey came to tea.

Monday 2 May
It is very hot today. We sat on the Close and a duck was sitting on its eggs a few yards away. At 8.30 p.m. I went to a talk by Glanville Williams on "Morality and the Law".

Wednesday 11 May
Women – two of them – dined in Hall at the undergraduates' table for the first time.

Saturday 21 May
We went to Epsom to stay the night with Humphrey and Betty Playford. Ian Fairbairn and his wife Margaret came to dinner. She talked "very posh" on such subjects as how they had spent their honeymoon "chamois-hunting in Roumaniah!"

Sunday 22 May
We went to Woolpit School near Ewhurst where, at their Chapel Service, I spoke on the merits of the Authorized Version of the Bible and Book of Common Prayer.

Monday 23 May
We went to Holmbury St Mary and had coffee with Bill and Olive Narraway. In his "workshop" we saw an oil painting of myself in my Boat Club blazer.

> [This was the Brittains first intimation that Narraway had painted another portrait of FB, for exhibition purposes, from the photographs he took on his first visit to Mimms. After FB's death it was purchased anonymously and given to Muriel.]

Tuesday 24 May
Cambridge. A so-called sculpture called 'Mortal Man' was set up in Pump Court yesterday. It is awful.

~ 1966 ~

Thursday 26 May
We went to the Pike and Eel and saw our four boats on their way to Clayhithe coached by P. N. Carpmael. We continued on to Milton and across the fen to near Baitsbite where we walked along the towpath and talked to the crews carrying the boats round the lock. Then back to Milton and on to Waterbeach and Clayhithe where we saw the four boats arrive and watched them start a bumping race on their way back.

Friday 27 May
Murie and I dined at the Arts Theatre and then went to see Somerset Maugham's play *The Sacred Flame* with Gladys Cooper in the cast.

Monday 2 June
About twenty choirboys from Linton arrived with the Vicar. Murie took them round the College and gave them tea in the Prioress's Room. They then came to 13 Chapel Court for ices and to see the cockerels and me.

Monday 6 June
In the Combination Room I entertained the Master and others with stories, especially the one about Red Morgan making a collection for the wife of a friend of his who had died and then marrying the widow.

Tuesday 7 June
We went to the Footlights Revue *This Way Out*, some of the best items being a parody of the life of the Brontes, a parody of 'Land of Hope and Glory', a sentimental song with pleasant words and tune – 'Understand Me' – admirably sung by Christine Mohr of Newnham, and a parody of a Shakespeare play.

Corpus Christi, Thursday 9 June
Attended sung Eucharist at Linton where I sat in the chancel in scarlet and then unlocked the door of the new extension to the church school and asked the Bishop of Huntingdon to bless it.

Saturday 11 June
David Fairbairn and his wife and others came to my rooms.

> [David, Steve Fairbairn's great-nephew, a Minister in the Australian government and afterwards their Ambassador in the Netherlands, was chided by his wife for not having subscribed to FB's portrait. He replied "I expect that got put into the TBD drawer". We all asked what that stood for. "Too bloody difficult", he said. We asked if he really meant it and he went on to say that most government offices in Australia had another

~ 1966 ~

drawer too, labelled LBW. At this Ruth begged him, "You can't tell them that Dave, it's one of our crude Australian expressions", but we all persisted thinking it might be something to do with cricket, but the abbreviation stood for "Let the Buggers Wait"]

Monday 13 June
We had tea with the Roosters on their way back from Bottisham in the launch Viscountess Bury and I taught them to sing:

> We go down to the river, that's all we have to do
> We go down by the hundred and we come back two by two
> And when the Lents are over to Baitsbite still we go
> From lunch till after teatime we sit in boats and ROW

(To the tune 'The flies walked up the window')

Friday 1 July
Staying at the King's Arms, Cookham, for Henley Regatta. Followed our Ladies' Plate crew in the launch which, after it had started, came back to pick me up. We beat 1st and 3rd Trinity after a fine race.

Sunday 3 July
South Mymms. Evensong at the Patronal Festival of Flowers at North Mymms then walked round the glorious gardens of North Mymms Park, roses superabundant and superb. Not a sound to be heard except a dove cooing.

Tuesday 5 July
At Potters Bar Vicarage I addressed the clergy of the Ruridecanal Chapter on "The Episcopal Underworld".

Wednesday 6 July
We had a wine party for local people. The Archdeacon of St Albans [the Venerable Basil Snell] asked me, "Have you always lived in this house?" I said, "No, only since I got married, but Muriel was born in the house and her parents and grandparents lived and died in it". "Oh!" said the Archdeacon, "I see, you took her on with the house".

Wednesday 13 July
Cambridge. We went to Westminster College for the Hymn Society Conference lecture by Adam Fox on "The place of Keble and Neale in Church History". After lunch we looked at the gardens and the new building at St John's.

~ 1966 ~

Saturday 23 July
South Mymms. Frank rang up to say that Elsie died last night. Murie and I left for East Grinstead to stay for the centenary celebrations of J. M. Neale.

Sunday 24 July
Attended Sung Eucharist at East Grinstead church, which was very beautiful. The Archbishop of Canterbury [the Most Revd Michael Ramsay] who preached was magnificent and venerable in a gold mitre. Afterwards we went to Neale's tomb where the Archbishop dedicated a memorial to him, and then on to Sackville College for a reception of about 150 people.

> [The Archbishop came up to FB and asked after the Roosters. A knot of people surrounded him and he turned to them and said, apropos of nothing, "I've known Fred Brittain for, let me be accurate, *43 years*" upon which they all turned and looked at FB. He then said "Mrs Brittain is a more recent creation, I've only met her to*day*, but it's a great *pleasure*", at which they all stared at Muriel.]

Wednesday 27 July
Five cats walked round the garden at 8 a.m. We picked up Mog and went to West Herts Crematorium where I conducted Elsie's funeral service. Then the congregation came back to Ingham Lodge for tea.

Wednesday 10 August
Winifred and Elizabeth Lang called to say that Gerard is going into Virginia Water Hospital tomorrow. From 7–10 p.m. we had a supper party for old members of the staff of Westminster Children's' Hospital.

Thursday 18 August
We left Ingham Lodge for Southwold where we stayed four nights at the Swan Hotel before going on to Aldeburgh.

Tuesday 23 August
We visited Snape, Tunstall, and Ufford where the church was very "extreme" with plenty of Walsingham and rosary literature, and lunched (after wanderings) among the furze high up on Kitson Point.

Wednesday 24 August
We went home via Stoke-by-Nayland (with its fine, big church with grand tall tower), Coggeshall, Braintree and Dunmow after a most delightful holiday, during which we visited 24 churches.

~ 1966 ~

Friday 9 September
We set out for Petersfield and called at Virginia Water to see Gerard and to take him out to lunch.

Saturday 10 September
We explored some of the Edward Thomas country, including a lovely drive round a hair-pin "hanger" to Wick Green but were unable to get to his monument because of the steep climb. We saw his last house, Yew Tree Cottage, Steep, and accidentally discovered his previous house, Berryfield Cottage, Ashford. The owner happened to come out at that moment and took us into the garden and showed us a memorial tablet over the door. Attended my godson Stephen Lance's wedding at Steep church and the reception at Bedale's School. Afterwards we went to South Harting where George Giri met us, showed us the church and then took us to dinner at his house, Cross Dykes.

Monday 12 September
We came home via Hindhead, Staines and Uxbridge. At Harefield we looked into the delightful church. It might be 100 miles from any town, a real village church with many monuments of the Newdegate family.

Friday 30 September
We dined sumptuously at the Middlesex Arms with Alan and Enid Hill.

> [The Middlesex Arms, the public house at the bottom of Greyhound Lane, South Mimms, between the Hatfield and St Albans roads, was demolished when the A1 road was upgraded to a motorway in the 1970s.]

Tuesday 4 October
Cambridge. Murie and I went to the housewarming of Lucy Cavendish College, Northampton Street.

Sunday 23 October
At an Old Elizabethans gathering in my rooms one of the party recalled how a boy at school had given the Headmaster's name on a form as E. H. Jenkins, MA Oxen.

Sunday 30 October
Just after lunch the Master arrived with the sad news that Frederic Raby had been found dead in his bed this morning.

~ 1966 ~

Saturday 3 November
Murie and I went to Linton where we jointly opened the Christmas fair as follows:
    FB: "When you saw"
    Murie: "or heard"
    FB: "that this Christmas Fair"
    Murie: "was going to be opened"
    FB   "by TWO people"
    Murie: "some of you probably said"
    FB   "what a nuisance, two speeches to listen to", (etc . . .)
until the last sentence when we said together, "We have much pleasure in declaring this Fair open".

Friday 4 November
I gave evidence at Frederic Raby's inquest. The Coroner returned a verdict of accidental death.

Thursday 10 November
Murie and I drove round Madingley. The colours of the foliage under the brilliant sun were wonderful, particularly the various shades of the copper beeches. Later we drove up to the Gogs and into Wandlebury, the first visit for either of us. The leaf colours again were gorgeous and it was an entrancing sight.

Saturday 17 December
Douglas Law from Johannesburg called with his wife, two daughters and future sons-in-law. I was delighted to see them. He modestly said that he owed his degree to me. "I sat for the papers", he said "but Freddy wrote the answers".

Monday 19 December
The marriage of Duncan McKie and Christine Kelsey of Girton took place in the College Chapel today. The bride and bridesmaids came to my rooms to dress. The marriage was in the outer chapel, the remainder of the service in the inner chapel. Then we went to the reception, lunch and speeches in Hall.

Tuesday 20 December
South Mymms. When we were just going to eat our already overdone supper carol singers called. They sang awhile at the door, we gave them some money for their tin and a humbug each and they went away.

Friday 23 December
We put the Christmas cards in the lounge on long strips of coloured paper as usual.

                [No further entries for December]

~ 1967 ~

Sunday 5 February
Cambridge. There was a short Roost followed by a pancake party in my rooms for about 23 men. Murie must have fried fifty or more pancakes.

Monday 13 February
At the AGM of the Amalgamated Clubs in the Junior Parlour I presented my annual report and then resigned from the office of Senior Treasurer, which I had held for twenty-five years. I was then presented with a pair of three-branched candlesticks. I made a reply in which I sketched the origin and history of the Amalgamated Clubs with some anecdotes. I was elected to the new office of Vice President of the JCAC.

Sunday 19 February
We took Jimmy Stephens (Papist President of the Roost) to the Sung Eucharist at Linton. He found it most impressive. As we got back to the Cambridge streets he said, "This seems unreal now. Linton church seems reality".

Tuesday 7 March
Went to see H. C. Fleming, our former Acting Head Porter.

> [When he was about to retire, Fleming, an ex-Marine, conceived the idea that he should be the subject of an article in *Chanticlere*, the College magazine, under the heading "Cocks of the Roost", which was devoted to personalities well known in the College (but had nothing to do with the Roosters). He therefore came to see FB about it but was told that it had an undergraduate editor. "Yes, Sir", said Fleming "but I understand that you run it". FB said that he would approach the editor and if he agreed they would get someone to write it. Fleming then revealed that, to save time, he had written the article himself. It included such phrases as "He is ready at all times to do everything which makes for the good of the College". Handing it to FB he said, "I think that's got it about right, Sir". When FB said that he would suggest that the article might be published the following term Fleming's face fell. "Well, Sir", he said, "I'm going to my old comrades' reunion in Portsmouth soon and I was hoping to take the magazine with me so that I could show them what the College really thinks of me". Needless to say the article appeared that term.]

~ 1967 ~

Monday 20 March
South Mymms. At 2 a.m. Muriel called the doctor to me as I had shivering fits and stoppage of the front bowel.

Tuesday 21 March
The doctor came again and I was taken to Barnet General Hospital.

[A week later FB was anointed by the Rector of Barnet before his operation for prostatectomy, performed by Mr Nick Downey who lived at the Grange, South Mimms.]

Saturday 25 March
Abbey Gate House
St Albans

Dear Freddy,

This letter may reach you before your operation tomorrow. May it, whenever you read it, remind you of the truth that every moment you are in God's all competent care and anointing is a visible pledge of this comforting strength.

God keep you tomorrow – we'll remember you and Muriel and please thank her for writing.

> Your affectionately
> (signed) Michael SA
> [Bishop of St Albans]

[FB stayed in hospital for about six weeks and Brian Wicks penned these two poems for him.]

Keep Brittain Tidy

> "Keep Brittain tidy" was what the man said,
> But that doesn't mean tidying a piece off our Fred.
> The surgeons performed with clawfull dexterity
> By preserving a piece of ff.B for posterity.
>
> Operation is over; anaesthesia weak;
> The tension declines, the patient doth speak
> The words pouring forth, a torrent, a glut,
> Though incision's completed he sounded half-cut.
>
> But Roosters unite; praise be to the Grainsack,
> The dean is recovered with all of the faculties back to normality, let's raise a cheer
> And pray he continues for many a year.

So here's to our ffreddy getting better and better,
For B is for Brittain, a capital letter
But mmuriel is angry, the surgeons turn pale,
"Who gave you permission to open my mail?"

Oh! what have they done to our ffreddy?

Oh! What have they done to our ffreddy?
Is he back on his perch of good health?
Have they now put him back altogether?
With catgut and nylon and stealth?

For DUE TO a horrid occlusion –
Or should it be OWING TO, eh?
But whatever it was they removed it
And took it away on a tray.

Yes, whatever it was they removed it
To prevent it from getting much worse.
It was done with the help of three surgeons,
One scalpel, and Flossie, the nurse.

So praise to the good Barnet General,
Its skill and its kindness intact.
They've given new life to our ffreddy,
So Prosperum iter fac.

The Lord helps him, so they tell us
Who doesn't mind helping himself;
But when the Lord needs a bit of assistance
Thank God for the National 'Elf.

Friday 12 May
South Mymms. Tom and Mary Blake arrived to stay the night for a presentation party before his ordination.

[Tom was the only son of FB's and Muriel's old friends Charles and Florence Blake. His whole life was spent in the caring professions, first as Master of Children's Homes, then as Area Secretary for the Church of England Children's Society and finally, after ordination, to the priesthood in parishes and old people's almshouses in the diocese of Worcester.]

Sunday 14 May
Early this morning I dreamt that Christine Kelsey McKie and I were at a lecture given by J. M. Edmonds. He told us to write something down. Then after looking at what Christine had written he said to her, "Hold out both your hands" and hit them several times rather savagely with a stick. She took it without turning a hair but I stood up and said, "This is disgraceful. There has been no corporal punishment in this University since Milton's time – even for undergraduates and she is a Fellow of a College. You ought to be ashamed of yourself". I was wondering whether this historic scene would get into the newspapers when I woke up.

Sunday 21 May
We went to Worcester Cathedral for Tom Blake's Ordination to the diaconate. It was very impressive and beautiful. Afterwards we met the Bishop in the Cloister and then went to Tom and Mary's lunch party.

Hangover Sunday 12 June
The Roost celebrated its Diamond Jubilee (founded in 1907 by John Hugh Allen) with a Back-to-the-Roost Roost, which was attended by about twenty ex-Presidents.

Thursday 6 July
I addressed the Annual General Meeting of the Alcuin Club at Church House, Westminster on "The Church and its services today: one layman's view". It had an enthusiastic reception.

> [The following are some excerpts:
> "... One thing that has not changed in my lifetime is Establishment (except in Wales). I have been a convinced Disestablishmentarian ever since I was about 18 years of age. I can remember when Welsh churchmen, led by the militant Bishop of St David's, marched through the streets of London to protest against the threatened disestablishment of the church in Wales. All sorts of calamities were to follow it; but it came about ... I sometimes think of the dictum of Father Stanton of St Alban's, Holborn: "We are told in the Epistle to the Hebrews that we are strangers and pilgrims on the earth; but did anyone ever hear of established strangers and endowed pilgrims?"
> Some years ago I was in Peterborough Cathedral on St Peter's Day. The service in that staggering building was most beautiful. It moved me greatly until the end of the procession came in sight, when I was moved in a very different way; for there, immediately in front of the coped and mitred bishop of the diocese, stalked a lawyer in morning dress, gown and wig, breathing establishment from every pore. I presume he was the Bishop's

Chancellor, perhaps a member of the firm Lee, Bolton and Lee, at least an ecclesiastical lawyer – one of those who get what is vulgarly called a rake-off from almost everything that takes place in the way of church appointments. The fees are considerable at times, I believe . . .

As far as my memory serves, church music has improved wonderfully since the days of my youth, but in some ways it has deteriorated. A regrettable custom, which has undoubtedly increased, is the visible conducting of anthems and canticles by choirmasters. In some places it has reached gigantic proportions with the choirmaster frantically gesticulating, flinging his arms about, beckoning, rebuffing, nodding and mouthing. The choir meanwhile turn towards him and essay the impossible task of trying to watch him and the music at the same time. Such a performance converts what should be an act of worship into a concert item and nothing more. The excuse is sometimes raised that for unaccompanied singing this visible conducting is essential. It was not so when Paderewski visited England. He was delighted to find that in Anglican cathedrals the most elaborate unaccompanied music was sung without any conducting at all. An unpleasant habit that nearly all choirs seem to have adopted in recent years when singing music of the sixteenth and seventeenth centuries is to sing "genera-ci-ons", "imagina-ci-on", and "salva-ci-on". . . I would deny that these words were ever so pronounced in the past . . . Another malpractice is the pronunciation of the word "alleluia" in an English context as "ah-lay-luia". It has been an English word for centuries and should be pronounced as such. A worse feature still in some cathedrals is the intruded "H" like this: "He hath put down the mi-hi-hi-hi-highty from their see-he-he-he-heat". This seems to me an insult to the English language and the last word in vulgarity. I am aware that Italian opera singers do it but that is no justification. Perhaps they feel an irresistible urge to introduce aspirates into their singing to compensate for the absence of them from their own language . . . A practice has sprung up or grown bigger, in recent years of announcing the name of the composer of an anthem during the course of the service. This seems to me an abominable practice. Like visible conducting it converts an act of worship into a concert item; it is music for the sake of music. No officiant says, "The Collect Almighty and Everlasting God is by Thomas Cranmer from the Gregorian Sacramentary" – why shouldn't he? Isn't the Collect the culmination of the whole Office and the anthem merely an unessential ingredient of it? It is evident that choirmasters do not take that view and the clergy, in some places at least, are afraid of them . . . Someone once asked me if I like plainsong. I replied that I adore it except when it is sung in the so-called "typewriter style" – staccato, making all the notes exactly equal in length, weight and emphasis and making a long pause at the end of the even lines. I do not know anything more likely than this to make people hate or ridicule plainsong for life. Closely allied to this is the practice of singing the psalms to "typewriter" plainsong with a ludicrously overlong pause at the colon and no pause at all between the verses . . .

Why are so many of the clergy, in the prayers which they introduce after the Third Collect, so often longwinded, and why do they go into such details? They seem, as I once heard Canon Wilfred Knox say, unable to credit the Almighty with any imagination. And why do some of the clergy habitually go about dressed as laymen? Is it that they are ashamed of their calling? . . .]

Sunday 16 July
John Morrison, who had spent the night at Ingham Lodge, gave us an interesting account of how he had attended the Vatican Council at the instigation of the Cardinal-Archbishop of Lille.

[John, a Jesus first boat cox, after several important livings, was appointed Archdeacon of Buckingham in 1988 and later Archdeacon of Oxford.]

Tuesday 1 August
Cambridge. It is very hot. Mr Kenworthy of Stearns came in and took a colour photograph of Murie and me in the Keeping Room.

Thursday 3 August
After dinner Bill Thorpe [Professor W. H. Thorpe] recalled that, during the Second World War when there was talk of WAAF women taking meals in Hall, Duckworth described the proposal as a "satanic mockery".

Tuesday 12 September
South Mymms. Buddy and Betty Bryant, and their daughter Lesley came from Cambridge to Ingham unexpectedly. We were delighted to see them.

[A. Parker Bryant was now running a real estate business in the United States. They reminisced about Parker's undergraduate days when he had been put in FB's care after firing a pistol at High Table for a joke.]

Thursday 12 October
Cambridge. A meeting of the Society was held in the Prioress's Room. There were some surprising events.
    (a) M. A. C. Warren and J. Bronowski were elected Honorary Fellows.
    (b) All discussion about the Deanship was ruled out until AD 2002 or *sine die*.
    (c) A small committee was appointed to draw up the proposed revision of the Statutes in general.

(d) It was agreed that scarlet may be worn in Hall on Scarlet Days and at Exceedings.

Saturday 28 October
Winifred Lang rang up to say that Gerard died yesterday morning. RIP.

Tuesday 31 October
There was a High Requiem Mass at the Spanish Fathers' Church, Potters Bar for Gerard Lang. *Cujus animae propitietur Deus.*

[FB wrote an appreciation of Gerard Lang for the *Barnet Press* in which he said, "Gerard Lang was a shining witness to the falsity of the oft-repeated assertion that the National Health doctor is only a pale shadow of the family doctor of the so-called good old days ... He was not merely a doctor to his patients but was also a friend to every one of them. When they ceased to need his services he continued to visit them regularly for the rest of their lives. Gerard was a religious man without being goody-goody or narrow-minded in any way. A staunch Roman Catholic, he would discuss ecclesiastical matters for hours without prejudice or bias ... His literary interests were very wide ... Those who saw him in University surroundings speedily realized what an admirable don he would have made and he could have followed an academical career without foregoing his undoubted vocation to medicine ..."]

Friday 3 November
Cambridge. We went to the Pike and Eel where Pat Delafield had just won the Colquhouns [Sculling Race].

Tuesday 7 November
Dick Ladborough and Miss Ramsay (the Archbishop of Canterbury's Aunt Lucy) came to lunch.

Thursday 9 November
The Linton CEMS, ten in total, came for a buffet supper after which I told them stories about the College.

Monday 20 November
Murie and I went to tea with Miss Lucy Ramsay at 13 Mount Pleasant.

Thursday 30 November
The University Heraldic society came to my rooms for sherry before their Annual Dinner in the Prioress's Room. The company included Brooke-Little (Richmond Herald) and Scott-Giles (Fitzalan Herald Extraordinary). It was a very pleasant evening.

Saturday 2 December
Went to Chapel where there was much conducting of canticles and anthem even though there was an organ.

Monday 4 December
We drove in exquisite warm sun to the Gogs and collected privet berries.

[No further entries for December]

~ 1968 ~

Saturday 6 January
We went to Cambridge for the wedding of Rosamund Page [the Master's daughter] in the College Chapel. The bride wore a white Russian fur-edged dress and a white round hat, which I unfortunately knocked off when kissing her, so I did the business again (without knocking her hat off). Ju-Ju, the bride's twin sister, was so overcome with emotion that she kissed me for the first time. The groomsmen were Felix Borchardt and John Birkhead, who looked very smart. [Both became doctors, as did Juliet.] At lunch in Hall we sat with David Butterworth who had played the organ. [He was a former Organ Scholar of the College and at that time was organist at St Mary's, Nottingham.] He was very communicative about his work at Nottingham. He acknowledges that D. R. Feaver is most able and that he likes him but says that he is very rude and the choirmen can't stand him.

Tuesday 9 January
South Mymms. Heavy snow fell. The doctor called in to see me during the night and again very early on.

Wednesday 10 January
An ambulance arrived. Mr Hawkins and Dr Graham had to shovel and dig the snow away to get it to the door. I was taken to Barnet General Hospital.

[FB was in hospital for five weeks with asthma, bronchitis and pneumonia. The diary contains a list of his numerous visitors, which included eight different clerics. Muriel spent most of very day with him and stayed the nights at the hospital when he was at his worst.]

~ 1968 ~

Monday 4 March
Murie took me out for the first time. Our snowdrops are at their peak, in great masses to my great delight.

Wednesday 27 March
We drove to Water End Ford, Pulmer Water and Codicote Mill, all lovely with daffodils and aubretia. We lunched in the car back at Water End Mill and watched the sparkling water and the emerald buds on the weeping willows and the great bank of daffodils between the river and the Duchess of Marlborough's house.

Ascension Day, Thursday 23 May
Cambridge. Dined at Trinity Ascension Day Feast as the guest of R. Y. Jennings.

Bank Holiday, Monday 3 June
We went to Cliffe Regis [King's Cliffe, Northants] to open the church fete in aid of finishing the repair to the church spire. Murie and I made a joint speech like the one we made at Linton with suitable alterations.

Thursday 8 June
Joe Bailey called and took us in his silver Rolls Royce right to Nevill's Court at Trinity for the Chancellor's Garden Party.

Tuesday 11 June
We went to the May Week Ball, walked round the Cloister a bit, had supper in the marquee in Second Court, attended a short Midnight Roost in Peter Allen's rooms on D Staircase as ours are being redecorated, and after a further stroll went to bed. It seemed to be a very good ball.

Monday 17 June
South Mymms. Sorrowfully we heard that Mr and Mrs Hawkins are selling their house next door and moving to Potters Bar.

Thursday 20 June
We dined at St Michael's Manor, our first visit. It has very beautiful gardens with Cedars of Lebanon, swans on the small lakes and one can catch glimpses through the fence of the Ver flowing just on the other side of it.

Friday 16 August
Went by car to Hitchin and with some difficulty we managed to discover the source of the River Oughton, "Oughton Head", approaching it by driving along the Pirton Road and walking along a footpath till we came to a dell in

the bottom of which the water came trickling very slowly out of the ground. We went back to Hitchin and Ickleford where we saw the pleasant Oughton and its two bridges near the big flour mill.

Monday 17 August
We went to Ayot St Lawrence and looked over George Bernard Shaw's house, which is very interesting and attractive.

Sunday 28 August
We were going to church but became absorbed in the television broadcast of the Lambeth Conference and the Sung Eucharist from St Paul's with +Michael Cantuar as celebrant and several concelebrants. The newly introduced primatial cross with two crossbars, looking like a TV aerial was used. De Mel, Metropolitan of India delivered a very moving sermon.

Wednesday 4 September
[The Brittains set out on what was to be their last holiday together, via Winchester through Salisbury and Sherborne to Trent where they called on Archbishop Lord Fisher but no one was in. They stayed with friends in Crewkerne, exploring the district and attending Evensong at East Coker. This led to several careful readings of T. S. Eliot's poem of that name, but they were not a great deal wiser afterwards. They received the following card from Lord Fisher when they got home.]

Trent Rectory,
Sherbourne
Sept. 22

So sorry that we were out when you called on us. I should have greatly enjoyed and valued a talk with you. Better luck if and I hope there is a next time.
    (signed) Fisher of Lambeth

Monday 9 September
We moved on to the Royal Hotel, Weymouth for a week.

Wednesday 11 September
We spent some time in the Osmington field "looking lazy at the sea" then went to lovely Cerne Abbas and looked round the charming church. After some miles of motoring we found the HQ of the Society of St Francis at Hilfield.

~ 1968 ~

[Brother Denys Marsh, who spotted their arrival, called out to his brothers, "Look! It's Freddy and his female relation". They were invited to join in the evening office in the Chapel, during which the prayers of St Radegund, patroness of Jesus College, Cambridge were invoked. Brother Denys whispered to Muriel at the end, "I was praying that he would mention St Radegund.]

Sunday 29 September
Cambridge. Numerous men up for last night's JCCS dinner called to say goodbye.

[L. N. Battersby and I. E. Gray were persuaded to stay for a casserole lunch. FB told them that they might call it a ragout or a ghoulash or anything they liked but it was, in fact, a stew. Irvine Gray wrote afterwards thanking Muriel for her "kindness and stew".]

Monday 30 September
Went to Heffers and talked with Reuben and Frank Collieson. As we sat in the car outside Muriel Bradbrook came along. She came up and kissed me through the car window. She is being installed as the Mistress of Girton this evening.

Saturday 12 October
At Evensong in Chapel the reader twice referred to Job as Jobb. After Hall, Fish Harries and P. Gardner-Smith came back to my rooms and we read some of T. S. Eliot's *East Coker* to them for a laugh.

Sunday 13 October
We went with Frank Bown [a freshman at Jesus, later the Rev Francis Adrian Charles Simon Bown], to the Sung Eucharist at Ely. It was superbly done but we didn't like Series 2 or Arthur Wills's gesticulations, or the "typewriter" plainsong.

Sunday 20 October
There was a Roost in my rooms with a debate deploring the increase in student power. R. Y. Jennings and Peter Glazebrook spoke.

Thursday 24 October
South Mymms. Two engineers from Herts County Council came to discuss the proposed diversion of the A1 road and its effect on Ingham Lodge.

[It was proposed to divert the road so that it would have cut across the paddock to within 25 ft. of the house. In the event, after years of enquiries, appeals and fresh enquiries, the road was widened on its existing site and Ingham Lodge and its land was preserved intact.]

Tuesday 29 October
Cambridge. We went to Walden and thence to Howe Wood and had a very clear view today including King's Chapel, the University Library tower and the new tall double chimney of Addenbrooke's Hospital. Murie picked a nosegay of 14 wild flowers in bloom: harebell, scabious, purple vetch, red deadnettle, white deadnettle, knapweed, scentless mayweed, ragwort, yarrow, yellow toadflax, dandelion, charlock, white campion and mallow.

Friday 27 December
Malcolm Graham called and said I had better spend a day or two in bed. Murie and I watched the astronauts return from the moon on television.

[No further entries for December]

~ 1969 ~

The first part of the year was spent at Ingham Lodge until, the Lent term having half gone, FB became anxious to get back to College. In early March the Brittains returned to Cambridge and the usual routine was followed. On Sunday 9 March, after an undergraduate sherry party, FB went for his afternoon rest saying, "Gosh! I *did* enjoy that party". But he had picked up a virulent infection and died in his rooms on 15 March, the last day of term.

The funeral was held at South Mymms, the Bishop of St Albans pronouncing the Blessing. FB's ashes were divided into two parts as he had wished, one half being buried in his parents' grave at South Mymms and the other half outside the east end of the Chapel at Jesus College, Cambridge by kind permission of the Master and Fellows. The simple inscription 'FB 1893–1969' is cut into the Chapel wall.

OBITUARY

The College Chapel was filled to capacity for the Memorial Service on 26 April. The service was conducted by the Dean and the Blessing was pronounced by the Visitor. The Master read the Lesson and the

~ 1969 ~

Ven. J. du B. Lance, Archdeacon of Wells, gave the Address which follows:-

"This is the third eulogy of Freddy Brittain that I have spoken or written. The first was in 1929, when I wrote one of those mock obituaries which used to appear in *Chanticleer*, the college magazine. The second was in 1966, when a great number of his friends presented him with his portrait. I have dared for the third time to accept this honour by reflection only because I am fairly confident that Freddy himself would appreciate the oddity of the panegyric for a Doctor of Letters being spoken by one who once held the degree of B.A., in brackets, failed, and him an unhorsed archdeacon.

"You will see that I hope that you will not want me to call this third occasion a sad one, for, before all else, Freddy was a Christian, anchored firmly in the Christian hope, which is that the life in Christ, which we can live now, is to be immeasurably filled up and enriched in the company of the Saints and in the close presence, and transcendent glory, and active service, of our loving God. For him death was not an end, but a gate; the gate of life and not the gate of death.

"But though the Christian hope has a future, it also has a present. The life in Christ is something to be lived now as well as then; and it is to be lived both in the ordered fellowship and worship of believers and as a transforming quality in the daily life of mankind.

"So Freddy was a devout practising member of his own Church of England, though a friendly critic of it, as is so characteristically shown in the famous pamphlet which he wrote with Bernard Manning (an equally devout practising Independent) called 'Babylon Bruis'd and Mount Moriah Mended'. He gave his special lifetime love and loyalty both to this chapel and to his parish church of Saint Giles, South Mymms.

"But though he had an unashamed interest in ecclesiastical affairs, even to writing a book about Latin in Church, his life in Christ showed itself most clearly, as it always should, in a transformation of character. I want to draw your attention to only two aspects of that Christian character, its vitality and its friendliness.

"His published books alone show the remarkable range of his interests, from a fairly abstruse study of medieval Latin, through lively biographies of Q and Bernard Manning, to light-hearted literature about rowing and the Roosters. But those of us who knew him personally know that there was hardly a subject of human concern which did not attract his interest. I suppose that he did occasionally sit in an easy chair, but I never saw him in one, and the characteristic picture of him will always be that of his portrait, sitting in an upright chair at his desk, busy and interested about some aspect of life, though never too busy to put down his pen and give his attention to a visitor. Human life to him was a gracious gift of God, and therefore fascinating, enjoyable, and important. That was the secret of his vitality, which kept him joyfully at work to the very end and carried him, with Muriel's help, through illness after illness.

"But to a Christian man all men are brothers under the fatherhood of God, and therefore of the highest possible value and interest; Freddy will be remembered most of all for the enormous number and variety of his friends from bedmakers to bishops, with whom he delighted to talk merrily in their own tongues, whether in plain Latin, as we used to suppose, at high table, or in ornamental English with the Boat Club. As they are all equally sons and daughters, brothers and sisters, in the eyes of God, so they were all equally of value and interest to Freddy, all the more interesting and valuable because of their variety. As we know, he kept meticulous records of the doings of all old Jesus men, but for him they were never mere names, but always persons, whom he always hoped to meet again.

"We all of us here give great thanks to God for having been numbered among Freddy's friends, but especially she whom I would like to call the blessed Muriel; blessed in the bliss she shared with our dear and mutual friend. To her we give our love and thanks and sympathy.

"How easy it is for Christian to speak to Christian about death. To Muriel I could and did simply write "Thank you for letting me know that the trumpets are sounding on the other side".

"That will do for my message to you."

The Published Works of Frederick Brittain Litt.D.

Saint Radegund, 1925.
The Lyfe of Saynt Radegunde (edited), 1926.
Saint Giles, 1928.
The Jesus College Boat Club (with H.B. Playford), Vol. I 1928, Vol. II 1962.
Slowly Forward (with S. Fairbairn), 1929.
Oar, Scull and Rudder, 1930.
South Mymms, the Story of a Parish, 1931.
Latin in Church, 1934 (revised edition 1955).
The Medieval Latin and Romance Lyric, 1937 (new edition 1969)
A Short History of Jesus College, 1940.
Babylon Bruis'd and Mount Moriah Mended (with B. L. Manning), 1940.
Bernard Lord Manning, 1942.
Q – A Biographical Study 1948.
'Q' Anthology, 1948
Tales of South Mymms and Elsewhere, 1952.
Mostly Mymms, 1953.
A History of Jesus College (with A. Gray), 1960
Guide to Cambridge.
The Penguin Book of Latin Verse (edited), 1962.
It's a Don's Life (The Autobiography of Frederick Brittain, Litt.D. Heinemann, 1972 (posthumously).

Index

Abbey of Christ the King 105–6, 119
Abbot, Edwin 6, 25, 100. 105,193
Abbot, Eric 245
Aconites 77, 103, 107, 129
Adamidi, Paul 269
Adelstrop 235
Aida 6
Aladdin 201
Alcuin Club 172, 206, 214, 218, 296
Alexander, Fraser 244
All Saints' Convent, London Colney 273
Almonds 209
Anson, Peter 234–5, 252
Archdeacon's Horse 62–7
Archibald, Edith 179, 180
Ashwell 15
Austin, Capt. 163, 222
Assizes, Judge of 157

Babylon Bruis'd & Mount Moriah Mended 125–6
Backs, frozen 261
Baelz, Peter 245
Bailey, Joe 301
Bainbridge, Richard 228
Balme, David 130
Barbour, Joan 193
Barnes, Henry 117
Banks, Simon 257
Barnet
  Fair 6, 85
  General Hospital 294
Barton, C.B.R. 170
Bates, H. E. 271
Battersby, Leslie 43, 303
Bebbington, B.N. 160, 182
Belloc, Hilaire 18
Benbow, Mr. M.4
Benbow, Elsie 17
Bernstein, C.A.B. 164, 171
Betjeman, John 200, 278–9, 284
Beveridge, W.I.B. 172

Birkhead, John 300
Blackhorse Sermon 81
Blake, Mrs F. 230
Blake, Tom and Mary 295–6
Blood, Janet 194
Bogus Universities 234
Boot, John (1st Baron Trent) 234
Borchardt, Felix 300
Bouquet, A.C. 54
Bradbrook, Muriel 142, 224–5, 248, 256, 303
Braunholz, E.G.W. 7
Brittain, Elizabeth 24, 42, 48, 184
Brittain, Frank 23, 98, 148
Brittain, Frederick
  Fellow 115
  Steward 162
  Litt. D. 172–3
  Portrait 285
Brittain, William 1
Brown, J.W. 4
Brown, Bishop Leslie 186, 201
Bryan, Revd. John 279
Bryant, A. Parker 70, 298
Bull, Elsie 4
Bullock, Percy 76
Bullough, E 30
Burns, Sir George 266–7
Burrough, Alan 121, 123, 206
Butterworth, David 300
Byng, Julian 195
Byrnell, J. 190

Cambridge as she is visited 207–9
Cambridge Review 142, 165
Casson, Sir Lewis 269
Chadwick, Prof. Henry 236
Chadwick, Sir Owen 149, 210, 227, 247
Charkham, Jonathan 190
Chase, Mary Ellen 142
Chelsea Arts Ball 206
Chesterton, G. K. 38
Christ Church School 1

309

Index

Church Enabling Act 11
Churchill. Sir Winston 10, 131
   Funeral 277–8
Civil Service 1, 3, 4, 6
Clinton-Baddeley, V.C. 280
Cockerel Collection 49, 178, 199
Codex Gallorum 83
Coldstream, Sir William 261
Coleridge, Gilbert 156
Comber, H. G. 43
Cooke, Arnold 253
Cottrell, Sir Alan 265
Coulton, Brian 118, 220
Coventry Cathedral 282
Cox, Vivian 110, 134, 232
Creswick, H. R. 41, 269
Crichton, Revd. Harry 260
Crocuses 11, 39, 270
Cunnington, Hilda 54
Cunnington, Muriel 226, 229–30

Daniels, Rt. Revd. Henry 175
Dart, Robert Thurston 202, 273
Dawson, Margaret 237, 244, 270
Deansley, Dr. Margaret 186
Death Silver 280–1
Dickins, Bruce 193
Dodd, C. H. 127, 178
Duckett, Eleanor 194
Duckworth, Canon J. N. 110
Duckworth, Dr. W.L.H. 63, 126, 131, 142, 298
Dyrham Park 5

Eastham, Nancy 259
Ecclesiological Society 175
Edleston, Mr. 7, 23, 28, 68, 70, 88, 104, 279
Edmonds, J.M. 16, 102, 168, 228
Egypt, The 6, 31
Egyptonian, The 6
Eleven days see UGBED
Elliott, C.A. 7, 97
Essex, Rosamund 216
Everlasting Club 3, 27
Exceedings 220, 280

Fairbairn, Sir David 117, 288–9
Fairbairn, Ian 78, 287
Fairbairn, Steve 9, 10, 72, 118, 262
Fairbairn, Sydney 78

Fairey, Michael 245
'Fairless, Michael' 204–5
Farjeon, Eleanor 238
Feaver, Rt. Revd. Douglas 191–2
Fergusson Ian 257
Ferrar, Nicholas 85, 166
Fielding, Sir Leslie 246
Finch, Flo 237
Finley, M.I. 225
Fisher, Most Revd. Geoffrey 142, 216, 302
Fleming, H.C. 293
Fleming, Rt. Revd. Lance 175
Foakes-Jackson, Dr. F.J. 23, 79, 132, 138
Footlights Club 97, 103
Footlights Revue 97, 288
Foot-the-Ball match 168
Forster E.M. 88–9, 223
Foster, Idris, 226, 235, 236
Fraser, Arthur 104
'Freddy Feast' 176, 239
Fuller. A.R.B. 20, 148, 277–8
Furze, Bishop Michael 31, 54

Gardner, Revd. Ralph 141
Gardner Smith, Revd. Percival 34–5, 49, 116, 210, 251
Gaselee, Sir Stephen 148
General Strike 63
Gershevitch, Ilya 276
Giddins, Guy 80–81
Gilbertson, Sir Geoffrey 127
Gilbey, Mgr. 146, 205
Giri, George 158, 291
Gittings, Robert 85, 112
Godinton Park 239, 281
Gombrich, Prof. Ernst 250
Gordon, Emma 258
Gore, Bishop 9, 10
Gowar, Mr 11
Granta, (river) 33
Granta, The 10, 12
Gray, Arthur 3, 27, 93, 128
Gray, Irvine 303
Greek Islands 262–4
Greenwood, Walter 183
Greer, Rt. Revd. William 153
Gresford-Jones, Rt Revd. Michael 185, 264
Grimes, John and Blanche 248

Index

Harcourt, Geoffrey 247
Harmsworth, Sir Hildebrand 35, 44
Harmsworth, Joe 35, 55–6, 73, 115
Harmsworth, Lady 51
Hardy, Thomas 151
Harries, S.G. 148, 303
Harriss, Desmond 170
Havard, J.D.J. ('Claude') 142, 152, 158, 210–11, 165
Hay, Revd. Allen 24, 25, 68, 210, 229
Hay, Katharine 46, 152
Hay, Monica 46, 91
Hayley, Sir William 240
Hazzard, V.B. 12, 15
Heaton, Eric 212
Heffer, Ernest 142, 144
Henson, Rt. Revd. Hensley 68
Heraldic Society 249, 299
Hill, Alan 94, 229, 256, 291
Hilton, Mary and Sidney 134
How, Revd. John 35
Hunkin, Rt. Revd. J.W. 59, 161
Hurford, Peter 260
Hutchinson, A.M. 110

Iacabucci, Frank 259
Iacabucci, Nancy see Eastham
Ignatius, Fr. 169
Inge, Dean 34, 79, 206
Italian Society 17, 30

James, June 213
Jenkin, Patrick 224
Jennings, R.Y. (Sir Robert) 124, 225, 286, 301, 303
Jesus College
   Boat Club 68, 79,
   Chapel 18–9, 19, 29
   Grace 106–7
   Lunch in Hall 76
   North Court 280
   Oriental Plane Tree 191, 271
   Small Combination Room 180
Johnson, Very Revd. Hewlett 185
Jones, Trevor 123, 218
Judo Club 179

K.D. (Kitty Drackett) 13, 37, 40, 42, 46
Kemp, Rt. Revd. Eric 182
Kennedy, Studdert 22
Keynes, John Maynard 36

Killanin, Lord 98–9, 113
Knightsland Farm 86, 110, 148
Knox, E.V. 107
Knox, Revd. Wilfred 48, 182

Labour Party 14, 58, 77
Ladborough, Dick 187
Lance, Ven J.B. 79, 285
Lang, Dr. Gerard 246, 255, 265, 270, 290, 299
Langton, M.J. 229
Langton, Tom 155, 253, 285
Lattimer, Mr 81
Law, William 247
Lawrence, Arnold 158
Lay Reader 64
Lent Races 1922 29–30
Lewis, C.S. 214
Linton Church 260, 288, 291, 293
Little Gidding 166, 227
Lloyd George, Gwilym 205–206
Lloyd-Jones, Hugh 248
Lockwood, J.H. 137–8
Lucy Cavendish College 291
Ludford, Geoff 177
Luxmoore, Lord Justice 144

Maidens, Matchless of Mimms 71
Manning, Bernard 33, 73, 138, 139
Martin, Sir Leslie 223
Mathew, Archbishop 29
Matthews, Very Rev. A.K. 267
Maundy Service 165, 226
May Races 32, 105, 256
Mayes, Harry 266
McKie, Duncan & Christine 236
Mew, Francis 195
Mills, Bernard 255
Milner-White, Eric 55
Mistral's birthday 217
Mitchell, Tiny and the Dame 120, 260
Mitchley, Mrs 96
Mitchell-Heggs, Peter 257
Moorman, Rt Revd. John 287
Moreton, Mark 253
Morgan E.H. 128, 288
Morgan, H.A. 117, 281
Morrison, John 244, 298
Mountbatten, Lord 10, 168
Mozarabic Mass 108
Muggeridge, Malcolm 48, 213

311

Index

Nairne, Alexander 23, 34, 37, 110, 111
Narraway, William 281, 283
Natives, The 80
Neale, J.M. 190
Neale Society 140, 193, 272
Needham, Joseph 44
Nicholson, William 94–5, 96
Nitti, Signor 36, 39, 52, 56
Noel, Conrad 32

Okey, Thomas 30-1, 74, 103, 106, 109
Old Elizabethans 45, 53
'Old Sweetie' 78
Oratory of the Good Shepherd 36, 38
Ord, Boris 181, 244
Owen, Revd. James 252, 279
Oxford 57
Oxley, Clive 244

Page, Sir Denys 239
Page, Juliet & Rosamund 300
Pars, L.A. 102
Patriarch – See Allen Hay
Pavement Club 22, 23
Peacock, Sir Geoffrey 131
Pennyfather, R.R. 147, 203
Percival, Alan 119, 143, 216
Perrins, David 158
Peters, David 237
Phelp, Mr 165
Philpot, Dorothy 54
Picken, L.E.R. 154
Pilkington. Peter 255
Pitt Club 140
Playford, Revd. H.B. 13, 236, 285, 287
Plumley, Prof. M.J. 276, 283
Poole, Revd. J.W. 214, 282
Portway, Donald 264
Potter, Gilly 112, 212, 216, 250
Praelector 8, 211
Prawer, S.S. 257
Prior, Camille ('Pop') 264, 276
Prior, Oliver 72
Proctor, University 146, 150, 167
Proctorial Insignia 161

Queen Elizabeth's Grammar School 1, 44
Quiller Couch, Sir Arthur 41, 74, 76, 120
 Death of 155
 Going Down Ceremony 104, 113

Memorials 161, 162, 175
Teetotal Lunch 82–3

Raby, Frederic 218–9, 225, 291
Radegund, St. 50, 53, 55, 58, 107
Rainbow, G.A.F 182
Ramsay, Archbishop Michael 290
Ramsay, Ivor 221
Raven, C.E. 142, 170
Raven, E.E. 149, 158
Real Folklore Society 86, 87
Red Herring, Order of 37
Rhadegunds, The 265
Rhodes, Cecil 153
Richardson. Prof.A.E. 151, 155, 168, 214, 221, 244
Richardson W.H. 268
Richmond, Sir Herbert 102, 112, 142
Roberts, Rt. Revd. Edward 273
Roberts, G.F. 271–2
Roberts, Miles 253
Roberts, S.C. 100, 142
Robey, Edward 39
Robinson Bruce 202
Robinson, Vincent 50
Roosters Club
 ––First attendance 27
 ––Concert Party 159
Roseblade, Dr. J.E. 283
Rothermere, Lord 51
Rowse, A.L. 182
Rustat, Tobias 72
Ruston, Revd. Mark 203

Sage, Revd. George 212, 213, 214
Saines, Mrs 11, 20
Sankey, Revd. Paul 273
Savill, Jo 123
Schweitzer, Albert 219, 220
Schneider, Chris 253
Scott, Sir Harold 259
Scott, Joan 186, 188
Sebley, F.J. 89
Seeley, E.A. ('The Yak') 105
Senate House 19, 161
Shackleton Bailey, Dr.D.R. 227
Shepherd, Lambert 90
Sikes, J.B. 50
Simpson, Dr. Gordon 284
Sinker, Sir Paul 97, 112, 129, 250
Skating on the Cam 76

312

Index

Skillicorn Alice 188
Skinner, Conrad 91, 106
Smalley, Stephen 229
Smoking, giving up 147
Smyth, Revd. Charles 139, 142, 169
Snowden, Philip 21–22
Snowdon, Lord 242
Southcott, Joanna's box 69
Sparks, Bruce 255–6
Spectator, The 145
Spens, Will 114
Stammers, F.M.G. 105
Staples, Peter 281
Stephens, Jimmy 293
S.T.C. 9, 38, 69, 152
Stewart H.F. 138
Stewartby, Lord 261–2
St. Giles' Church, South Mymms 3, 100
St. Ives' Church 12
Streat, Ian 244
Styler, Revd. Geoffrey 183
Sutton, Rt Revd. Keith 277
Swallow holes 38, 179
Symondson, Guy 121
Szilagi, E.A. 124

Taunt, Derek 243
Thaxted Church 32, 57
Thicknesse, Very Revd. C. 259, 273
Thirkell, Angela 199
Thomas, H.H. 8
Thorndike, Dame Sybil 68, 269
Tibbatts, Revd. George 55
Till, Barry 205, 245
Tillyard, E.M.W. 102, 163, 255
Timins, Zelie 244, 279
Traill, Sir Alan 278
Trench, Sir David 111
Trevor-Roper, Hugh 268
Trotter, Mrs 141
Troubadours 54, 221
Turner, John 244, 274
Tyndale-Briscoe, Canon 87

UGBED 58, 59–61
Union Society 10, 12, 167

Varsity Boat race 21
Venn's *Alumni Cantibrigiensis* 137, 211
Vicar, see Allen Hay
Victorian Evening 276
Vidler, Alec 226

Waggon and Horses 40, 58
Wallman v Brittain 215–6
Ward, J.S.M. 105–6
Ward, Revd. Percy 140, 212
Watt, J.C. ('Tommy') 20, 24
Welch, John and Diana 271
Westminster Children's Hospital 233
Whale, J.S. 124
Whalley, John 259
Whalley, Larry 170
Wheatsheafs, The 74–75
Whibley, Charles 45
Whiteley, Lynton 216
Wicks, Brian 157, 203
Wilkinson, Denys 142, 156, 186, 228–9, 265
Williams, A.K. 5
Williams, Glanville 287
Williams, Raymond 247
Wilson, Charles H. 119, 149, 268,
Wilson, J, Cameron 283
Women,
  Academical dress 171
  Dined at Supervisors Dinner 285
  Dined at undergraduate table 287
  Members of University 26, 168, 171
Wood, James 145
Woods, Hilda and Gerald 189
Woods, Jennifer 194
Wyndham Green, Alan 205, 239, 271
Wyld, Revd. E.J.M. 19
Wynn, Rt. Revd. Edward 15, 43, 137, 147

Yates, Eric 173
Yates, Rt. Revd. John 183

Zander, Michael 224
Zinkin, Maurice 276–7